Trails to Texas

TRAILS TO TEXAS

Southern Roots of Western Cattle Ranching

Terry G. Jordan

University of Nebraska Press
Lincoln and London

Parts of Chapters 1, 3, and 4 have previously been published, in somewhat different form, as "The Origin and Distribution of Open-Range Cattle Ranching," *Social Science Quarterly* 53 (1972): 105–21; "The Origin of Anglo-American Cattle Ranching in Texas: A Documentation of Diffusion from the Lower South," *Economic Geography* 45 (1969): 63–87; and "Early Northeast Texas and the Evolution of Western Ranching," *Annals, Association of American Geographers* 67 (1977): 66–87, reproduced by permission.

Library of Congress Cataloging in Publication Data

Jordan, Terry G
  Trails to Texas.

  Bibliography: p. 191
  Includes index.
    1. Ranch life—Texas—History   2. Cattle trade—
Texas—History.   3. Texas—Historical geography.
  I. Title.
F391.J69   976.4   80-14169
ISBN 0-8032-2554-7

To my father,
Prof. Gilbert J. Jordan,
ranch-born and ranch-bred, whose J4 cattle brand was
registered in Mason County, Texas, before his retreat to
academe. His model led me to the academic life—surely
the best of all possible worlds.

Contents

List of Tables and Figures

Preface

"OH MY GOD, NOT ANOTHER ONE!" J. Frank Dobie reportedly quipped when confronted by a newly published book about cattle ranching, and it is true that the western lore shelves of our libraries already groan beneath a heavy load of "cowboy books." I hope, however, that Mr. Dobie would have excused me for adding to that weight, because I bring to the study a fresh perspective: that of the cultural geographer. I do not mean to imply that cultural geographers have previously ignored cattle ranching. Indeed, one-third of the secondary sources listed in my bibliography were written by geographers. Rather, I suggest only that the rise of Texas and western cattle ranching has not previously been explored in depth by any member of the small, hardy fraternity of cultural geographers. Our perspective, I believe, is both unique and valuable.

Cultural geographers study culture from a spatial, ecological viewpoint. We are primarily concerned with the distribution and spread of elements of culture through geographic space, and many of our best contributions to knowledge have come in studies of cultural diffusion. Moreover, we remain constantly attentive to the crucial interrelationship between people as bearers of culture and the physical environment that houses them. Against the current sweeping all scholars toward ever narrower specialization, we have swum to preserve our particular cultural-ecological perspective.

My interest in cattle ranching stems from several sources. I am a sixth-generation Texan with ancestral roots among herders and ranchers. My paternal great-grandfather ran a herd of four hundred longhorns on the open range of Mason County in the 1870s, and some of my maternal ancestors followed the trail to Texas, driving their small herds westward in a series of migrations from the Carolina back country through Georgia and Alabama to East Texas in the early 1800s. Possibly, too, the movie cowboy cult of the 1940s—in which I as a city boy gleefully immersed myself on many a Saturday morning at the local picture show, watching Gene, Roy, and the others—originally spurred my interest. As a graduate student at the University of Texas, I had a history class under Walter Prescott Webb, and his ideas on the origin of western cattle ranching both fascinated and disturbed me. Without question I was greatly influenced by the teachings, writings, and conversations of humanistic cultural geographers such as Fred Kniffen, Don Meinig, Gary Dunbar, Carl Sauer, Lauren Post, Don Brand, and Andrew Clark. I borrowed many thoughts from them, providing grist for my own ideas. At the same time, I have tried not to be academically parochial—a fatal flaw in any geographer—and my bibliography also includes the works of professional and local historians, linguists, folklorists, economists, archaeologists, soil scientists, foresters, and journalists, among others.

Over the last two decades, the span of my academic interest in ranching, I have received generous aid, both financial and personal. Ready cash was first provided by Arizona State University in 1967-68, in the form of a faculty grant-in-aid. The Faculty Research Committee at my present academic home, North Texas State University, never seemed to tire of my obsession with ranching, having awarded me grants in 1971-72, 1975-76, and 1978-79 (nos. 34266, 34259, and 34370), covering released time and travel expenses. Three of the six chapters in this book were the results of those grants, and preliminary published versions have appeared in *Economic Geography, Social Science Review,* and *Annals of the Association of American Geographers.* The last-named grant from North Texas State University, in 1978-79, provided me the released time necessary to put this book in final form.

My personal debts are to Don Stallings and Pete Kosinski, my students at North Texas State, who served as research assistants; to Mr. V. T. ("Cowboy") Williams, Jr., of rural Navasota, Texas, a gentleman breeder of East Texas "cow dogs," who generously provided information and photographs concerning his business; to Jim Hurst, a Houston photographer, who took several of the pictures used in chapter 5; to Katy Caver, curator of the Texarkana Historical Society Museum, who kindly acquired for me copies of several old photographs of Piney Woods cattle from the society's archives and granted me permission to use them; and to Lonn W. Taylor, former curator of history at the Dallas Historical Society, who called my attention to a remarkable drawing of southern cattle drovers (fig. 2.2).

I am also indebted to Prof. John D. W. Guice of the University of Southern Mississippi, who organized a stimulating special session on open-range herding in the South at the 1979 annual meeting of the Organization of American Historians. I profited much from this session and was pleased to be an invited participant. Fred Kniffen, Boyd Professor Emeritus at Louisiana State University, served as a reader when this book was in manuscript stage, and his suggestions were of great value. Any errors or misinterpretations are, of course, solely my fault.

Trails to Texas

1
A Traditional Lifestyle

THE OPEN-RANGE SYSTEM of cattle raising, precursor of present-day livestock ranching, was a colorful form of frontier economy that has long fascinated students of Americana.[1] This herding system, complete with its own customs, lore, and vocabulary, its own material culture, constituted a whole way of life not duplicated before or since, a *genre de vie*, or "lifestyle," in the true sense of the French human geographers.[2] The distinctiveness of this method of cattle herding lay not only in the absence of fencing, but also in such practices as periodic stock roundups, marking and branding of cattle, large scale of operation, long overland drives to market, careless treatment of livestock, and lack of controlled breeding. Man was pitted against semiwild animals in an epic, annually repeating drama played out in a raw physical setting beset with hazards. It was the stuff of which folk heroes were made.

Perhaps nowhere else in the world did open-range cattle herding attain greater importance or generate more legend and lore than on the American Great Plains in the late nineteenth century. As the native grazing animals of the Plains, notably the bison, were quickly and efficiently decimated, huge herds of cattle replaced them. Simultaneously, cowboy replaced Indian. The land stretching eastward from the foot of the Rockies, all the way from Texas to Canada, suddenly became home to an open-range ranching empire. And just as suddenly, scant decades later, the machine age with its barbed wire, steel windmills, and iron rails heralded the end of this traditional lifestyle on the Plains. Scarcely had the first generation of Plains cowmen retired to write or

1

dictate their reminiscences than the system was gone, so
that their recollecting often took on the character of lamenta-
tions for a way of life that had disappeared. The twentieth
century had claimed one of its many victims.

This book is an inquiry into the origins of the Great
Plains cattle empire. As such, it joins an extensive body of
professional literature. Academic speculation and controver-
sy concerning the beginnings and spread of traditional open-
range cattle ranching in the United States date back almost
ninety years, to the time when such ranchers were still active
on the Plains.[3] Historians and cultural geographers have
participated in this still-unresolved debate, and in recent
years an increasing number of publications have appeared.[4]
In the spring of 1979, a special session at the annual meeting
of the Organization of American Historians was devoted to
open-range livestock herding in the antebellum South.[5]

The ongoing debate has produced divergent ideas and
theories concerning origins and diffusion. Some scholars
have probed distant lands and alien peoples in search of the
explanation; others have sought the answer in the physical
character of the land. Essentially, six schools of thought
have developed concerning the evolution of open-range cattle ranching: (1) the European origin thesis; (2) the African
origin thesis; (3) the environmental determinist view; (4) the
Hispanic-American origin thesis; (5) the frontier stage theory; and (6) the market accessibility model. Those who support the European or African origin thesis point to similar
herding economies once found in the Old World, perhaps
most notably in medieval Iberia, the Celtic highlands, and
West Africa. The environmental determinists view ranching
as an economic response to semiaridity, a necessary adaptation by farming peoples to inadequacy of rainfall. Supporters
of the Hispanic-American thesis argue that cattle ranching
in the American West is simply a surviving New World Spanish colonial institution. Frontier stage theorists regard the
system as a logical and widespread pioneer livelihood common to most frontiers, one of several stages in the transition
from wilderness to completed settlement. Proponents of the
market accessibility model feel that ranching is the inevitable product of remoteness and poor access to market, an
extensive form of land use forced to occupy zones on the far

peripheries of the world system of commercial agriculture. By no means are these six schools of thought necessarily mutually exclusive, a point proponents of the several theories often acknowledge.

The Frontier Stage Theory

Perhaps the best known of the ranching origin theories attributes open-range herding to frontier conditions. According to this theory, ranching arose when European colonists entered wilderness areas devoid of the conveniences known in the Old World homeland. In the short run, it was not feasible for the pioneers to fence the land, produce fodder crops, or construct adequate barns and sheds. The labor shortage typical of nearly all frontier zones discouraged or rendered impossible the hiring of herdsmen to tend the livestock. In such a situation, the European pioneers had no choice but to allow their cattle, hogs, and other animals to run loose and untended on the open range. For example, as early as 1611, the few head of cattle in the Jamestown colony in Virginia were out of necessity left to forage for themselves all winter in the woods.[6] To their surprise, the European settlers discovered that the livestock could usually fend for themselves quite well, that cattle were willing and able to revert to the wild. The "habitual" practice of the Portuguese, as early as the 1400s, was to unload and abandon livestock prior to colonization in new lands, so that stock would be on hand when the first settlers arrived. The Portuguese used this method in the Azores, the Cape Verde Islands, and Madeira before colonizing Brazil in the 1500s. Spaniards also employed this practice, with varying degrees of success.[7]

Impressive support can be marshaled for the frontier origin thesis. Cattle ranching arose on many overseas European frontiers.[8] At one time or another, open-range cattle herding flourished in lands as diverse as Latin America, the eastern seaboard of the United States, South Africa, and Australia. It thrived in the tropics and the mid-latitudes, in grasslands and forests, among diverse European ethnic groups.

The concept of the frontier as a reshaper of European culture and economy was first proposed by the noted historian Frederick Jackson Turner, who described an Anglo-American herder frontier moving westward from the colonial seaboard colonies, always on the outer perimeter of the crop-farming areas. In Turner's view, other distinct economies preceded and followed ranching in the march westward. "Stand at Cumberland Gap," Turner advised, "and watch the procession of civilization, the fur trader and hunter, the cattle-raiser, the pioneer farmer.... Stand at South Pass in the Rockies a century later, and see the same procession."[9] Turner, in explaining the origin of the Great Plains cattle industry, proposed that "the experience of the Carolina cowpens guided the ranchers of Texas."[10]

Nor was Anglo-America the only frontier to witness the evolution of cattle herding. In South Africa, colonists of Dutch ancestry engaged in open-range ranching on the frontier of the Cape Province by the late 1600s, less than half a century after the founding of the first colony there. One writer referred to "the moving pastoral frontier which pulled the Boers away from governmental control and European ideas into a self-sufficient and isolated life in the interior."[11] By the early eighteenth century, these *Trekboer* cattle ranchers were pressing on into the interior and along the east coast, the beginning of a major areal expansion which had, by the 1780s, seen South African ranching spread to the banks of the Orange River, nearly five hundred miles from Capetown.[12] The majority of the Boer ranchers owned large pieces of property, adapting "themselves to economic and geographical circumstances by improvising a pastoral economy with a 6,000-acre farm as its typical unit."[13]

The European settlement of Australia began much later than the similar occupation of Anglo-America and South Africa, but open-range cattle ranching was present almost from the beginning of colonization. Cattle were imported from a variety of sources in the 1790s, and soon many were running half-wild on the open range. In the county of Cumberland in New South Wales, the original nucleus of Australian settlement, farmers occupied the lands along rivers and streams in the Cumberland Plain by 1820, while cattle and sheep ranchers dominated the interfluvial areas.[14] There were 26,000 cattle in New South Wales by 1814, a total which increased rapidly to 68,000 in 1821 and to nearly 250,000 by 1828. As early as 1813, ranchers probed through a gap in the Blue Mountains into the interior of the continent. Westward expansion began in earnest after 1820 and continued for several decades, with ranchers in the vanguard.[15] In a passage inspired by Turner, W. K. Hancock asked his readers to "stand at this gap," Australia's equivalent of Cumberland Gap, "and watch the frontiers following each other westward—the squatters' frontier," which filled the outback with livestock, "the miners' frontier," and "the farmers' frontier." "Stand a few hundred miles further west on the Darling river," he continued, "and see...the pastoralists and prospectors pass by."[16] As in South Africa, then, open-range ranchers were the typical Australian frontiersmen. They developed a system of cattle raising remarkably like that of North America.[17] A student of comparative frontiers, H. C. Allen, noted that "branding, ear clipping, mustering [table 1.1], and the technique of handling stock with horse and rope were common to both" the Australian cattle country and the United States. "On both frontiers," Allen continued, "was bred a race of horsemen."[18] Only the vocabularies employed by ranchers differed in these open-range systems (table 1.1). In the Australian cattle ranching country were found such typical open-range traits and practices as overland drives to market, roundups, rustling, and the use of spurs. On both ranching frontiers, one reaction to aridity was for ranchers to establish ownership of the water, thereby eliminating possible competitors.

The culture area perhaps most closely identified with open-range ranching is Latin America.[19] In almost every colony, the Spaniards and Portuguese established open-range ranching, and their colonial cattle frontiers reached as far north as Florida, Texas, New Mexico, Arizona, and California.[20] Not infrequently, the pioneer ranchers of Latin America were mission fathers, who used Indian herders to tend the stock. Open-range ranching began in the 1500s in Latin America, a century or more before similar economies appeared in the United States and South Africa and over two hundred years before the Australian development. Moreover, it is mainly in the disease-infested tropical savannas of

TABLE 1.1
COMPARATIVE OPEN-RANGE VOCABULARIES

Anglo America	Australia	Spanish Latin America	Portuguese South America
cowboy	musterer, herdsman	vaquero, gaucho, llanero	sertanejo vaqueiro
cow hunt, roundup	muster	vaquéria, rodeo	vaquerjada
stock farm, cowpen, ranch	station	hacienda, estancia, rancho	fazenda
pen, trap	stock yard	corral	curral, manqueira
drive, trailing	overlanding		
drover, driver	drover	reseros, curreteros	boiadeiros
brand		hierro, marca marcado, herrado	marcacao
maverick	cleanskin	cimarrón	chimarrão
rustler	bushranger, duffer		
trail	track	trillos, huellas	estradas boiaderas
open range		campos generales	campos gerais

Latin America that open-range ranching survives today, though even there it is fast disappearing.[21]

In all of these zones of overseas European colonization, say the proponents of the frontier thesis, the lack of fencing and adequate labor supply led to most of the other traits associated with traditional ranching. Controlled breeding was impossible, branding or marking became essential, the declining domesticity of the stock necessitated management from horseback, and the lack of adequate transport facilities produced the overland drive. Struggle for survival in the wilderness produced tough, wily creole breeds of cattle, while an abundance of forage in the emptiness of frontier fringes encouraged a rapid multiplication of the animals. Large herds running loose on the open range required the periodic roundup.

Turner's frontier stage model, depicting a mobile zone of herders shunted ever westward by encroaching farmers, has been accepted by a variety of distinguished scholars. The Southern historian Frank L. Owsley, for example, described herders as "the typical pioneers," forming the vanguard on the frontier of the American South.[22] The model, however, also has critics. Some have pointed out that not all overseas European frontiers experienced a herder phase. More recently, historians Forrest McDonald and Grady McWhiney have claimed that open-range herding in the American South, far from being a transitory pioneer economic phase, persisted long after the frontier had passed to the west.[23]

The European Origin Thesis

The spatial correlation between cattle ranching and overseas Iberians, British, Dutch, and other western Europeans leads naturally to a study of Europe itself. Was open-range cattle herding part of the European cultural heritage? Were the ranchers of the Great Plains merely latter-day perpetuators of an ancient European lifestyle? Certainly the far-flung distribution of cattle ranching among the children of the European diaspora suggests a common prototype in the mother continent. Nor is evidence of European origin lacking. Even classical mythology and the world view of the ancient Greeks and Romans are suggestive. The citizens of the classical world perceived themselves to be surrounded by a pastoral fringe, the domain of wild men of the forest and steppe, livestock-tending folk who worshiped Pan—the herder god of fertility. Sometimes the classics ascribed to the Scythians and other such fringe peoples an idyllic character. They were seen as noble savages, free of the burdens and demands of civilization, living comfortably from their abundant herds without an undue exertion of labor. There, on the periphery, the barbarians led a carefree life in humankind's "natural" condition. If the sale of dime novels is any accurate measure, the civilized easterners of the nineteenth-century United States had a similar opinion of Great Plains cowboys.

A much less romantic view of the borderland herder folk was held by some Europeans. Englishman Edmund Spenser was unfavorably impressed by sixteenth-century migratory

Irish cattle raisers. Comparing the Irish to the Scythians of classical times, Spenser described how they lived "the most part of the yeare... pasturing upon the mountaine and waste wilde places... driving their cattle continually with them."[24] Spenser deplored the lawlessness of the cattle Irish and held no illusions about the noble savage. But whatever their opinion of the herder, the civilized Europeans knew they were out there where civilization ended, in the Celtic highlands, on the steppe grasslands, in the semidesert of the Iberian Meseta, in the Saharan fringe, in the fastness of wooded hills and mountains.

How similar were these "barbarian" herders to the ranchers of the American Plains, South African veld, and Australian outback? Some scholars who have studied the faint trace left by these pastoral peoples on the historical documents of Europe have concluded that the peripheral cattle folk were indeed the cultural forerunners of the overseas ranchers. Historian Charles Julian Bishko, for example, has spoken of "the enduring influence of medieval Iberian cattle ranching upon the history of the Americas."[25] Bishko argues that cattle ranching, a possible prototype of the later Latin American type, evolved from sheepherding in the eleventh and twelfth centuries on the Castilian Meseta of interior Spain, between the middle Duero River and the central Sierras to the south—on the frontier of Christian Iberia. From this early base in Old Castile and León, he maintains, cattle ranching spread in late medieval times southward to the Andalusian plain and Portuguese Alentejo, advancing as the Moors withdrew. Conceivably, these fledgling Spanish ranchers could have learned many techniques from the retreating Arabs, a herder folk from ancient times. From the southern bases in Andalusia and Alentejo, Bishko proposes, many elements of Iberian ranching spread to the Western Hemisphere.

Similarly, cultural geographer Lauren C. Post has pointed to the cattlemen of French Camargue, a district at the mouth of the Rhône River on the Mediterranean shore, as possessing a herder economy rather like that of French Louisiana.[26] Semiwild cattle tended by mounted herdsmen roamed the deltaic marshes of Camargue until recent times.

Others have looked to the Celtic highlands as a likely source of overseas European cattle herding, particularly in the United States.[27] Historians McDonald and McWhiney, Celtic in name and sympathy, champion "Celtic characteristics that predated both the South and the American frontier by many centuries" as a possible prototype for southern Anglo-American herding.[28]

Certainly, the European herder peoples displayed many traits later evidenced by the overseas ranchers. The practice of driving cattle overland to market along well-established trails, for example, was once typical of lands as diverse as Spain and Britain. One such route, the Gallowaygate, was mentioned in Westmorland, northern England, as early as 1186. This particular drove road served to bring cattle from Scotland to the markets of English Yorkshire. The stock were driven on the hoof in approximately seven-mile stages between resting places, or stock stands. The last day's move brought them to Thornton-in-Lonsdale, just across the Yorkshire border, where a famous cattle fair was held. Scotland was crisscrossed by a maze of cattle trails, leading from the Highland producer areas to Lowland markets,[29] and similar trails, called *cañadas*, were very common in Spain. Branding and earmarking of livestock were also widespread in Europe and can seemingly be traced to the prehistoric Middle East, the site of original herd animal domestication. Both overland droving and branding imply the use of open range, where the animals of different owners mingled, as they foraged in unfenced tracts of forest, marsh, and moor, as well as on fallow fields. As recently as the nineteenth century, open-range grazing was very common in the British Isles, the Netherlands, France, Spain, and Portugal—the homelands of every major group of overseas European ranchers—and some traces are yet in evidence, particularly in the Mediterranean lands. Since open-range grazing was typical of nearly all Old World peoples who raised herd livestock, the practice can in no sense be regarded as uniquely European. It is reasonable to suggest, however, that Europeans were responsible for introducing the open-range system to the overseas colonial areas.

Some techniques of herd management seem also to be derived from Europe. By the fifteenth century, Britishers had perfected the use of herder dogs, a practice which spread slowly to the European mainland in later centuries and was carried overseas to various English colonies.[30] Iberians, by contrast, learned to tend cattle from horseback, a method well suited to the grassy tablelands of the Meseta and one which may have had roots in Moorish practices. European, too, was the custom, especially common in Britain, of deliberately burning grazing lands to induce a fresh growth of grass, a procedure also noted among some North American Indians.

Yet another ranching trait possibly derived from Europe is *transhumance*, a system in which a few herders migrate with stock from summer pastures in the mountains to lowland home pastures in the winter. Transhumance has been practiced historically by various peoples in Europe, and in some areas the custom can still be observed today.[31] In the 1700s, the century in which Northern Ireland sent tens of thousands of Scotch-Irish to eastern North America, Ulstermen in the Mourne Mountains south of Belfast still annually drove their cattle to the *booley*, the highland summer pastures.[32] Iberia was also a noted scene of transhumance. This custom of seasonal movement of cattle herds spread to most of the overseas ranching areas, including the United States. In South Africa, for example, the Karroo district of the interior was early utilized by Boer cattlemen to pasture stock in the winter season. In Latin America, transhumance occurs in numerous localities, such as the Brazilian Serra do Mar, the Plateau of Mexico, and Neuquen province in the Argentinian Andes.[33] Admittedly, the practice was never common in Texas.

The livestock breeds of open-range ranching were also derived from Europe. Small, hardy British breeds and wiry Iberian longhorns became particularly common in the overseas herding economies.

Departures from European Tradition

But while the similarities between European cattle herding and overseas ranching are numerous and unmistakable, there were also some notable differences. One of the most fundamental traits of open-range ranching among overseas Europeans was a general neglect of the livestock. Cattle were obliged to forage pretty much for themselves and to do without such niceties as housing, winter feeding, and protection from predators. In the process, the livestock inevitably became semiwild. A greater contrast to the typical European way of doing things, past or present, can scarcely be imagined. In Europe, animals are above all thoroughly domesticated and scarcely ever out of sight of their diligent human stewards. To the American, they seem spiritless and overly docile, more like household pets than agricultural animals. The open-range in Europe was integrally related to the use of herders who kept constant and careful watch on the livestock. Straying and loss of stock to predators was rare, and every effort was made to feed and house the animals during the winter. In medieval Spain, for example, "the herds were not left to roam at will, but kept under standing guard to avoid both stock losses and the heavy penalties imposed for trespass against the...orchards, grain fields, vineyards, ox pastures, and mown meadows."[34] The herders defended the cattle from the perils of drought, storm, and stampede, often memorizing each animal's physical appearance in order to detect strays and find lost cattle. Such practices suggest that the Spanish livestock raisers of the medieval period were rather different from the ranchers of New Spain in later centuries. They were undeniably cast in the European mold, dedicated to the careful tending of their stock.

Neglect, in part, was the product of abundance. The rapid natural increase of stock on the frontier quickly brought the overseas European ownership of hundreds or even thousands of cattle and prompted his abandonment of careful herding practices. Just as overabundance of land destroyed the colonials' interest in conservation, so overabundance of livestock rendered unprofitable and unnecessary any immediate attempt to reestablish the careful European system of livestock husbandry on the overseas frontiers. Indeed, the large scale of operation typical of open-range ranching provides another departure from Old World tradition. European peasants rarely owned more than a few head of livestock or used in excess of several tens of acres of land. Ranchers, by contrast, typically owned hundreds or

thousands of animals that ranged over vast areas of public
and private domain. The immensity of colonial cattle holdings rarely failed to impress visitors from Europe.

European travelers visiting the overseas colonies often
noted in their journals that the colonial livestock were more
feral than the European. In a delightful passage, Crèvecoeur
described the semiwild cattle on the open ranges of the back
country of the seaboard colonies in Anglo-America during
the 1770s, noting particularly that the animals were self-
reliant, proud, and healthy. In contrast, he observed, "the
slavery, the solitude, the harshness with which the Europeans treat...[their cattle] have abused them, degraded
them."[35] Indeed, one might argue that only thoroughly
docile, completely "degraded" domesticated stock could have
tolerated the inactivity of the long, difficult sea voyage to the
overseas colonies. The Iberian ancestors of the proud, bellig-
erent longhorn cattle so common on the frontiers of New
Spain and the American Southwest were comparatively
docile, subdued animals, a consequence of daily tending by
their stewards. The open range and human neglect provided
nothing less than a bovine emancipation.

Emigrants newly settled in the colonies, writing letters
back to friends and relatives in Europe, frequently commented on the fundamental differences between European
stock farming and colonial open-range ranching. Typical is
a letter written by a German-born immigrant who became a
cattle rancher in the hill country of Texas, explaining to a
relative in his home village in Europe that "things are different here; you [Germans] tie your cows to the feeding trough
with chains, but we do not have any stables for the cattle.
They stay outside in summer and in winter."[36]

European travelers also remarked these basic contrasts,
generally heaping scorn on the colonial method of raising
livestock. The anonymous author of *American Husbandry*,
writing in the 1770s, described open-range cattle herding in
the back country of Pennsylvania, North Carolina, and
Georgia, where he noted that stock were poorly tended and
the herders "inattentive" to winter feed, the result being
"herds of half-starved, stunted beasts." "They let them run
through the woods not only in summer, but also in winter,"
he wrote of the Pennsylvania cattlemen.[37] Some years ear-

lier, another observer described the open-range system in South Carolina, where "the Planters are freed from the Charge and Trouble of providing for their Cattle, suffering them to feed all Winter in the Woods."[38] In a similar vein, a British traveler in Texas during the early 1840s, disgusted by the methods employed by Anglo-Texan ranchers near Galveston Bay, recorded in his journal that the cattle were "suffered to roam at large in the wilderness," as a consequence of which they were "nearly as wild as the...buffaloes."[39] The frequency with which such comments appear in the letters and journals of the Europeans who observed colonial agriculture lends further support to the notion that in Europe there was nothing akin to the careless methods and semiwild livestock of open-range ranching.

The vocabulary of livestock raising also differs between Europe and the overseas areas, providing additional evidence for the notion that the colonial system was unique. Word meanings changed. For example, *corral* in Spain refers to the courtyard of a farmstead, an open space surrounded by workrooms, stalls, wagonsheds, and dwelling, a place where draft animals, swine, cattle, and sheep are brought for feeding and protection. Poultry and playing children are at home in a Spanish corral.[40] In Latin America, on the other hand, a *corral* is typically a fenced pen where horses or cattle are confined.

Even in the choice of livestock, the overseas ranchers often departed from their Old World tradition. Cattle became the major ranch livestock in most Spanish and Portuguese colonies in Latin America, yet this animal was historically of relatively minor importance in the greater part of Iberia and the Mediterranean region as a whole. It is true that small numbers of cattle were found throughout southern Europe and cattle even attained a sacred status in Minoan Crete, playing a religious role that was still evident in the time of Homer and is possibly echoed yet today in the Iberian ritual of bullfighting, but sheep, goats, and swine were the principal livestock in traditional Mediterranean agriculture.[41] One expert on the history of Spanish livestock raising wrote of the "striking reversal" which occurred when the overseas Spaniards in Mexico and other colonies substituted cattle for sheep and goats in their herding economy.[42] The decline of

sheep in overseas Iberian ranching areas may have been
largely a function of livestock neglect. Perhaps cattle sur-
passed sheep on the ranges of Latin America because they
were better able to survive the attacks of predators, better
able to revert to the wild and fend for themselves.

In short, Europe provides only a partial antecedent for
open-range cattle ranching. The origins are not to be found
exclusively there, and we must look to other sources and
causal factors.

The African Origin Thesis

Historian Peter H. Wood has recently proposed that cattle
herding in Anglo-America owes a cultural debt to Africa.
Noting that the southern colonies, particularly the Carolinas, were an early center of the open-range cattle industry,
Wood has suggested that the presence of large numbers of
slaves there may have been partially responsible. He be-
lieves that many slaves entering South Carolina after 1670
had previous herding experience. "People of the Gambia
region," he observes, "the area for which South Carolina
slave dealers expressed a steady preference, were expert
horsemen and herders."[43] Cattle-raising nomads abound in
Africa, and some of them living along the southern Saharan
fringe may have acquired the skills of horsemanship through
contacts with the Arabs. Moreover, traders on occasion
transported both slaves and cattle from Africa to the
Americas.[44]

Blacks developed and tended Carolina herds as early as
the 1670s and 1680s, and servant and beast were listed
together in estate records. A 1741 estate described in the
South Carolina Gazette mentioned "a Stock of Cattle ... said
to be from Five Hundred to One Thousand Head ... Also a
Man used to a Cow Pen and of a good Character."[45] In view of
the well-known nineteenth-century importance of black cowboys in Texas and other western regions, the early Carolina
experience may be of considerable significance.[46] Even the
word "cowboy" may have begun as a term for a slave cow
herder. Similarly, the western American word "buckaroo,"
long assumed to be a corruption of the Spanish *vaquero*, may

instead have its origin in the Gullah *buckra*. A South Carolina variant of this African word is *bockorau*. Among southern blacks, this word acquired a secretly derisive meaning, roughly "white trash," and was possibly used, contemptuously, to describe Piney Woods "Cracker" herders and, later, Anglo and Mexican cowboys in Texas.[47]

The problems with accepting an African origin of cattle ranching are several. First, blacks were not present in the formative stages of Latin American ranching and never appeared on the Australian scene. In addition, the type of livestock husbandry found in West Africa was rather different from ranching. The cattle cultures of Africa, in common with the pastoral life of the Eurasian steppes and deserts, can be classified as nomadic herding.[48] Unlike ranchers, nomads were organized into tribes, exhibited a high level of communalism, lived in tents with no fixed place of residence, and practiced a subsistence economy little dependent on the world system of money and markets. Still, individual African herding skills could easily have been transmitted from a nomadic to a slavery setting in North America. A similar transferal could have occurred in Dutch South Africa.

The Environmental Determinist View

Rather than seeking the origins of ranching in Old World hearths and cultural diffusion, some have looked to the nature of the land and climate for an answer. To the climatic determinist, livestock ranching represents the reaction of overseas European farmers to aridity. Historian W. K. Hancock, for example, emphasizes "the environmental conditions, which, in South Africa as in Australia, had produced a pastoral economy with a tendency to sprawl indefinitely."[49] Another champion of environmental determinism was the late American historian Walter Prescott Webb, who argued that a semiarid, treeless, and flat "Great Plains Environment" forced fundamental modifications in Anglo-American culture and livelihood when pioneers left the humid, forested East. Webb felt that ranching was a logical and necessary adaptation to semiaridity, and he argued that Anglos began engaging in cattle ranching only after they encountered the Great Plains environment in the brush country of South Texas.[50] According to Webb, Anglos entered Texas without any significant ranching heritage and adopted this herding system in a diamond-shaped area south of San Antonio and west of the Guadalupe River. He felt that the period between 1840 and 1860 witnessed most of the metamorphosis from farmer to rancher in the Anglo-Texan culture. The Plains environment made herders out of tillers.

Webb's thesis has been widely accepted by other writers. His friend, the folklorist J. Frank Dobie, wrote that Anglo-Americans came to Texas "without any conception of ranching" and that they did not practice this form of economy until 1836 at the earliest.[51] Francis L. Fugate has placed the birth of the Anglo-Texan cattle industry in the quarter-century between 1840 and 1865, the period during which Anglos entered semiarid South Texas, a move, Fugate says, that gave them "no choice but to discard their Eastern habits, get on a horse, and learn to handle cattle."[52]

The environmentalist outlook, although beautiful in its simplicity and appealing in the lyrical prose of Webb and Dobie, simply will not hold up under close scrutiny. While it is true that ranching thrived in semiarid and arid portions of all the overseas European colonization areas, about the most that can be said for the environmental factor is that dry conditions provided a refuge for ranchers after they were driven out of more desirable areas by farmers. The important fact is that European emigrants developed open-range ranching in varied overseas environments—wet and dry lands, mountains and plains, tropics and mid-latitudes, forests and grasslands. Cattle herding once flourished in the forests of humid eastern Anglo-America and the well-watered pampas of Argentina and Uruguay. The only major tribute paid by the overseas European herders to aridity was the abandonment of forest-loving swine as ranch animals.

The Hispanic-American Origin Thesis

Webb himself did not rely solely on the environmentalist explanation. Instead, he attributed the development of Great Plains cattle ranching to the Hispanic people, a group with long experience in the American drylands. From the Hispanics, believed Webb, the techniques of ranching passed to the Anglos.[53] He argued that Anglos first learned the rudiments of this economic system from Mexican ranchers in the South Texas "diamond," an area from which many Hispanic cattlemen were expelled as a result of military conflict in the decade 1836–46. The Anglos simply picked up where the Mexicans had left off, confiscating their land, stealing their cattle, and adopting their methods. Given his environmentalistic outlook and Hispanic origin thesis, Webb naturally chose the South Texas "diamond" as the cradle of Great Plains cattle ranching. Only there did he find combined the three elements necessary—a demanding physical environment, a long-established Hispanic ranching economy, and frequent Anglo-Hispanic contacts in antebellum times.

The Hispanic origin thesis has drawn many supporters.[54] No one has stated the argument more concisely and convincingly than Sandra Myres, a Texas historian.[55] Myres points to the widespread use of corrupted Spanish vocabulary by Anglo cattlemen, words such as "ranch," "lariat," "lasso," "bronc," "dally roping," and "corral." She documents Mexican prototypes for the roundup, the overland drive, branding, stockmen's associations, and mounted herdsmen; and she finds Hispanic antecedents for the dress, saddle, large scale of operation, and horseback herding techniques of the Great Plains cowmen.

The Hispanic origin thesis, particularly in this age of awakening Chicano pride and consciousness, has great appeal. When linked to the equally enticing environmental theory—one well suited to the increasingly popular environmental protection movement—the Hispanic-American origin proposition is almost irresistible. Reading Walter Prescott Webb's eloquent description of an Anglo-Saxon people, humbled by semiaridity, learning a new, ecologically appropriate economic system from desert-wizened Hispanos, any sensitive person who sympathizes with ethnic minority causes and favors harmony with the physical forces of nature will surely be converted. It is a powerful emotional combination.

But even when combined with environmental determinism, the Hispanic origin thesis leaves too many questions unanswered. The mounted cattle keepers of interior Australia surely owe no Hispanic debt, nor does an Iberian heritage stand behind the Boer cattle tenders of South Africa. And, as will be described in chapter 2, Anglo-Americans developed a thriving open-range livestock economy on the colonial eastern seaboard, seemingly without Spanish or Mexican help.

Indeed, the ranching vocabularies of the several overseas cattle herding European peoples differ, suggesting multiple origins (table 1.1). The Anglo-American *cowhunt* and *pen* are the Australian *muster* and *stock yard*; the Mexican *rancho* is the Brazilian *fazenda*; the Argentinian *gaucho* is the Anglo-American *cowboy*. The variations in vocabulary also imply that open-range cattle ranching evolved overseas rather than in Europe. Spaniards in the South American pampas preferred *estancia* and *gaucho*, but Spaniards in Mexico used *rancho* and *vaquero*. What to Anglo-Australians were *cleanskins* and *tracks* were to Anglo-Americans *mavericks* and *trails*. Clearly, vocabulary argues for multiple, independent development of cattle ranching. The Hispanic-American origin thesis by no means provides a full explanation.

The Market Accessibility Model

Economic spatial forces were also at work in the evolution of livestock ranching. These were concisely expressed a century and a half ago by the German scholar-farmer Johann Heinrich von Thünen, who proposed that more intensive forms of agriculture would be located nearest to the market, since farmers could place almost all of their investment in the land in the form of labor and capital rather than in transportation.[56] With increasing distance from market, farmers would spend progressively less per unit of land because they would have to spend progressively more on transporting produce to market. Thus, they would be forced to use their land less intensively. In addition, according to von Thünen, higher land prices, taxes, and labor costs in areas near the market would require farmers in those regions to maximize production and income per acre of land.

The von Thünen model suggests that highly intensive commercial forms of land use, such as market gardening and feedlots, would be located nearest to large urban-industrial markets. Successive belts of progressively less intensive agriculture, represented by dairying, livestock fattening operations, commercial grain farming, and livestock ranching, would extend beyond this region. Livestock ranching, being the least intensive commercial type of agriculture, would therefore be relegated to the regions most remote from markets. Figure 1.1 diagrams an adaption of von Thünen's model.

Research in economic geography has provided ample support for the von Thünen model, both in contemporary agriculture and in past times.[57] Geographer Ronald J. Horvath made a detailed study of the African region centering on the Ethiopian capital city of Addis Ababa. While noting disruptions caused by ethnic and environmental contrasts, Professor Horvath found "remarkable parallels between Thünen's crop theory and the agriculture around Addis Ababa."[58] Similarly, German geographer Ursula Ewald applied the model to the farming patterns of colonial Mexico during the period of Spanish rule, concluding that even this culturally and environmentally diverse land provided "an excellent illustration of von Thünen's principles on spatial zonation in agriculture."[59]

On a broader scale, von Thünen's model can be applied to the world as a whole. Much of the world map of commercial agricultural regions has been shaped by the development of the huge, discontiguous urban-industrial complex in northwestern Europe and northeastern Anglo-America, that global economic core region which arose in the 1700s and has been dubbed the "Thünen World City." Most of the commercial agriculture in the world is keyed to the demands of the urban-industrial core, and the result is a series of fairly well-defined agricultural zones or belts situated at different distances from the core. Each of these agricultural zones produces the commodity which it is "best fitted to export by virtue of location relative to the markets" of the great urban-industrial complex.[60] Nearest the "World City" are zones of dairying and market gardening, intensive forms of agriculture which yield a high income per acre and produce perishable commodities which must have quick access to market. Following at increasing distances from the "World City" are (1) a region producing feed grains and fattened meat ani-

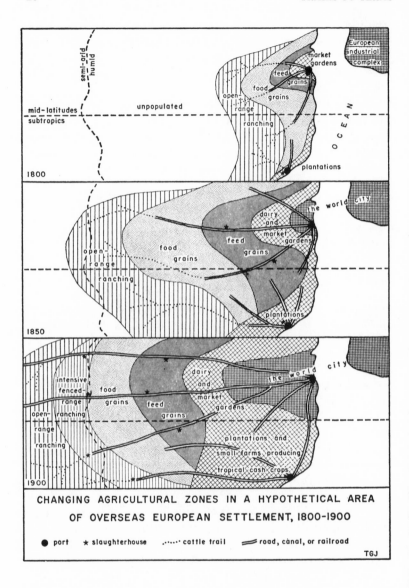

CHANGING AGRICULTURAL ZONES IN A HYPOTHETICAL AREA

OF OVERSEAS EUROPEAN SETTLEMENT, 1800-1900

● port   ★ slaughterhouse   ·······cattle trail   ⚏road, canal, or railroad

Fig. 1.1 The theoretical basis of the patterns shown is provided by von Thünen. Less intensive forms of agriculture, such as open-range livestock ranching, will occupy peripheral frontier locations due mainly to difficulty of access to market.

mals, (2) a commercial food grain zone, and, on the outermost periphery, (3) a ranching region producing lean animals, hides, tallow, and other herd animal products (figure 1.1). The intensity of land use decreases steadily with increasing distance from the urban-industrial core, reaching its lowest level in the ranching zone, where, in the open-range era, "only by concentrating the feed from many acres into a few valuable pounds of commodity" could the inhabitants join the international economy.[61] Because livestock were self-transporting and not subject to spoilage en route to market, inhabitants of the remote fringe regions could, by becoming herders, participate in the commercial agricultural system. By converting the cattle into cured hides and tallow at transshipment points, further reduction of transport costs was possible.

An equilibrium might have been reached, in which the open-range system could have become fixed in this peripheral position, had the urban-industrial core in northwestern Europe and northeastern Anglo-American not continued to grow and spawn new technology in the nineteenth century. However, growth and innovation in the economic core were continuous after 1800, with far-reaching effects on open-range cattle ranching. The demand for agricultural produce rose spectacularly, new farming techniques allowed intensification of farming further and further from the core, and dramatic innovations in transportation greatly lessened the time and expense required to ship goods to the economic core region. As a result, the open-range ranching zone became mobile, retreating steadily before the advancing agricultural technology and the spreading transportation tentacles emanating from the "World City." On its inner periphery, ranching gave way to commercial food grain farming, which in turn was being shunted outward by an expansion of the feed grain–livestock-fattening zone. In the United States, in Australia, and eventually in South Africa and the pampas of Argentina, cattle ranchers retreated before advancing waves of wheat farmers, a retreat which halted only when the ranchers found refuge in lands too dry for the "sodbusters." In effect, growing demand and improved technology made more intensive forms of agriculture economically possible and even necessary in areas once dominated by open-range ranching.

Markets other than those of the "World City" also stimu-
lated commercial open-range ranching. Perhaps most notable among these was the mining industry, which operated on
most of the frontiers of overseas European settlement, but
particularly in Mexico and the western United States.

In time, even the last refuges of open-range ranching
were invaded as demand and technology continued to
increase. The inevitable result was the end of the open-range
system and its replacement by modern, more intensive
methods of livestock raising. Barbed wire, a new invention,
allowed the fencing of ranges in the treeless, semiarid ranching refuges; the American windmill, a new technical modifi-
cation of an ancient machine, increased the carrying capacity of the grassland refuges by dispersing the stock; and
penetration by railroads ended the need for overland drives.
These changes allowed, indeed virtually demanded, the
introduction of improved livestock, which in turn required
greater care and supervision than had their tough creole
predecessors.[62] In effect, the changes which eliminated open-
range ranching might be viewed as a sort of "Europeaniza-
tion" of overseas animal husbandry, a reversion to intensive,
careful European methods of tending livestock. The imprint
of the frontier on men and livestock alike is fading rapidly
decade by decade in the overseas settlement areas, and
before long the process of re-Europeanization will be complete.[63] "Ranching" in the fenced-range era has in fact
become synonomous with an advanced, intensive form of
livestock raising, as is evident in the use of the term in some
recent geographical publications.[64]

Viewed from the economic perspective of market accessibility, the presence of open-range cattle ranching on various
overseas European frontiers becomes more understandable.
While we may at first recoil from the notion that the "wild
men" of the pastoral fringes were firmly enmeshed in the
economic system of the Western world, that they were behav-
ing in accord with the dictates of market and functioning as
rational, profit-maximizing entrepreneurs, we must ultimately concede the validity of the von Thünen model. Open-
range cattle ranching cannot be properly understood outside
the context of economic location theory.

The economic logic of the spatial pattern of cattle ranching should not, however, blind us to the role of culture. Herd-

ing systems differed from one group to another, as did lore, material culture, and herding techniques.

The Present Study

Regardless of which of the six viewpoints concerning origins they advocate, most writers on the subject of the Great Plains cattle industry consider the state of Texas to be a pivotal region. For the Hispanic-American origin proponents, Texas is the place where Anglos learned ranching from Mexicans. For defenders of the frontier thesis, Texas is the meeting point for the separate cattle herding traditions of Anglo and Hispano frontiersmen. For those who prefer the environmental explanation, Texas represents the Anglo farmers' first encounter with the problems posed by semiaridity. For these reasons, Texas will be the focus of the present study.

In concentrating upon Texas and the routes leading to it from the East, I do not mean to imply that all ranching in the American West was derived from a Texan model. Southern Arizona and California housed a distinctive cattle-ranching system that owed little if any cultural debt to Texas, a system that also played a role in shaping western ranching. Too, the early nineteenth-century Ohio Valley "cattle kingdom," described in chapter 2, may have had a considerable direct impact on herding in the central and northern Great Plains. Still, Texas was a key center in the evolution and spread of cattle ranching.

Specifically, the theses to be defended in the following chapters are (1) that a form of open-range cattle herding evolved among colonial Anglo-Americans and Afro-Americans on the eastern seaboard in South Carolina and diffused westward along two principal routes; (2) that this colonial Carolina herding system reached Texas and initially took root in three major districts in the eastern part of the state; and (3) that the Carolina cattle-herding culture blended with that of the Hispanic people, producing a hybrid ranching system that spread through much of the Great Plains. Thus the Anglo-American made a major cultural contribution to western cattle ranching.

It will become apparent, I believe, that none of the six origins theses discussed earlier in this chapter, taken alone, explains the evolution of Great Plains ranching. Instead, each provides part of the answer, and I will draw upon them all, in varying measure.

2
Anglo Cattle Herding in the East

ANGLO-AMERICAN CATTLE HERDING arose simultaneously with the establishment of colonies on the eastern seaboard. Cattle accompanied the earliest colonists in most cases, and systematic herding became common within a decade or two of initial settlement.

The Anglo colonial herder economy, well developed even in the late seventeenth century on the Atlantic seaboard, consisted of a complex of traits that were, to some degree, distinct from those characteristic of the Spaniards in Latin America, though many similarities existed between the two herding systems. These traits included (1) the use of open range, unrestricted by fences or natural barriers; (2) the accumulation by individual owners of very large herds, amounting to hundreds or even thousands of cattle; (3) the neglect of livestock; (4) the marking and branding of cattle; (5) the collection at regular intervals of herds at established cowpens; (6) the use of hired, indentured, or enslaved cowhands, constituting a labor force beyond the owner's immediate family; (7) in some instances, absentee ownership; (8) a heavy reliance on shepherd dogs in cowhunts and herd management; (9) the use of salt in herd control; (10) the use of whips to help manage stock; (11) the occasional use of horses in cattle tending; (12) overland cattle drives to feeder areas or markets along regularly used trails, performed by professional or semiprofessional drovers; (13) transhumance, or seasonal movements of the stock; (14) the periodic burning of the range; (15) the combination of cattle and hogs on the same range; (16) a predominance of cattle breeds of British origin, typically rather small animals; and (17) the raising of some field and garden crops, though livestock were the principal products of the system.

The open-range method was employed in the American colonies from the very first. Both European tradition and frontier conditions dictated the use of free range. It had not been the custom in Europe to enclose pastures, and the labor shortage typical of the early colonies simply would not have permitted extensive fence construction. An observer in Pennsylvania, writing only five years after the beginning of English colonization, in 1686, reported cattle running loose in the woods, and similar accounts exist for other colonies.[1] Typically, as in colonial Georgia, the range was public domain, or "king's land," rather than the private property of the herder.[2] In the immediate coastal area, some effort was made to prevent excessive straying by ranging cattle on islands or by building barriers across the necks of peninsulas, as occurred in the Virginia Tidewater.[3] But when the herder economy spread inland, these restraints were necessarily abandoned and a completely open range prevailed.

Neglect of the cattle herds was very early evident, perhaps owing to the shortage of labor. Colonial South Carolinians provided little for their cattle, allowing them "to range wild in the woods," and early Pennsylvanians similarly neglected the livestock.[4] North Carolina herds were neither fed nor watched, as a consequence of which the cattle were "half-starved, stunted beasts," while livestock in Georgia roamed "freely in the woods without herdsmen."[5] A natural consequence of neglect was a reversion of the stock to a feral or semiferal condition. As early as 1652, residents of Maryland were ordered to cease and desist from killing or capturing "wild unmarked Cattell ... and not any further meddle therein."[6] A South Carolina estate inventory of the early 1680s mentions "thirty head of Cattle ... wild in the woods."[7] Another consequence of neglect was widespread rustling. A 1741 North Carolina document laments that "many Wicked Men in this Province ... make it their Business to ride in the Woods and steal Cattle and Hogs, and alter and deface the Marks and Brands of others, and mismark and misbrand Horses, Cattle and Hogs."[8]

In spite of neglect and the resultant losses to predators, poaching Indians, rustlers, and straying, colonial herds multiplied rapidly. As early as 1674, cattle were beginning to be plentiful in South Carolina. Eight years later in that colony, an observer noted that "severall in the Country have great stocks of Cattle," including some herds of as many as 700 or 800 head.[9] A few decades later, a contemporary witness in the same colony described how the cattle "have mightily increased since the first settling of the Colony, about Forty Years ago: It was then reckoned a great Matter for a Planter to have Three or Four Cows: but now, some People have a Thousand Head of Cattle, and for one Man to have Two Hundred is very common."[10] In another description of colonial South Carolina, cattle were said to be "extremely plentiful, many Gentlemen owning from five Hundred to fifteen Hundred Head."[11] Some Pennsylvanians at the time of the American Revolution owned "400 or 500 head of horned cattle, oxen, cows, bulls, calves, and young cattle," while in North Carolina it was not uncommon "to see one man the master of from 300 to 1,200, and even to 2,000 cows, bulls, oxen, and young cattle." A Georgian cattleman in the same era was said to own 440 cattle.[12]

Branding and marking of cattle was the normal practice among eastern seaboard colonists.[13] Regulations for branding stock were introduced before 1700 in South Carolina, and a branding iron dating from the "early days of the settlement" was excavated at Jamestown, Virginia (fig. 2.1).[14] Indeed, it would have been curious if branding and earmarking had not appeared among British settlers in North America, since both practices are common in Great Britain and Ireland. Marking and branding of calves was typically done twice each year, in the spring and fall.[15]

Neglected cattle running free on the open range naturally necessitated periodic roundups or "cow hunts."[16] Pens were built for the purpose of holding the assembled cattle. "Cowpen" was a Virginia term as early as 1634, and the place name "Cowpens Branch" was mentioned in a 1692 document. Marylanders were warned in 1652 that any "unmarked Cattell" they had "gotten up" in "their penn or custody" should be released immediately. In North Carolina, a place called "Cowpenpoint" on Currituck Sound was mentioned in 1692.[17] The name "cowpen" acquired widespread notoriety as a result of the Battle of the Cowpens, fought

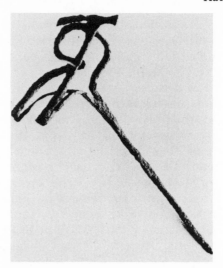

Fig. 2.1   A brand excavated at Jamestown, Virginia, dating from
the early years of settlement. The brand is typically British in
design and differs greatly from Spanish brands (see fig. 4.3). This
Jamestown brand design is very similar to many used by Anglo-
Texans on the Great Plains in the nineteenth century. (Photo copied
from John L. Cotter and J. Paul Hudson, *New Discoveries at
Jamestown: Site of the First Successful English Settlement in
America*, Washington, D.C.: Government Printing Office, 1957, p.
87.)

during the American Revolution in the South Carolina back
country. Another early name for livestock pens, used mainly
in South Carolina, was "craul" or "crawl," perhaps derived
from the Dutch-Portuguese-African *kraal* and imported with
Angolan slaves.[18] The colonial Anglo use of "crawl" could
have facilitated the later adoption of Spanish *corral* in the
West.

In South Carolina, "cowpen" early took on a distinctive
meaning, perhaps best rendered as "ranch" or, more precisely, "ranchstead." The Carolina cowpen consisted of a
clearing or grassy savanna containing several large stock
pens, the dwellings of the manager or owner and his
cowhands, and a garden tract for provisions.[19] A traveler in
1734, for example, came upon "a little sort of settlement,
which proved to be a cow-pen" near the South Carolina-

Georgia border.[20] Contemporary observers clearly perceived "cowpens" and "plantations" to be different types of enterprise in colonial South Carolina.

The owners, managers, and cowboys associated with cattle raising in the South Atlantic seaboard colonies were variously called "cowkeepers," "cowpenkeepers," "pinders," "hands," or "rangers," and they were sufficiently skilled at their work that, according to a South Carolina document, only a "very few" were needed to manage large herds.[21] Both whites and blacks worked as cowhands in colonial times. Crèvecoeur described the former, the prototypical "Crackers," as "a very peculiar class," who had "not enough industry to undertake a lucrative profession or cultivate the earth," a description that could apply equally well to many of the Anglo drifters who became cowboys on the Great Plains after the Civil War. Their surnames were mainly British, a mixture of English and Celtic. A white named Barker was in charge of the cowpen at Savannah, Georgia, in 1738, while others named Brandon, Burnet, Clark, Comming, Lee, and Noland plied their trade in British Florida in the 1760s. In the eighteenth century, white squatters in the southern Appalachians were hired by cattle owners as summer herders.[22]

However, as was mentioned in chapter 1, a great many colonial cowhands were African slaves (fig. 2.2). The use of blacks as cowboys was most common in South Carolina, where the practice was noted throughout the colonial period, beginning in the 1670s.[23] A century later, in the same colony, a newspaper mentioned "2 negroes, excellent cattle hunters, used to the stock," and a 1755 South Carolina document referred to "negroes, to look after the ... kine, hogs, etc."[24] As has been suggested, herding vocabulary such as "cowboy," "buckaroo," and "crawl / corral" may have African and slave roots. But white or black, the herdsmen were not part of the cattle owner's family; the open-range livestock enterprise was not a middle-class, family-farm enterprise. It was, in common with the plantation system, a large-scale operation dependent on labor outside the family unit. Indeed, herding typically served as an adjunct to a plantation in the colonial South, run as a subsidiary of the cash crop operation. The "cattle baron" of the nineteenth-century Great Plains is per-

Fig. 2.2 "The Droves," a cattle drive in the antebellum Appalachians. A black man guides the lead ox while whip-cracking,
mounted drovers follow the herd. This scene was sketched in the
early 1850s in Bath County, Virginia. The cattle were being driven
"from the rich pastures of Monroe and Greenbrier" counties in
present West Virginia to an eastern seaboard market. (Reproduced
from Porte Crayon, [pseud. for David Hunter Strother], "Virginia
Illustrated," *Harper's New Monthly Magazine*, 10 [February 1855]:
303).

haps, in this sense, a direct descendant of the aristocratic planter of the colonial seaboard. Not infrequently, the owner of the cowpen was absentee, resident on a tidewater planta-tion or in a port town.[25] A North Carolina law of 1741 specifi-cally mentioned absentee cattle owners, requiring that "if any strange Cattle shall go into the Cowpen of any Person in this Province, the owner of the Cowpen, if he resides there, or the Overseer or Manager, where the Owner does not reside," must give public notice.[26] A similar pattern of absentee ownership of cattle ranches was typical of West Texas in the late nineteenth century.

Colonial cowboys employed a variety of techniques to manage the semiwild cattle under their care, but the key to herd control was the dog (fig. 2.3). The use of shepherd dogs had ample British, particularly Celtic, precedence. Herding dogs date back to at least the fifteenth century in the British Isles, and the custom seems to have originated there.[27] Writ-ing of the eighteenth-century golden age of open-range cattle raising in the Scottish Highlands, A. R. B. Haldane noted that "dogs were extensively used in droving," and the twentieth-century visitor to the Celtic highlands can still observe such canines at work with sheep.[28] The term "bull-dogging," used at least since the late 1700s in Britain, refers to holding or working cattle and hogs with bulldogs.[29] The British custom spread to the American colonial South, prob-ably in the early eighteenth century. German-speaking immigrants may also have introduced such dogs into Geor-gia and the Carolinas, and it is likely that the Highland Scottish settlers who occupied a portion of eastern North Carolina brought cow dogs from Europe. The descendants of colonial herder dogs can still be found in some parts of the South, particularly the pine barrens of southern Georgia, Alabama, northern Florida, Louisiana, and East Texas. This canine, variously called a "Catahoula," "leopard dog," "bulldog," or "Tennessee brindle," is a medium-to-large hound, often unevenly spotted (merled) or striped (brindled), with light-colored eyes. These are the only dogs consistently able to bring down running wild cows and hogs, an attribute that made them indispensable in rounding up open-range livestock in wooded country. Their technique was to grab the animal by the nose, lip, or ear and pull it down. Artist Fred-

Fig. 2.3 Frederic Remington's "A Cracker Cowboy," Florida, about 1890. This pine barrens herder, an Anglo, is mounted but not equipped to rope. His cow dog accompanies him on the cow hunt. Remington described such Crackers as poor and violent people who earned a scant living herding cattle that belonged to wealthy men. The Cracker herders probably differed little from their eighteenth-century South Carolina ancestors. (Reproduced from Frederic Remington, "Cracker Cowboys of Florida," *Harper's New Monthly Magazine* 91 [1895]: 340.)

eric Remington observed such dogs at work in nineteenth-century Florida, "fierce cur-dogs, one of which accompanies each cattle-hunter, and is taught to pursue cattle, and to even take them by the nose" (fig. 2.3).[30] The better-trained cow dogs were also capable of "cutting" one cow out of a herd.[31]

The modern rodeo event called "bulldogging," both in its name and technique, commemorates the southern canine method. Significantly, "bulldogging" was introduced into rodeo by Bill Pickett, a black Texas cowboy of South Carolina ancestry whose people were no doubt familiar with southern herder dogs from generations of firsthand experience. Pickett imitated the leopard dog to the extent of using his teeth in bulldogging, biting the upper lip of the animal in order to help bring it down—a technique too daring for most of Pickett's rodeo successors.[32]

Horses were also used by cattle herders in the American colonies, but more as transportation than as a control device. In Britain, men on horseback ordinarily accompanied cattle drivers, so it is not surprising that Crèvecoeur found cattle drovers "on horseback" in the back country of South Carolina (fig. 2.2). Roundups, too, required horses. An early Georgia account, from 1739, described a "Pindar" at Savannah "who was to be furnished with Half a Dozen Horses, to enable him at the usual Seasons to hunt for, and bring home to a Cow-Pen, all such Heads as lay scattering many Miles wide, and not to be turned out again without being regularly branded and marked by the rightful Owners." As early as 1712, a resident of South Carolina reported that each spring the practice was "to ride out in search for [cattle] in the woods," and a 1779 document from the same colony mentioned seven horses at one cowpen "kept for hunting the cattle."[33] As was mentioned above, some Gambian slaves in the South may have had African experience as mounted cattle tenders. However, the eastern cowboys lacked the roping skills and techniques associated with the Spanish-American ranching complex, as is evidenced by the absence of the horned saddle (fig. 2.3). Dogs instead of horses bore the brunt of stock control, and even the horses used by the Anglos were taught canine methods. The typical Anglo cutting horse was often a quarter horse, bred by colonial southerners to race short distances and subsequently trained by herders to move and

control stock in a canine manner. Anyone who has watched
the antics of shepherd dogs in Ireland or Scotland cannot
help but be impressed by the similarity to the back-and-forth
movements of a well-trained cutter. The rider astride a cutting horse is superfluous. A quarter horse trained as a cutter
is well named—it is three-quarters dog.

Another effective herd control device widely used by
colonial Anglo herders was salt. Crèvecoeur dealt at length
with this technique, concluding that "salt is an absolute
necessity for governing cattle." "Salt makes up for the lack of
fences," he noted, because it served to keep the semiwild
stock reasonably close to the cowpens. On Saturday, the
normal salting day, the salt was either strewn by handfuls
on the grass near the pens or placed in tree trunks and on flat
stones. Prior to overland drives, the cattle were deprived of
salt, then lured along the trail with it.[34]

Whips (fig. 2.2) were also an important control device, to
some extent taking the place of ropes. Contemporary
sketches of stock drovers, whip in hand, attest to the popular-
ity of the practice in the American Southeast, and the term
"bullwhip" likely derives from this technique. Made of
rawhide, fifteen to twenty-five feet in length, and equipped
with a plaited lash, the bullwhip in a skilled hand was most
effective and intimidating. The word "Cracker," describing
white residents of the Georgia-Florida pine barrens, may
have derived from some popular notion of their whip-
cracking abilities, though such an explanation is unlikely.
Bullwhips were being used to manage range cattle in central
Texas as recently as about 1920.[35]

The lack of roping skills and techniques meant that
colonial Anglo herders had to work their stock by hand in
pens. Frederic Remington, describing the practices of their
Cracker descendants in late nineteenth-century Florida,
noticed that "these men do not use the rope, but work their
cattle in strong log corrals, which are made at about a day's
march apart all through the woods." Somewhat contemptuously, Remington, who had seen and painted cowboys in the
American West, told how a Florida Cracker "goes into the
corral, grabs a cow by one horn, and throwing his other arm
over her back, waits until some other man takes her hind leg,
whereat ensues some very entertaining Graeco-Roman
style" wrestling (fig. 2.4).[36]

Fig. 2.4 Frederic Remington's "Cowboys Wrestling a Bull," Florida, about 1890. Lacking Hispanic roping techniques, these Crackers had to hand-wrestle their cattle in cowpens enclosed by sturdy split-rail fences. The method may have been developed in colonial Carolina. (Reproduced from Frederic Remington, "Cracker Cowboys of Florida," *Harper's New Monthly Magazine*, 91 [1895]: 345.)

Transhumance, the ancient British highland custom of organized movement of herds between summer and winter pastures, appeared at least by the middle eighteenth century in the American South. The early settlers had been quick to recognize the value of the "balds," grassy regions near the summits of many ridges and peaks in the southern Appalachians, as summer pasture, and by the time of the American Revolution, a lowland-to-highland movement, almost identical to that in Scotland and Ireland, was well established between the Atlantic coastal plain and the southern Appalachians. In the late 1700s the mountains of Tugaloo, in the northwestern corner of South Carolina, were supporting 20,000 head of transhumant livestock during the summer months. Typically, hired herders or "keepers" accompanied the livestock to the Appalachian pastures, and one such cowboy could reportedly manage 1,500 head of stock through the proper use of salt, leading the herd back to the plantation in autumn by judicious salting of the trail. Lowland-to-highland cattle transhumance recurred as Anglo frontiersmen spread westward, most notably in the Ozarks and the Rockies, while a variation on the pattern, by which cattle herds were brought seasonally into the Carolina tidewater marshes for pasturage and which had begun even earlier, perhaps by 1700, is still in evidence today in South Carolina.[37]

The seasonal movement of stock, as well as transportation to feeder areas and markets, demanded overland drives of cattle along well-established trails. Initially, these drives were probably directed by cowpen hands, but at least by the middle eighteenth century a class of professional or semiprofessional drovers like that in Britain had arisen.[38] Sizable herds were driven to market at colonial port towns such as Charleston, Philadelphia, and New York, often hundreds of miles distant from the herding districts. Way stations and feeder areas developed along the more important trails.[39] Cattle driving was still being practiced in the southern seaboard states long after the frontier had crossed the Mississippi River, even to the time of the Civil War. For example, many tributary trails funneled into the Asheville Basin of western North Carolina, a feeder area in the middle nineteenth century, and the fattened stock were then driven via a cattle trail of great importance, the Buncombe Turnpike, from Asheville to Warm Springs, Georgia.[40] In this manner, range cattle from Tennessee and Kentucky reached markets in South Carolina and Georgia. On such drives, the traditional use of dogs and whips was in evidence (fig. 2.2). As many as several hundred dogs maintained order among an equal number of cattle on a drive. Drovers, following British custom, rode horseback or went on foot. One or two men led the herd with oxen, while other whip-cracking drovers walked or rode at the rear. Meeting such a trail herd, "one of those monstrous herds of cattle wending their way...eastward" along a southern Appalachian road in antebellum times, one traveler heard "the hoarse bellowing of the beeves, mingled with the oaths and whoops of the drivers"—the same sounds that echoed a generation later on the cattle trails from Texas to Kansas.[41]

Another custom possibly of British origin was range burning. Mention was made of firing savannas to improve forage as early as the 1730s in coastal Georgia, and a group of Highland Scots may have introduced the practice into North Carolina a few decades later.[42] Possibly, too, range firing may have derived from American Indians. In any case, burning became an important element in the Anglo herding system and was widely practiced in savannas, marshes, and woodlands. Writing of the mountains of western South Carolina, Crèvecoeur described such firing: "In order that the pasturelands in these mountains may become more abundant and more nutritive, it is necessary to burn some of the leaves every year toward the end of March," on an appointed day.[43]

Few if any colonial Anglo stockraisers produced only cattle. Typically, large droves of swine shared the range with cattle, as part of the same operation. Similar control techniques were employed for both kinds of stock. In fact, the previously mentioned herder canine of the American South is often called a "hog dog." Certain ethnic groups, such as North Carolina's Highland Scots, devoted less attention to hogs, but most stockmen kept sizable droves.[44]

It would be tempting to link the importance of swine in southern herding to the German colonists of Georgia and South Carolina, since pork consumption in the Old World is much greater in Central Europe than in the British Isles. The fact is, however, that large-scale swine raising was established in the southern colonies long before the Germans arrived. The first settlers of South Carolina, largely of English origin, gained their "chief subsistence" from "Hoggs & Cattle," according to an early observer.[45] This viable livestock combination persisted throughout the open-range era.

Nor were crops ignored. Normally, stockraisers attempted to be largely self-sufficient in food production. A 1779 description of a cowpen in South Carolina mentions acreage adequate "to raise provisions for the negroes."[46] Often this was little more than a kitchen garden, and livestock were clearly the principal products of the system.

The cattle raised on colonial Anglo-American ranges were largely British in origin. In the more southern colonies, primarily the Carolinas, this British character was diluted by an infusion of Iberian stock imported from the West

Indies and run wild from the abandoned Spanish colonies in
Florida and possibly also by some African cattle, but the
prevalent strain was apparently British. These small, tough
animals proved well suited to the American open range,
though a cattle disease in the late 1700s destroyed huge
numbers of stock in the Carolinas.[47]

While similar to the Spanish-American ranching complex, the colonial Anglo system was nonetheless distinctive
in several ways. Typically Anglo traits included the use of
shepherd dogs and bullwhips; the combination of cattle and
hogs on the same range, a contrast to the typical Spanish
cattle-sheep-goat association; range burning, a practice uncommon in the semiarid domain of the Hispanic Americans;
the use of salt in herd control; the prevalence of British-
derived cattle breeds; and the absence of roping skills and
associated paraphernalia, such as the horned saddle and
double cinch. Also, Anglos apparently rounded up cattle less
frequently than did the Spanish-Americans. An Anglo-
Texan, writing of his experiences in the 1850s, referred to a
"Mexican plan" of herding which involved roundups "once a
week or oftener" for purposes of doctoring, branding, and
marketing.[48] Anglos, by contrast, rarely held roundups
oftener than twice a year.

A Carolina Hearth

The Turnerian concept of a herder fringe along the entire
Anglo-American frontier has some measure of validity.
Pennsylvanian and Georgian alike kept open-range livestock. However, herding was unevenly developed along the
frontier; in some colonies stockraisers were of minor significance, in others they attained great importance. Perhaps it is
possible, as several scholars have concluded, to pinpoint a
specific source of large-scale Anglo-American cattle herding.
That source, or hearth area, I believe, lay in the colony of
South Carolina.[49] It is no accident that so many of the references in the preceding section of this chapter are to that
colony.

Contemporary observers had little doubt that the southernmost English colonies were paramount in livestock rais-

ing. Four decades after initial settlement, South Carolina, said one of its residents, "abounds with black Cattle, to a Degree much beyond any other English Colony; which is chiefly owing to the Mildness of the Winters, whereby the Planters are freed from the Charge and Trouble of providing for their Cattle." As early as 1712, "many men" in South Carolina had reportedly "by their stocks of cattle and hogs ... become rich," and by the middle of the eighteenth century, the number of black cattle in the colony was estimated at 80,000 to 100,000, with the annual slaughter of about 12,000 head.[50]

Besides mild winters, South Carolina also boasted extensive pine barrens, many grassy savannas, and numerous cane-filled marshes, which provided good year-round forage for cattle. "A savannah is a large spot of clear land...,
nothing but grass," wrote a visitor to South Carolina in 1734, "exceeding good for a stock of cattle, and on which [people] frequently settle their cow-pens." Wooded, "spacious tracts of higher lands" adjacent to the coastal marshes also served "no other use than for their cattle to range in," even as late as the 1730s. The leaves and sprouts of marsh cane, as well as a "long sort of green moss, which the wind shakes off the trees," provided winter forage for the cattle.[51] The abundance of savannas may have been the work of Southeastern Indian tribes, who had relied on agriculture to a greater degree for their livelihood than did Indians to the north, producing as a result many grass-covered oldfields.

So early did large-scale stockraising achieve dominance in South Carolina that the London proprietors of the colony became dismayed. It was "our designe to have Planters there and not Graziers," they lamented. A 1687 document declared that the "chief subsistence" of the early South Carolina settlers was "by Hoggs & Cattle," and not even the introduction of rice as a plantation crop in the 1690s brought immediate change. As late as 1720, the export of livestock products apparently remained more important than the rice trade. The "Beef Market" acquired a prominent place on the map of colonial Charleston.[52]

The South Carolina nucleus of Anglo cattle herding appears to have lain in the coastal fringe between the Santee River and Port Royal, in the area of earliest settlement, and

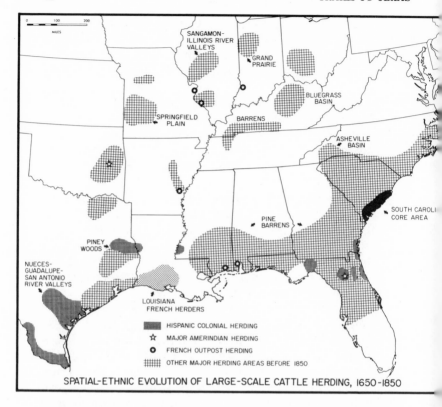

Fig. 2.5 Spatial evolution of cattle ranching in the eastern half of the United States before 1850. (In part after Sauer, Post, Israel, Doran, Dunbar, Arnade, Henlein, Wheeler, Prunty, and Mealor.)

the formative period seems to have been 1670 to 1690 (fig. 2.5). Certain placenames from the coastal area, such as Bull Island and Cow Savanna, are perhaps relics of that era. By about 1720, most of the cowpens were located "southward" of Charleston, though an Indian war seriously disrupted the herding economy of that region for a time. Initially, cattle herds were probably confined mainly to islands and peninsulas—a 1692 estate appraisal, for example, mentioned a herd of 134 cattle on James Island—and the largely black inhabitants of Daufuskie Island, South Carolina, retain an open-range system of raising cattle to the present day. Spread to the interior came quickly, however, and by the middle eighteenth century the focus of cowpen activity had seemingly shifted to the inner coastal plain, west and southwest of Orangeburg.[53]

The principal market for Carolina beef, even as early as 1682, was the West Indies. Barbados, the source of many early South Carolina settlers, "and the several Leward Caribbee Islands, the Bahamas, [and] Jamaica" were of key importance in the trade. The export beef was put up in barrels in late August and September, the season of slaughtering and butchering in South Carolina. "Many thousand barrel" of beef were reportedly shipped to the West Indies each year by 1712. Tallow, tallow candles, cowhides, and some tanned leather also reached foreign markets from South Carolina.[54] A thriving Indian trade in deerskins very early focused on Charleston, with the result that local merchants became accustomed to dealing in large volumes of animal hides. Deerskins and cowhides could easily be shipped together to the British market.

Prior to the middle eighteenth century, it seems, no other English colony rivaled South Carolina in cattle raising. Virginia had been settled earlier, but Wesley Laing's exhaustive study of early cattle raising there revealed no notable large-scale open-range herding activities—in fact, Virginia cattle herds rarely exceeded fifty or seventy-five head. Nor was North Carolina a major ranching colony. The "cowpen complex," according to geographer Roy Merrens, was nowhere present in eighteenth-century North Carolina.[55] As will be documented later, Merrens's claim is not entirely accurate, but his statement is likely true for the greater part of the colony. Georgia was settled much later than South Carolina, beginning in the 1730s, and could not have been an early center of herding.

Early observers and modern scholars seem to agree, then, that colonial South Carolina had no major rivals as a center of open-range livestock herding. Most likely, the key to South Carolina's preeminence lay in a fortunate combination of mild winter weather; abundant pine barren, savanna, and marsh pastures; a hardy breed of mixed British-Spanish cattle; a link to the lucrative West Indian beef market; a British-African heritage of cattle raising; a mercantile group early conditioned to skin and hide exports; and Gambian slaves familiar with herding techniques—a combination found in no other colony. Germans and Scottish Highlanders in and adjacent to South Carolina probably contributed minor elements to the evolving herder system. The surnames of colonial cowpen owners and operators, such as Musgrove, Bellinger, and Macpherson, suggest that a mixture of English, Germans, and Scots were active in the business.[56] Nor should we dismiss the fact that South Carolina was the nearest English neighbor of Spanish Florida, where a notable cattle-ranching industry thrived until about 1700.[57] True, a wide, unpopulated swath separated Carolina from Florida, diminishing the chance for significant cultural exchange between the two colonies. However, during Queen Anne's War, from 1702 to 1704, South Carolinians took part in several invasions of Florida. These raids effectively destroyed the ranching industry in Florida, but it is possible that the invaders could have observed and learned from the Hispanic herders. Still, as mentioned above, the South Carolina cowpen system differed in some fundamental ways from the Spanish-American style of ranching and was already well established a decade or more prior to Queen Anne's War.

South Carolina's leadership in large-scale cattle raising ended between about 1750 and the time of the American Revolution. Cattle disease, range deterioration, expanding cotton acreage, and increasing population density diminished both herd size and open range.[58] About 1750 a local resident complained that "a distemper very fatal to the black cattle and for which we have never been able to find any remedy, has raged here for several years, and has carried off vast numbers," though some parts of the colony were still free of the malady at mid-century. A North Carolina document of 1766 protests against "distempered" cattle brought in from South Carolina. Some observers also felt that overgrazing had partially "exterminated" some canebrakes by 1750. Outlaw bands took an additional heavy toll, particularly in the interior districts. A 1767 petition by hard-pressed cattlemen in the South Carolina back country complained that "our large Stocks of Cattel are either stolen and destroy'd—our Cow Pens are broken up—and all our valuable Horses are carried off... by these Rogues."[59]

The Carolina cattle industry never recovered from these setbacks. By 1840, when the first agricultural census of the United States was taken, only one South Carolina county—

Horry, in the coastal pine barrens at the North Carolina border—had more than twice as many cattle as people.[60] The cowpen keepers had departed, along with a sizable part of the population of South Carolina. Remarkably, in 1850 over 41 percent of the people claiming South Carolina birth resided in some other state.[61] It is among these children of the South Carolina diaspora that the bearers of the Anglo cattle-ranching culture will be sought.

Diffusion along the Coastal Corridor

Large-scale open-range cattle raising seems to have spread from South Carolina along two principal routes. The more important of these stretched southward and westward along a coastal corridor, following the belt of longleaf pine forest that parallels the shore all the way to East Texas (fig. 2.6).[62] Through repeated burnings, these pine barrens, like those in South Carolina, had taken on an open appearance devoid of underbrush, with fine stands of grass growing among the trees. Also reminiscent of Carolina were streamside cane-brakes and scattered prairies, which provided still more for-age for the herds of cattle. Moreover, these piney lands were poorly suited for cash crops, freeing the herders from compe-tition with farmers and planters. As early as 1741, for exam-ple, governmental authorities in Georgia recognized that "Pine Barren Land" was poor for agriculture.[63]

The South Carolina cowpen culture apparently began its westward diffusion in adjacent Georgia. Only several years after the founding of Georgia, the colony's trustees pur-chased herds from South Carolina cowpen owners, including 150 cattle driven to the trust's Savannah cowpen in 1734. By 1738 the trust also owned a "Cow-Pen" at Old Ebenezer, including "a great Stock" of cattle. The pinder there, together with his counterpart at the trust's Savannah cowpen, was ordered to round up the "near a Thousand" cattle estimated to be running loose in the "North Part of the Province." The Georgia trustees continued for some years to maintain a large cowpen. In 1747, for example, they instructed "that the Cowpen Keeper be ordered, that as the Season for Hunting and Driving up Cattle is near at Hand, He immediately puts all his Fences in good Repair." Purchases from the govern-ment cowpen were mentioned as late as 1752. Another

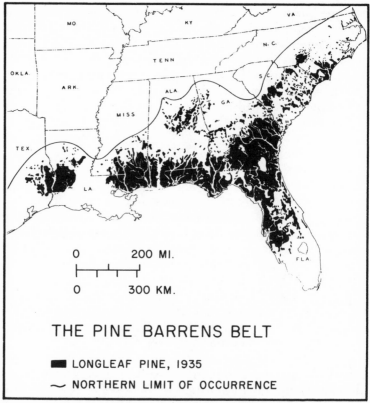

THE PINE BARRENS BELT

■ LONGLEAF PINE, 1935
∼ NORTHERN LIMIT OF OCCURRENCE

Fig. 2.6 This corridor, or belt, provided a major natural route for the westward expansion of the Carolina cattle culture (compare this map to Fig. 2.7). (Copied from W. G. Wahlenberg, *Longleaf Pine: Its Use, Ecology, Regeneration, Protection, Growth, and Management*, Washington, D.C.: Charles Lathrop Pack Forestry Foundation and the U.S. Dept. of Agriculture, 1946, p. 44.)

cowpen, privately owned, had been established by 1734 on the Georgia side of the border "about six miles from Savannah."[64]

Because of Oglethorpe's policy of maintaining Georgia as a slaveless smallholder haven, the South Carolina herder intrusion progressed slowly at first. Only after 1752 did the immigration begin in earnest, with cattlemen in the vanguard. "To make room for the yearly immense Increase" of cattle in South Carolina, wrote contemporary observer William DeBrahm, "great Herds...have been driven...into the

Neighbouring Province of Georgia...since 1757," particularly into the frontier lands between the Savannah and Ogeechee rivers. There, he continued, the cattle were "kept in Gangs under the Auspicie of Cowpen Keepers which move ...from Forrest to Forrest in a measure as the Grass wears out, or the Planters approach them." The planters' smaller herds, reported DeBrahm, were "prejudicial to the great Stocks, from among which the former draw the Bulls, and sometimes the Calves...and as the Cows follow the bulls also, great Gangs are apt to be misled to the Pasturage near the Plantations, which not affording sufficient Range for a great stock, the Cattle are in Danger to grow poor and sick, for which reason the Cowpen Keepers prefer their Solitude to the Neighbourhood of Planters."[65]

By the time of the Revolutionary War, the cowpens of Carolina's children were scattered through much of the Georgia coastal plain. An anonymous observer in the 1770s described the scattering of rural population in Georgia, noting that "they generally plant themselves at a distance, for the sake of having an uncultivated country around them for their cattle to range in." Some Georgians in more thickly settled districts near the coast sent their cattle and cowkeepers back into the interior for grazing.[66]

From Georgia, Anglo cattlemen soon expanded into Florida, where the place name "Cowpen" and the profession of "cow keeper" occurred as early as the 1760s. Eventually, in the latter part of the nineteenth century, these "Cracker Cowboys" reached Lake Okeechobee and the Everglades (fig. 2.3).[67]

A larger, more significant prong of diffusion reached westward across southwest Georgia, the Florida Panhandle, southern Alabama, southeast Mississippi, and the "Florida Parishes" of eastern Louisiana. Leapfrogging the Mississippi River, a vanguard of Anglo cattle herders, well mixed with French Cajuns, exploded into the tall grass coastal prairie of southwest Louisiana to reach the borders of Spanish Texas.[68] The census of 1840 showed the pine barrens-coastal prairie route of diffusion to be intact all the way from the Atlantic coastal plain of Georgia to the southeastern corner of Texas (fig. 2.7). By mid-century, South Carolinians were well distributed all along the chain of coastal states, and the pine barrens no doubt housed a substantial share of them. Over 30 percent of the natives of South Carolina lived

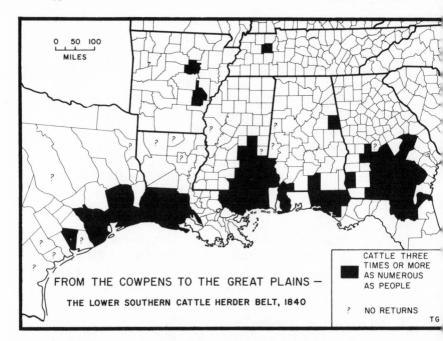

0   50   100
MILES

FROM THE COWPENS TO THE GREAT PLAINS —

THE LOWER SOUTHERN CATTLE HERDER BELT, 1840

CATTLE THREE
TIMES OR MORE
AS NUMEROUS
AS PEOPLE

?   NO RETURNS

TG

Fig. 2.7 In 1840, the coastal southern cattle herding belt was
intact all the way from the pine barrens of eastern Georgia to the
Coastal Prairie of Southeast Texas. Virtually the entire length of
the crucial diffusionary link between South Carolina and southern
Texas was occupied by cattle raisers in 1840, and some cattlemen
had migrated the entire length of this belt. (Sources: *Compendium...of the Sixth Census, 1840*, 1841, and MS Texas tax lists,
Republic of Texas, 1840, in the Texas State Archives, Austin.)

in Georgia, Alabama, Florida, Mississippi, and Louisiana in
1850, and one contemporary account names Carolina and
Georgia as the principal sources of herders in the pine
barrens of southern Mississippi.[69] So rapid was the westward thrust that a man who had learned the cattle business
in colonial South Carolina could have ended his days raising
cattle in Louisiana or even Texas.

What began as a distinctly South Carolinian ranching
system east of the Savannah River was considerably inter-
nationalized and somewhat modified by the time it reached
the Sabine River border of Texas.[70] Hispanic and Franco-
American elements were incorporated between the Savan-

nah and the Sabine, with increasing frequency to the west. Anglo herders encountered French cattle raisers as far east as Biloxi and Mobile, where remnant French populations were still present in the 1790s, finding "their chief employment is raising of cattle and stock, and making pitch and tar."[71] Far more important was the cattle-herding complex in French Louisiana. One plantation there boasted 300 head of cattle by 1724, brands were registered as early as 1739, and sizable herds were common by mid-century. The period 1750 to 1775 in south Louisiana witnessed a large-scale cattle boom.[72] Acadian immigrants contributed to this rapid rise, and French-speaking free blacks, variously described as "hommes de couleur libres," "quarterons libres," or the like, also registered cattle brands in eighteenth- and early nineteenth-century Louisiana. Access to the expansive coastal prairies of southern Louisiana was also a key in the development of large-scale cattle raising by the French. By the 1770s, the Cajun parishes in the coastal grasslands housed five to seven times as many cattle as people, increasing to fifteen to one by the early nineteenth century.[73] In heritage, the Louisiana system of *vacheries*, or ranches, owed a cultural debt to the longstanding importance of cattle in France and in Franco-American settlements (fig. 2.8).

The French cattle herding around Arkansas Post, on the lower Arkansas River near its confluence with the Mississippi, is best regarded as an offshoot of the Louisiana complex. Crèvecoeur referred to these herders as Acadians, noting that, aside from a few small fields, "their riches consist only in the number of their cattle," which grazed on the open range provided in the summer by the Grand Prairie of Arkansas and in the winter by river bottom canebrakes.[74] By the late 1700s, the French cattlemen at Arkansas Post were using salt as a herd-management device—a technique generally indicative of Anglo influence. When the area around Arkansas Post began acquiring Anglo-American settlers after about 1820, the newcomers perpetuated and enlarged upon the French cattle economy. By 1840, the prairies from Arkansas Post north into White County were the principal focus of the state's cattle herding. Arkansas County, which included the old Post, had over four times as many cattle as people, and the ratio in White County was three to one.[75] A tie to French Louisiana is suggested by the practice of driving

Fig. 2.8 Vacherie, Louisiana, commemorates in its name the importance of cattle ranching in eighteenth- and early nineteenth-century French Louisiana. The town lies on the Mississippi River between Baton Rouge and New Orleans. In France, *vacherie* means "cow barn," but in colonial Louisiana it came to mean "ranch." (Photo 1979 by author.)

cattle from the Arkansas Grand Prairie to market at New Orleans.[76]

The contact of pine barrens Anglos with Hispanos began well east of the Mississippi River. Florida, under renewed Spanish rule until 1819, housed a diverse population. Around Pensacola in the 1790s, cattle herds of 200 to 1,000 head were common, and the local population included both Anglos and Hispanos. In southern Mississippi, also, Spanish influence could be detected. The Anglos' typical "Florida cow" was largely of longhorn blood, and Iberian stock were also prevalent in southern Mississippi.[77]

Hispanicization of herding was greatest in southern Louisiana, perhaps as a result of the lengthy Spanish rule there, spanning the last third of the eighteenth century, but more likely because of contacts between Spanish ranches in South Texas and Cajun herders in Louisiana. Texas longhorns were driven in large numbers to southern Louisiana at the time of the American Revolution and perhaps even earlier. The material culture of Louisiana French cattle herding cleary reflected Hispanicization. Cultural geographers Fred Kniffen and Lauren Post found, for example, Hispanic-style brands (see fig. 4.3) and a whirligig, or horsehair spinner, of Spanish origin in southwestern Louisiana. The spinner, called a *tarabi* by the Cajuns, is an apparent borrowing of the Mexican *tarabilla*.[78] This device was unknown in the Anglo pine barrens cattle complex.

In addition to Anglos, French, blacks, and Hispanos, the pine barrens cattle belt also housed American Indian herders. Even as early as 1734, an Anglo-Indian mixed-blood owned a cowpen near Savannah, Georgia, and in the early 1700s, individual groups among the Five Civilized Tribes began developing large herds. Colonial Georgia records mention a Seminole Indian chief named "Cowkeeper" in 1757. William Bartram, sojourning among Cowkeeper's people near modern Gainesville, Florida, in the 1770s, saw "innumerable droves of cattle" on the expansive Alachua Savanna. While Bartram watched, "a party of Indians on horseback appeared upon the savanna, to collect together several herds of cattle which they drove along near our camp." Muddying the ethnic waters still more, Bartram reported that Cowkeeper's clan appeared "tinctured with Spanish civilization" and had many blacks among their number.[79] Indeed, the Seminole and Creek Indians may have preserved Spanish ranching techniques in Florida and Georgia, later passing Hispanic horseback skills on to pine barren Anglos.

The Creeks in eastern Alabama owned some large cattle herds at least by the 1790s, when Colonel Benjamin Hawkins observed certain individuals who owned 100 to 400 head in the Tallapoosa River Valley. Even earlier, several Indian groups in Louisiana had adopted open-range cattle herding, apparently in imitation of the Cajuns, and had registered their brands in the record books of the districts of Opelousas and Attakapas. Some of the Cherokees and Chickasaws, too,

eventually acquired large cattle holdings, though the Cherokees initially resisted the acceptance of domestic bovines.
Later, in the middle nineteenth century, Indians of the Five
Civilized Tribes transplanted the coastal cattle culture to
eastern Oklahoma.[80]

The end product of ethnic mixing along the belt of pine
barrens and coastal prairies was a thoroughly creolized
herding system, one with roots in South Carolina, Spanish
America, and New France. By the time cattle herders following this coastal routeway entered the forests and grasslands
of East Texas after 1815, they were bearers of a mixed tradition. South Carolinian ancestries and traits still abounded
among them, but Hispanic horseback skills had been acquired and more Iberian genes were in their livestock. Rom-
ance language words had entered their herding vocabulary.
Some loanwords in the Anglo-Texan ranching speech long
assumed to have been adopted from Hispanos in South
Texas—words such as "lasso," "lariat," and "calaboose"—
may instead have entered English in Louisiana or even Georgia and Florida, in which case the words may have passed
from Spanish to Creole French and then to English. Quite
possibly, a ranching lingua franca borrowed from English,
Spanish, French, and even Amerindian tongues was spoken
along the coastal corridor.[81] The bloodlines of the herders
themselves had become more diverse in transit through the
pine barrens and prairies, a result of intermarriage with
Cajuns and Indians. A few herder families crossing the
Sabine into Texas were "redbones"—a mixture of white,
black, and Indian.[82]

But in spite of the creolization of this herder culture,
many South Carolina traits reached the borders of Texas
intact. All across the coastal belt, Carolina practices and
vocabulary were implanted. Nineteenth-century Florida, for
example, abounded with "cowpens" and "cow dogs," and
range burning was a common practice there. Pine barrens
herds were often, or even typically, owned by absentee planters whose homes were in the cotton and sugar cane districts,
a duplication of the pattern in colonial South Carolina. Black
cowhands, so instrumental in shaping the Carolinian system, plied their trade all through the coastal belt. One traveler said the blacks there were "among the best horsemen in
the world."[83]

As the pine barrens–coastal prairie ranching complex expanded, Gulf ports eclipsed Charleston and other eastern seaboard towns as major terminals of cattle trails. Punta Rassa and Pensacola in Florida, Mobile, Natchez, and New Orleans became important "cow towns."[84] As had been true of colonial Carolina, a major market for pine barrens cattle was the West Indies.

Diffusion through the Upper South and Midwest

The second possible routeway of diffusion of the Carolina herding system led northwest across the Piedmont, through the Appalachians, and into the great interior lowland of North America (fig. 2.5). This second pathway apparently also led eventually to the borders of Texas.

The first steps along the interior route were taken about 1750, when South Carolinian cowkeepers spread onto the Piedmont in the western part of their native colony. "Horned cattle" were being driven into the upper regions of South Carolina at least by 1756, and likely earlier.[85] The Revolutionary War Battle of the Cowpens, fought on the South Carolina Piedmont near the modern town of Cowpens in 1781, commemorates in its name the prevalent colonial economy of the region. About the same time, transhumant cattle herders from around Orangeburg began using Appalachian mountain summer pastures near the Tugaloo River in the far western tip of South Carolina.[86] In the back country, the lowland Carolina system of large-scale open-range herding spread quickly among settlers of Scotch-Irish descent, who had filtered south from Pennsylvania. The Scotch-Irish had a long tradition of livestock herding in Europe, though their most recent British experience had been with sheep raising. They took readily to the cattle-hog combination.

Only briefly did the cowpen culture thrive in the South Carolina back country. Cattle disease and a large influx of war veterans to Piedmont bounty lands after 1782 quickly ended the heyday of the ranchers there. New lands were necessary, and the result was a surge to the continental interior.

The next steppingstone on the path westward was provided by North Carolina, though the Tarheels never seriously rivaled their neighbors to the south in scale of cattle raising. Some South Carolinian herders had expanded their operations into their adjacent sister colony as early as the first half of the eighteenth century. Initially, they were lured by the abundant pine barrens and marshes along the coast. North Carolina records dating from 1715 suggest that "cowpen" was being used at that time in the South Carolinian meaning of "ranch." A law passed in that year mentioned "persons that shall have at... their respective Cowpens or Plantations any stray cattle," a clear indication that the two were regarded as different types of enterprise.[87] In 1735 mention was made of "the Lands called the cowpen" on the Northeast Cape Fear River, north of Wilmington near the Holly Shelter Swamp. Acts passed in 1741 and 1766 in North Carolina made similar references. The early coastal expansion into North Carolina ultimately produced a significant cluster of cattle-ranching activity in the marshlands between Albemarle Sound and the Neuse River. The Pamlico River port of Bath became the major export depot. The absentee owner of a ranching operation in this area wrote in 1750 that he owned "two places... with tennants on Shares with what we cal Cowe Penns, in which way Cattle and Hogs are easily raised under careful Industrious People." Nearby, across Pamlico Sound, the Outer Banks shared the cattle culture of the coastal mainland. The importance of herding in the coastal marshes, pine barrens, and islands, involving "prodigious numbers" of stock, apparently misled one eighteenth-century observer, who assumed that the entire colony of North Carolina resembled its southern coastal fringe and concluded that "such herds of cattle and swine are to be found in no other colonies."[88] In the long run, however, this northward thrust along the coast of North Carolina proved to be a diffusionary cul-de-sac, similar to the expansion into the Florida peninsula to the south. Boxed in by the sea and the fertile farm areas, the coastal cattlemen could not continue their spread northward.

Instead, the more important diffusion occurred farther west, in the back country of North Carolina. The growth of the Piedmont as a herding area was mentioned in the colonial records of North Carolina in 1755, when an official noted that "the great increase of settlements in this Province of late in the Countries at a distance from the sea, has increased the

Breeding of Cattle and Hogs." Partially responsible for this growth were absentee South Carolinians, who began establishing cowpens managed by overseers on the public domain of certain border counties. One result of this intrusion was a 1766 law "to prevent the Inhabitants of South Carolina [from] driving their Stocks of Cattle from thence to range and feed in this Province." "Whereas of late years," read the act, "many of the Inhabitants of South Carolina have made it a Practice to fix Cowpens, and settle People with Large Stocks of Cattle (though they are not Owners of any Lands) in this Province, which destroys the Range, and greatly injures the poor inhabitants of several of the Counties bordering South Carolina," it was henceforth required that landownership would be a prerequisite for using North Carolina's public range. The fact that these cattle were owned by absentee South Carolinians would explain their absence from the tax rolls and estate inventories of North Carolina, an absence which led Merrens wrongly to conclude that interior counties housed few if any sizable ranching operations in colonial times.[89]

The most significant expansion into North Carolina apparently came during and after the Revolution. Perhaps the most important route of diffusion was Saluda Gap, later to become a traditional emigration route of South Carolinians, leading from the Piedmont into the Asheville area west of the Blue Ridge. Migrating cattlemen apparently used this strategic routeway to implant a large-scale herding economy in the Asheville Basin in the 1780s. About the same time, local Cherokee Indians also began to acquire sizable herds. Buncombe County, of which Asheville is the seat, initiated a cattle-brand registration procedure by the early 1790s. A micro-study of cattle raising in certain districts of western North Carolina, including the Asheville Basin, revealed persistent activity through the first half of the nineteenth century and documented such typical Anglo practices as droving, salting, and the use of slave cowhands.[90]

From the Asheville Basin, the presumed diffusionary path westward across the mountains has grown faint. Unlike the movement through the pine barrens of the coastal Lower South, where cattle ranching expanded through an elongated, contiguous belt and endured for many decades, the progression across the mountains and into the interior lowlands seems to have involved a leapfrogging from one district to another, leaving areas of minor herding importance in between (fig. 2.5). Large-scale open-range livestock raising apparently did not survive long in any of these scattered districts, giving way quickly to more intensive forms of agriculture. Tennessee, directly west of the Asheville Basin, seems not to have inherited the Carolina cowpen culture, for I have encountered no evidence that large-scale livestock raising was ever practiced in east or middle Tennessee. The problem may be the result of an absence of studies on the district and regional scales for the Volunteer State. Certainly the potential for cowpen activity was present in Tennessee, for over fifteen thousand South Carolinians resided there by 1850. Perhaps suggestive is the remark by a late-eighteenth-century traveler that "in the state of Tenasee cattle at present support themselves among the reeds, pea-vines, rye-grass, and clover."[91]

Kentucky, rather than Tennessee, seems to have housed the earliest clearly defined herding regions west of the mountains. There, in the glades and prairie barrens of the Pennyroyal and the Bluegrass Basin, a thriving cattle industry arose before 1800, though geographer Carl O. Sauer was overambitious in claiming that "the Pennyroyal was the first area in the country in which grazing developed on a large scale."[92] The early years of cattle raising in Kentucky were hindered by Indian wars. Daniel Boone, in 1776, lamented that he had lost an "abundance of cattle" to the Indians, and in attacks on the Bluegrass settlements, "most of the cattle around the stations were destroyed." The 1780s were better years, and herds multiplied rapidly. The key to this development in Kentucky may well have been the presence of sizable tall grass prairies, or "barrens," a vegetative type more common in Kentucky than in neighboring Tennessee. In any case, by the 1790s, a class of herder folk occupied much of central and southern Kentucky, a "people who have . . . long been in the custom of removing farther and farther back as the country becomes settled, for the sake of . . . what they call range for their cattle." Cattle herding in Kentucky peaked before 1830 and afterwards went into a decline. By 1840, in only three Bluegrass and Pennyroyal counties were cattle twice as numerous as people.[93]

From Kentucky, cattlemen spread across the Ohio River into the lower Midwest (fig. 2.5). By about 1810 Kentuckians had begun pasturing cattle herds in southwestern Ohio, and soon thereafter the districts along and between the Scioto and Miami rivers, containing some small prairies, became an important range.[94] Cincinnati rose to become a major meat-packing center. The path of Kentucky's cattle complex led next to the Grand Prairie of northwestern Indiana, where herding thrived by the mid-1820s. From there it was a short leap to the prairies along the Sangamon and Illinois rivers, where expansive grasslands were soon utilized by a number of notable Illinois cattle barons. Perry County, southeast of St. Louis, became the focus of another Illinois cattle district, and by 1840 the county boasted almost seventeen thousand head, over five times the number of people.[95]

Simultaneously with developments in Indiana and Illinois came the rise of open-range cattle raising in parts of Missouri. From a pre-1820 base in the Missouri River Valley between Boonville and Lexington, including the Boonslick country and the Peteatsaw (Petitsault) Plains, cattlemen from the Ohio Valley moved south to establish a cattle industry in the western part of the Ozark Plateau and adjacent prairie plains westward to the Kansas border. The Springfield Plain, as early as 1832, was a major cattle-herding area. Boonville retained its original importance and became a center for slaughterhouses serving the western Ozark counties.[96]

In the westward diffusion of Anglo cattle raisers through the American heartland, livestock fattening farms normally displaced open-range herding after a relatively brief interval. Usually, feeders shunted breeders out within a decade or two, creating the well-known "Corn Belt" type of operation. The model for this transition was perhaps the Asheville Basin, where herder-breeders scarcely held on until the end of the eighteenth century before being superseded by feeding operations. Kentucky range cattle were initially driven to Virginia or West Virginia for fattening. "The number of horned cattle is very considerable in Kentucky," wrote an early observer, adding the comment that dealers "purchase them lean and drive them in droves of from two or three hundred to [West] Virginia, along the river

Potomack, where they sell them to graziers, who fatten them." Shortly thereafter, feeder farms came to dominate Kentucky itself, spreading quickly from there across the Ohio River. In rapid succession, herder-breeders were displaced by farmer-feeders in the Bluegrass and lower Midwest.[97] Cattlemen retreated westward, abandoning ranges east of the Mississippi long before mid-century. By the time of the Civil War, Missouri, too, had joined the Corn Belt. The spatial pattern of herding / Corn Belt segregation was thus established. Frederick Jackson Turner's view of open-range livestock raising as a transitory frontier economy accurately describes the agricultural succession in the Ohio Valley.

The rapid displacement of herders by feeders likely reflects a Pennsylvanian–Middle Atlantic influence. Such influence would be expected in the Ohio Valley, considering the major flow of migration. Livestock feeding was a traditional Central European type of farming, possibly introduced to Pennsylvania by German-speaking immigrants. In much of the Ohio Valley, an early wave of settlers from the southern states was soon followed and in part displaced by people from the Middle Atlantic states. The early, southern wave bore the ranchers; feeders, such as Isaac Funk, followed close on their heels. Carolina hurried through the Ohio Valley; Pennsylvania abided there.

The question remains as to what degree the transitory herding system of the Ohio Valley and Missouri was influenced by the South Carolina tradition. The connection, if there was one, is unproven. But it is no great distance from the Asheville Basin through various mountain gaps to the Bluegrass and Pennyroyal. Only three thousand South Carolinians resided in Kentucky at the census of 1850, the first to enumerate birthplaces, but by then the pioneer cattlemen would have gone on west. Some evidence of a South Carolina connection with Ohio Valley herders comes from Texas. The Halsells, a famous Texas ranching clan, had family ties in both South Carolina and Kentucky. A similar migration pattern was followed by Francis Henderson, a self-declared "stockraiser" in Guadalupe County, Texas. Henderson, a 1780 native of South Carolina, which was also the birthplace of his wife, had children born in Illinois (1812) and Arkansas (1825). Also, Kentucky livestock were regularly marketed in South Carolina, likely along old paths of migration. Indeed, some Kentucky cattle in the early days were driven to the Asheville Basin for fattening.[98]

More significant, perhaps, was the appearance in Kentucky, the lower Midwest, and Missouri of certain herding traits associated with the colonial cowpens of Carolina. Range burning, branding, salting, overland drives to market, mounted drovers, hog raising, and the use of bullwhips all occurred along the path to the interior lowlands, and there were occasional black cowhands, though hired whites were more common (fig. 2.2).[99] Transhumance was practiced at various places along the presumed Asheville–Kentucky–Ohio Valley–Missouri route, and in fact the Kentucky ranges were probably used at first as summer pastures. Kentucky glades were being grazed in this manner at least by 1784. Conceivably, the descriptions brought back by transhumant herders could have prompted herders in the Asheville Basin and other Appalachian valleys to shift their headquarters to Kentucky. By the early 1800s, Kentucky stockraisers, in turn, were driving cattle to seasonal pastures in southwestern Ohio, a prologue to the development of open-range herding north of the Ohio River, and in later decades, Ozark cattlemen in Missouri drove herds south to canebrakes in Arkansas for the winter.[100]

While the herding culture of the coastal Lower South became considerably creolized during westward diffusion, the cattle raisers along the upper southern–lower midwestern route preserved a much purer British-American tradition. Apparently absent were the massive infusions of Spanish and French influence that occurred in the pine barrens and coastal prairies. Still, the Kentuckians and their progeny overran small French posts such as Vincennes, Cahokia, and St. Louis, where sizable herds of cattle were kept. A traveler in 1778 reported "large stocks of black cattle" at both Cahokia and St. Louis.[101] If we may judge from the success of these few French in transferring their word *prairie* into the Anglo vernacular, displacing "barrens" and "glade," they could well have exerted some influence. Perhaps the cluster of cattle herding revealed by the census of 1840 in Perry County, Illinois, owed a cultural debt to nearby French Kaskaskia. Without doubt, cattle of French and

French-Canadian ancestry mixed into the bloodlines of
Anglo herds in the Midwest.[102] A detailed study of the Mississippi Valley French herding economy is much needed.

Nor was Spanish influence totally lacking in the Ohio
Valley. Kentucky cattlemen acquired some longhorn stock
from the Chickasaw Indians in western Tennessee as early
as 1810, and longhorns from eastern Oklahoma and Texas
were found in Missouri by the 1840s.[103] Apparently the Spanish influence was confined to these stock introductions and
did not extend to herding techniques.

Conclusion

From a cradle in early colonial South Carolina, then, a distinctly Anglo cattle-herding culture seems to have spread
rapidly westward along two major routeways in a pincer
movement that converged on Texas from the east and northeast even as early as 1820. In the following chapter, attention
will be focused on Southeast Texas, where the creolized coastal southern cattle culture, shaped by Anglo, black, Hispano,
and French alike, first entered Texas.

3
The Coastal Prairie Corridor of Southeast Texas

By THE EARLY NINETEENTH CENTURY, the cattle-herding belt along the coastal Lower South, from Carolina through Louisiana, pointed like an extended finger toward Texas, toward the diamond-shaped area south of San Antonio where a ranching system had been implanted by Hispanic settlers in the eighteenth century (fig. 2.5).[1] If this finger did in fact reach farther westward, allowing the tip to touch the Hispanic diamond and link South Carolina to Mexico, the intervening space along the Texas coast would have to have been bridged. If, in short, the thesis of diffusion of herding traits from the East, from the Carolina core, to the Great Plains by way of the coastal South is to be validated, then abundant evidence of early cattle ranching by Anglos in Southeast Texas must be presented. Let us begin with brief descriptions of the Coastal Prairie environment and its settlement.

The Environmental Setting

The proposed crucial western link in the great route of diffusion lay along a corridor formed by the Texas Coastal Prairie, a narrow belt of grassland driven like a wedge between the sea and the interior forests. Stretching from the Louisiana border on the lower Sabine River westward beyond the Guadalupe and ultimately to the Rio Grande, the Texas Coastal Prairie offered a splendid natural setting for cattle ranching (fig. 3.1).

Two major subdivisions of the Coastal Prairie can be detected. Nearest to the coast is a narrow strip of marsh and

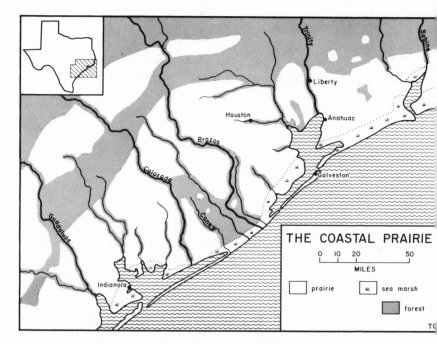

Fig. 3.1 The Coastal Prairie is an exotic vegetational wedge driven between the forests of East Texas and the Gulf of Mexico. (Sources: Various U.S. Geological Survey maps, soil surveys, and contemporary accounts.)

salt grasses, a zone subjected at intervals to inundations from the hurricane-aroused Gulf of Mexico. Adjacent to this strip of sea marsh, between it and the forests to the north, is a much broader zone characterized originally by tall, coarse grasses, mainly species of andropogon, panicum, and paspalum. Contemporary observers described "a dense mat of grass," decorated in the spring by "wild flowers... spread around... in the utmost profusion, and in wonderful variety." The wide expanse of prairie was often compared to the ocean, and some observers found the scenery "too monotonous to be agreeable." At times, the traveler completely lost sight of timber, but often scattered groves of trees, called "woods," "islands," or "motts," diversified the landscape. These groves, of oak, pine, gum, and cedar, generally had little or no undergrowth and presented "outlines perfectly well defined and often surprisingly regular."[2] Anglo-

American settlers, as early as 1824, followed Carolina custom and burned the prairies in the short period of vegetational dormancy, in order to destroy weeds and bushes and to make room for new grass. Soon after the fire passed, a lush green growth of grass would spring up on the blackened surface, reaching a height of six inches or so by March, and in the late summer, the grasses would have grown "nearly up to the horses' knees." In the salt grass marshes of Chambers County, intentional burning continued into the twentieth century.[3]

Slicing across the Coastal Prairie at regular intervals are numerous rivers, creeks, and bayous, trending generally in a northwest-to-southeast direction, each paralleled by a narrow ribbon of timber. In their native condition, these *galeria* forests contained a variety of trees. The more eastern streams, such as the Sabine and the Trinity, had bottom forests dominated by cypress, pine, magnolia, and ash; while along the Brazos, the Colorado, and other western rivers were live oaks, cottonwoods, pecans, hackberrys, and laurels ("wild peach"). A mournful growth of Spanish moss often bedecked the trees of the *galeria* forests. Canebrakes, some of immense proportions, also lined the streams, both as undergrowth in the forests and in open stretches with a few trees. The largest expanse of cane extended along Caney Creek for about seventy miles, with scarcely a tree to be seen in the entire distance. Sprouting annually from its perennial root stock, the cane was grasslike and low early in the year, but in maturing it took on a woody character and reached twenty or twenty-five feet in height. Generally, the *galeria* forests were narrow, only about one-half mile to six or seven miles in width, and the prairie reached the river banks in many places. However, in the area between the lower Brazos and Colorado, where repeated changes in the courses of the rivers had occurred, the alluvial forests extended the entire distance between the streams (fig. 3.1). The wooded areas did not reach closer than several miles to the coast, even along the largest rivers, ending instead at the fringe of the sea marsh.[4]

Climatically, the Coastal Prairie is a humid area. In the eastern part, over fifty inches of precipitation can be expected each year, while amounts decrease to twenty or thirty inches toward the west. Rainfall is well distributed through-

out the year, though many weather stations report a hurri-
cane-induced maximum in September. Temperatures range
from averages in the eighties for the warmest month to the
mid-forties in the coldest, and the growing season varies in
length from about 260 days in the interior up to 335 days on
the coast. The entirety of the Coastal Prairie lies within the
humid subtropical climate, as defined in the Köppen-Tre-
wartha classification.[5]

Cattle could graze for ten months or more each year on
the open prairies, taking refuge during the short winter in the
bottom forests to feed on canebrakes and Spanish moss.
Since the Coastal Prairie was humid, with many flowing
streams, the cattle had abundant water, and it was not even
necessary to put out blocks of salt for them, because the dew
on the grass was saline and the vegetation contained ample
amounts of salt.[6]

Settlement of the Coastal Prairie

The occupation of the Coastal Prairie west of the Sabine
began about 1820. At that time, Texas was a virtually empty,
poorly guarded outpost of Latin America, though its position
astride the path of the explosive westward surge of the southern Anglo-Americans might have allowed a perceptive contemporary observer to predict its future.

The pioneers who penetrated Southeast Texas were,
under Mexican law, of two types—legal and illegal. The first
type were Anglo-Americans who came as participants in
organized colonization efforts encouraged by the Mexican
government. The most important colony founded in this way
was that of Stephen F. Austin.[7] The colony embraced a sizable cross section of the Coastal Prairie (fig. 3.2), and many
settlers found homes in those grasslands. In fact, the combination of fertile bottomlands and lush prairie made the corridor the most desired settlement area in the colony. The
population attracted by Austin rose steadily from the initial
establishment in 1821 to reach 1,800 by 1826, 5,700 by 1831,
and perhaps 10,000 by the time of the Texan revolution.[8]
About one in every ten persons in the colony was black. At
the time of the first federal census in Texas, 1850, the counties containing the Coastal Prairie portion of the old Austin

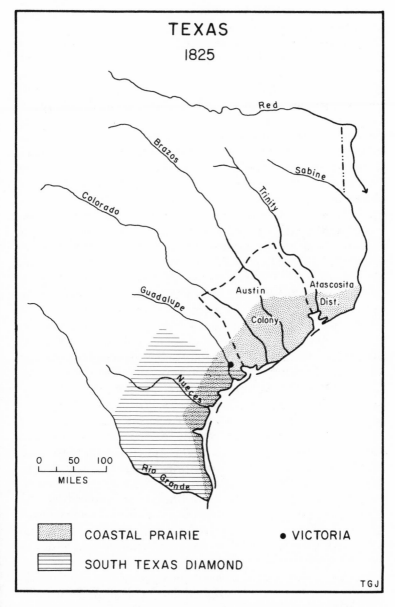

Fig. 3.2 The South Texas diamond-shaped area, center of early Hispanic ranching, lay beyond the zone of initial Anglo-American settlement east of the Guadalupe River in the Austin Colony and Atascosita District.

Colony reported a total population of some 20,000, including the cities of Galveston and Houston.[9]

The second type of Anglo-Americans to enter the Coastal Prairie of Mexican Texas in the 1820s came uninvited and had no legal footing. They simply drifted across the poorly guarded border at the Sabine and squatted on Texas soil. Clearly, Mexico had a serious problem with illegal Anglo aliens. In this way the section of the Coastal Prairie between Louisiana and the eastern border of Austin's Colony, an area first known as the Atascosita District, was initially occupied. A census in 1826 revealed a population of 407 persons in the district, including 76 slaves. Among these Atascositans, the oldest individual who had been born in Texas was only seven years of age, and over half of the native-born were just one year old, indicating that colonization began about 1818 and that the majority of the settlers had drifted into Texas in the mid-1820s. By 1834, after the area had been organized as the Municipality of Liberty (Liberdad), the population had swelled to about 1,000, and in 1850 the two counties Liberty and Jefferson, which by then encompassed the Coastal Prairie between the Sabine and Trinity, had 4,400 residents.[10]

The Anglo settlers and their black slaves did not have the Texas Coastal Prairie entirely to themselves. Instead, the ethnic diversity of the lower southern pine barrens was duplicated west of the Sabine. Louisiana French, in small numbers, were among the earliest settlers, bringing Cajun family names like Leblanc, Broussard, Arceneaux, and Hebert to Southeast Texas. The Ashworths, a "free black" extended family of mixed Anglo, black, and Indian ancestry with roots in South Carolina, settled near present Orange in the early 1830s, and they were not the only mixed-blood people to seek out Mexican-ruled territory in the decade preceding the Texas Revolution.[11] The more liberal attitude toward racial mixing in Mexico was perhaps the main attractive force, and the antislavery policy of the Mexican Republic was no doubt also a factor.

West of the Austin Colony, parts of the Coastal Prairie were colonized in the 1820s and early 1830s by Europeans and Mexicans. Martín de León brought several hundred settlers from Mexico to the Victoria area along the Guadalupe River, beginning in 1824, and Catholic Irish, many from

County Wexford, colonized nearby Refugio and San Patricio about 1830.[12]

Even though Anglos constituted a large majority of the Coastal Prairie population in the 1820s and 1830s, the presence of these various minorities should not be overlooked, particularly in view of the multiethnic character of coastal cattle ranching east of the Sabine. It is among the diverse peoples of the Texas coastal plain that evidence of the creolized, partially Hispanicized pine barrens cattle culture is to be sought, with a focus on the period between 1820 and 1850.[13] A logical place to begin is in a search for references to large cattle herds.

The Presence of Large Cattle Herds

Abundant contemporary records establish beyond any doubt that the Coastal Prairie of Southeast Texas supported many large herds of cattle before mid-century, and, indeed, before 1835. In the Austin Colony, most of the newly arrived settlers brought modest numbers of cattle with them, generally not more than five or ten. A few of the colonists apparently introduced larger herds, as for example a certain Mr. Tumlinson, who brought a herd of 200 to the colony in 1821 or 1822, and the Kuykendalls, who imported 70 cattle from Louisiana in 1822.[14] Herds of over a hundred cattle roamed the Coastal Prairie portion of the colony as early as 1824, and the stock multiplied rapidly in the humid grasslands. By 1826, a census revealed 3,500 cattle in the colony, just about double the number of people, and in August of that year Stephen F. Austin noted that beef was "cheap and abundant." By 1830, there were 20,000 cattle, including oxen, and a year later 26,000, in both cases over four times the human population of the colony.[15] In the latter year, 1831, the anonymous author of *A Visit to Texas* described herds of 600 and 700 belonging to a number of Anglo-Americans settled close to the Brazos River near the Gulf Coast. By 1837, another anonymous observer reported that several persons in the vicinity of the new town of Houston owned from 500 to 4,000 head. Near the Brazos were "immense herds of cattle," including one of over 2,000, and cattle raising dominated the economy of the Coastal Prairie.[16]

The settlers of the Atascosita District did not lag behind their neighbors to the west in the Austin Colony as cattlemen. Their census of 1826 listed no fewer than sixty-four "stockraisers." By 1831, one rancher near the mouth of the Trinity owned 300 to 400 cattle, and in the same year another near Anahuac, on Galveston Bay, had holdings totaling 3,000 head, which he increased to 5,000 by 1835. Just before the Texas revolution, a traveler on the Atascosita or Opelousas Road, which passed through the Coastal Prairie east of the Trinity, saw "immense herds of cattle." There is some indication that these herders operated on a larger scale than those in Austin Colony, for a Mexican official estimated in 1834 that the Department of Nacogdoches, including the Municipality of Liberty, had 50,000 cattle as opposed to only 25,000 in the Department of Brazos, which contained Austin's Colony. By mid-century, a traveler reported "herds of cattle of the finest kind, several hundreds together, and thousands in some places, are not an uncommon sight in the prairies between the Sabine and Trinity."[17]

Perhaps the most convincing evidence of large cattle herds on the Coastal Prairie comes from the tax lists of the Republic of Texas.[18] These figures reveal that the Coastal Prairie was, without serious challenge, the main ranching area of the Republic, whether the measure was number of cattle or the population: cattle ratio (figs. 3.3 and 3.4) (table 3.1). Some 50 percent of the 125,000 cattle in Texas in 1840 were found in only seven Coastal Prairie counties. By 1845, after five years of rapid settlement in other parts of the Republic, tax lists indicate that the humid prairies of the southeastern part of Texas still contained 40 percent of the 336,000 cattle reported.[19] The United States census of 1850 offers evidence that ranching remained concentrated in the Coastal Prairie corridor even at mid-century (table 3.1). At that date, cattle outnumbered people ten to one in the corridor, as compared to only three to one in the remainder of Texas, and about 30 percent of all cattle were found in the Coastal Prairie.[20] Contemporary reports cited earlier suggest that this concentration of large numbers of cattle in Southeast Texas was present, at least in rudimental form, by 1830 and perhaps even earlier.

Large herds, of course, required access to large amounts of land. For the Austin colonists, this presented no problem.

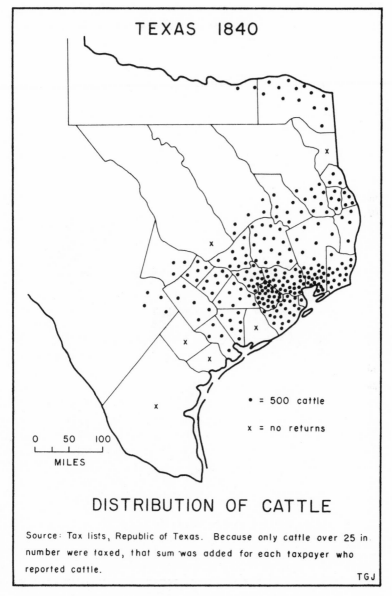

Fig. 3.3 The concentration of cattle in the Coastal Prairie counties is apparent.

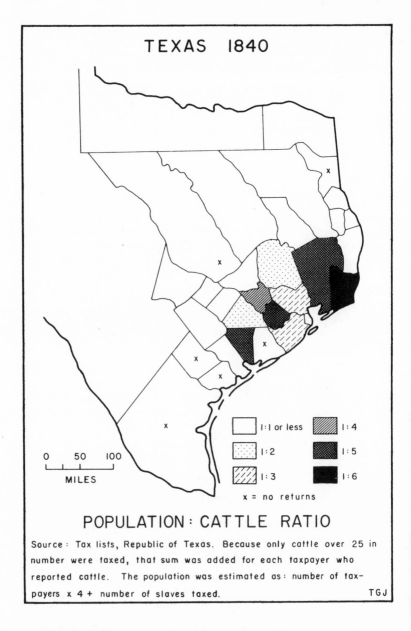

Fig. 3.4 The dominance of the Coastal Prairie in Texas ranching
by 1840 is strikingly revealed.

TABLE 3.1
CATTLE IN THE TEXAS COASTAL PRAIRIE, EAST OF THE GUADALUPE RIVER, 1840 AND 1850

County	1840[a]		1850[b]	
	Number of Cattle	Population: Cattle Ratio	Number of Cattle	Population: Cattle Ratio
Brazoria	9,625	1:3	50,192	1:10
Fort Bend	11,930	1:5	29,223	1:11
Galveston	535	1:1/2	13,328	1:2
Harris	13,709	1:3	29,123	1:6
Jackson	3,634	1:5	20,792	1:20
Jefferson	8,028	1:6	29,159	1:15
Liberty	14,058	1:5	45,670	1:17
Matagorda	(Tax records missing)		35,009	1:16
Wharton	(created in 1846)		15,668	1:8
Eastern Coastal Prairie Total	61,519	1:4	268,164	1:10
Remainder of Texas ..	62,878	1:1	649,360	1:3

[a] MS county tax lists, Republic of Texas, 1840, in the Texas State Archives, Austin. Only cattle above 25 in number were taxed, and, accordingly, that sum was added to the total listed for each taxpayer in order to provide more accurate figures. The county populations were estimated in the following manner: population = number of taxpayers × 4 + number of slaves taxed.

[b] *Seventh Census of the United States, 1850* (Washington, 1853), pp. 503–504, 514–15. The total for cattle represents a combination of the census categories of "milch cattle," "oxen," and "other cattle."

All the married settler needed to do to acquire title to over four thousand acres of land was announce his intention to be a stockraiser and pay a modest surveyor's fee. His bachelor neighbor could acquire half that much land by the same procedure. Some of the colonists obtained huge landholdings and lived in the midst of what amounted to private principalities. The settlers of the Atascosita District were not so fortunate, because initially they had no land titles. Eventually, however, the government bestowed that legal recognition upon them, and they attained a footing equal to the Austin colonists'.

In actual practice, how much land a herder owned was of no consequence. All he really needed was title to a homestead on the fringe of a woods, for he could then allow his cattle to range far and wide on the public range. A rancher near Houston who owned only 400 acres became, by his own account, the largest cattle owner between the Trinity and the Brazos, registering his brand in five adjacent counties to protect the far-flung livestock.[21] Such extensive land use was made possible by a very sparse population. The Coastal Prairie had relatively few rural inhabitants, less than two per square mile as late as 1850.[22] Even for a rancher of the postbellum West, that would have left a lot of elbow room.

Open Range, Roundups, and Branding

The open-range system, with its associated neglect of cattle, prevailed from the very first in the Texas Coastal Prairie. A visitor to the Austin Colony in 1831 wrote that "the whole business of raising cattle is ... reduced ... to the simple oper- ation of letting them care of themselves," and, on ap- proaching the home of one cattle herder who lived near the mouth of the Brazos, he noted "an almost boundless plain, or natural meadow, a large part of which ... is appropriated to grazing, and left unenclosed ... as a vast pasture ground for his cattle." A decade later, another traveler noted that cattle fed "upon the prairies or in the wooded bottoms during the whole year," requiring "almost as little attention as the wild deer." After foraging for themselves on the open range, the cattle became semiwild. This was especially true of "swamp- ers," cattle that drifted into the bottom forests and marshes. Only with difficulty could they be dislodged from their sanc- tuary, for these wily beasts came out on the prairie only at night. As late as 1884, all of Chambers County, on the east- ern shore of Galveston Bay, remained open range.[23]

Hand-in-hand with the open-range system went periodic roundups, called "cowhunts," "cattle hunts," or "hunt ups" by Coastal Prairie herders. A group of cowboys engaged in a roundup was known as a "crowd."[24] Following Anglo cus- tom, cowhunts took place only once or twice a year, depend- ing on the size of the herds. In Chambers County, one annual hunt swept the expanse of prairie, reaching even into adja- cent counties, while in Refugio County cattlemen held fall and spring roundups. The term "pen" was used to describe

the enclosures used at roundup, but no Coastal Prairie reference to "cowpen" has been found.[25]

Branding and marking were the principal purposes of
roundups. An observer in 1840 remarked that the Coastal
Prairie cattle herders "drive them into their pens once a year,
and brand the calves in order to distinguish them from [those
of] their neighbours." Nine years earlier, in 1831, another
traveler described an identical system of roundup and branding in various parts of the Coastal Prairie corridor. In 1835,
"vast herds of cattle...marked with the owner's initials"
were seen "roaming over the rich prairies," and a rancher
near Anahuac was said to have branded 2,700 calves in the
previous year.[26] Many other references to roundups and
branding, complete with accounts of disputes that arose
when a cow and her calf showed up wearing different brands,
can be cited for Southeast Texas, many of them from the
pre-1840 period.[27]

Cattle Driving and Transhumance

Already by 1831, drovers were coming each year from Louisiana to purchase cattle in the Coastal Prairie of the Austin
Colony and the Atascosita District and drive them overland
to New Orleans and ports on the Red River in Louisiana. In
that year, it was noted that "for the live stock a market is
found at New-Orleans; and drovers annually visit this part
of the country to purchase cattle, which they take back in
great numbers." Three years later, in 1834, a traveler described how cattle were "driven by land across the country to
Natchez or New Orleans" at a "trifling" expense. One
rancher near Galveston Bay drove 1,000 head of cattle to
New Orleans in 1834, a drive which took three weeks and cost
$4.12½ per head. His motivation for undertaking this long
and difficult drive can be understood when one considers
that his yearlings were worth $5.00 per head in Texas and
$12.00 or more at New Orleans.[28]

The major trail to Louisiana followed the old Atascosita
(or Opelousas) Road through the Coastal Prairie, crossing
the Sabine just above present Orange and continuing on
through Opelousas to the Mississippi River. Another route,

called the Beef Trail, led northeast from Liberty on the Trinity into the forests, crossed the Sabine at Belgrade, then forked into trails leading to Alexandria and Natchitoches. Ultimately, much of the Texas beef reached the West Indies, the same market served a century and more earlier by the original South Carolina cattlemen.[29]

A limited local market also existed. Drovers brought some Austin Colony cattle to market at San Antonio, and by 1840 the new capital town of Austin had become a cattle market.[30] In the early 1840s, slaughterhouses existed at Houston and Galveston to provide beef for those towns and to produce hides, tallow, and horns for export to Europe.[31] Some cattle hides were exported by sea through Galveston Bay in the mid-1830s.[32]

Other drives conducted by Coastal Prairie ranchers were for the purpose of transhumance. For example, cattle in the Velasco vicinity, near the mouth of the Brazos River, were driven into the adjacent woodlands for winter range in the 1830s, and still today some Matagorda County ranchers drive stock out onto the Matagorda Peninsula each fall after the hurricane season for wintering, a drive which requires three or four days and utilizes public highways for part of the distance.[33]

Cattle Breeds

The exact physical characteristics of the cattle raised by herders in the Coastal Prairie corridor will never be known, but it is certain that longhorn blood was dominant. As early as 1823, "Spanish Cattle" were accepted in place of currency in the Austin Colony.[34] To be sure, there was considerable mixing between the small, sturdy cattle brought from eastern Anglo-America and the Spanish-Mexican stock found in Texas, but the end product was more nearly longhorn than anything else. Typical, perhaps, were the cattle owned by a Mr. Stafford, east of the lower Brazos in Austin's Colony, who in 1833 had a steer measuring "nearly four feet from the tip of one horn to that of the other." Additional references mention cattle "larger than those common in the north, with longer and straighter limbs, broader horns and smoother coats";

cattle "of the horned kind"; and cattle which were "a mixture of American and Mexican." It is noteworthy, however, that a Mexican soldier in 1836, describing the sizable cattle herds near the Brazos River in Fort Bend County, recorded in his diary that "the hornless variety is abundant."[35]

That the Anglo-Texans of the Coastal Prairie owned dominantly longhorn stock is not surprising, for in many cases they bought cattle from Mexican traders. Further, Louisiana was a major source area of Texas cattle in the 1820s, and longhorns had spread into that state at least as early as the 1760s.[36]

Horsemanship

"In the final analysis," wrote Walter Prescott Webb, "the cattle kingdom arose at that place where man first began to manage cattle on horseback."[37] Webb believed that Anglos did not acquire equestrian skills until they entered the Hispanic ranching diamond in South Texas. In this assumption, he was wrong. Anglos, blacks, French, and Indians had been using horses in herd control far to the east, as was documented in chapter 2. The level of skill increased to the west and had flowered on the Louisiana coastal prairie, where the openness of the countryside made dogs less practical and the saline content of the grasses rendered salt useless for managing stock. Certainly by the time the lower southern herders reached Southeast Texas, they were skilled horsemen, well acquainted with Hispanic roping techniques.

Nor is evidence of these skills lacking. On the eastern shore of Galveston Bay, a traveler described in 1831 how, at branding time, "horsemen ride into the pen among them, and throw their lazos over the horns or necks of the young animals." The same observer, while visiting the lower Brazos area of the Coastal Prairie, was told that "a horseman can always readily separate such as he chooses from a herd." Near Houston in the 1840s, another Anglo-American rancher described how cowhands in his employ worked on horseback and used the lasso, mentioning that one of them had received his training in Louisiana. Still another writer commented, in 1840, that a couple of mounted men could manage a herd of a thousand cattle. With the lasso, of course, went the horned saddle. Clearly, Anglo-Americans managed cattle from horseback in the Coastal Prairie corridor, and they were doing so when they first came to the province. A resident of the region summed it up well in 1860, declaring that "the stockraisers of Texas are generally good horsemen ... and many of them are not inferior to the best Mexican vacqueros."[38]

Cowhands

The sizable herds typical of the Texas Coastal Prairie required labor beyond the immediate family. As had been true in colonial South Carolina, these workers were often black slaves. According to tax returns of the year 1840, 62 percent of all taxpayers in the Coastal Prairie counties who reported 100 or more cattle were also slaveowners, and the existence of this combination is documented in the late 1820s and early 1830s.[39] Specific references to black cowboys in this area are easy to find. Francis Lubbock, a rancher near Houston, used blacks to tend his cattle in the 1840s, and he allowed one of these slaves to own some cattle and register a brand. That particular man bought his freedom with the wealth he accumulated. Recently, the role of the black cowboy in the cattle-ranching industry of the West has received long-overdue scholarly attention, and, in that light, his presence in the Coastal Prairie corridor is particularly interesting.[40]

There were, however, other sources of labor on the ranches of Southeast Texas. Anglos often served as cowhands, and the region provides another possible origin of the word "cowboy." According to the antebellum lore of the Texas Coastal Bend, the term "Cow-Boy" was originally applied to ambitious young Anglos who, in the period between 1836 and 1845, ventured south of the Nueces River along the Coastal Prairie to round up longhorn cattle belonging to Mexicans forced to flee during the Texas Revolution. Some rode as far as the Rio Grande and stole cattle from Hispanic ranchers there. By 1860 the meaning had been altered to mean any Anglo cowhand. "The young men that follow this 'Cow-Boy' life," wrote a stockraiser in that year, "notwithstanding its hardships and exposures, generally become attached to it."[41]

Hired Mexican herders also worked on some Coastal Prairie Anglo ranches, at least those west of the Trinity River. Writing in the 1830s, a resident of the Austin Colony noted, "Mexicans... are employed by the settlers mostly as herdsmen, and are universally acknowledged to be the best hands that can be procured, for the management of cattle, horses, and other live stock." A decade later, a traveler mentioned that cattle raising was facilitated by "employing a Mexican or two as herdsmen, an occupation for which they are admirably fitted." In addition, some Louisiana French worked as cowboys in Southeast Texas.[42]

Crop-Livestock Combinations

The pine barrens herders of the Lower South, following the earlier example of Carolina cowpenkeepers, generally made do with a bare minimum of field crops, most commonly confining their efforts to a small enclosure of corn. However, as has long been recognized, the pine barrens cattle often belonged to wealthy cotton planters who lived in the more fertile parts of Georgia, Alabama, and Mississippi and hired herders or sent slaves to care for their stock. In Louisiana, many planters along Bayou Teche owned large cattle herds on the Opelousas prairies to the west. There were, then, two primary types of herding operations. One involved ownership of the cattle by the herders, in which case crops were very limited and usually raised only for subsistence purposes, and the other a planter-rancher who produced both cash crops and cattle in a territorially fragmented operation.

In the humid Coastal Prairie of southeastern Texas, operations essentially identical to each of these types could be found in the 1820–1850 period, and there was a certain amount of regionalization of the two. The planter-herder combination was common in the area of the old Austin Colony. Brazoria County, which was representative of the area, had 90 persons who reported ownership of 100 or more cattle in the census of 1850, and of these over one-third also reported cotton. The combination of cash crops, mainly cot-

ton and sugar cane, with large-scale cattle raising is documented as early as the 1820s in the Austin Colony.[43] In one
respect, however, the planter-herder of this part of Texas
differed from his prototype farther east in the Lower South. It
was not necessary for him to divide his operation territorially, because he could use the much-sought "peach and cane
lands" of the *galeria* bottom forests to grow cotton and the
adjacent prairies to pasture cattle.

East of the Austin Colony, beyond the Trinity, the
planter-herder was rather uncommon, and most of the people
engaged exclusively in cattle raising. In 1850, in Jefferson
and Liberty counties, which encompassed all of the Coastal
Prairie between the Sabine and Trinity, there were 143 persons who reported 100 or more cattle to the census marshals.
Of these, only eight grew cotton and nine sugar cane. In
keeping with the tradition of the pine barrens herders farther
east, 118 of them grew corn, but 25 reported no crops whatever. The difference was also evident in the fact that 70
percent of all persons taxed for 100 or more cattle in the
Austin Colony counties in 1840 owned slaves, as compared to
only 42 percent of those east of the Trinity.[44]

This contrast between the eastern and western parts of
the Coastal Prairie corridor had several causes, the most
significant perhaps being that the Austin Colony attracted a
higher economic class of settlers initially because valid land
titles were available there and not in the Atascosita District.
Also, the portion of the Coastal Prairie which lay in Austin's
Colony contained more of the fertile alluvial bottoms desired
by planters (fig. 3.1).

The prairie environment discouraged the Carolina custom of raising hogs on the same range with cattle, but the
practice nonetheless persisted in Southeast Texas. Of the 45
herders in Jefferson County who reported 100 or more cattle
in 1850, only three did not also keep swine. One of the most
important ranchers near Houston in the early days kept "a
large stock" of hogs, and the Brazos bottom forest near Brazoria in 1831 supported "many...hogs."[45] Scattered groves,
such as Hog Island and Pignut Island in Jefferson County,
also provided the necessary mast for the Coastal Prairie
swine.

Origins and Ethnic Makeup of the Coastal Prairie Ranchers

Obviously, then, cattle ranching thrived on the Texas Coastal Prairie between 1820 and 1850. But who were the ranchers, and where did they come from? Fortunately, a variety of records permit an answer. Particularly valuable is the 1826 census of the Atascosita District, a document superior to United States censuses of the same era because it listed the birthplace of each inhabitant. From it, we learn that sixty-four men in the district listed their occupation as "stockraiser" and that all but one of them had an Anglo-American surname. Nearly 60 percent of them claimed birth in the string of lower-southern coastal states from Virginia to Louisiana, and nearly one-fifth were natives of the Carolinas. Georgia had mothered four of them, Mississippi six, Louisiana seven, and Florida one. The census also recorded their last place of residence prior to settling in Texas, providing even more convincing evidence of the herders' pine barrens heritage. Fully 86 percent had migrated to Texas directly from Louisiana, Mississippi, and Alabama—the three states of the coastal herder belt closest to Texas.[46] Typical of these people was Micajah B. Munson, a stockraiser-saddler born in South Carolina about 1789, who was brought by his family as a small child to Mississippi, resided in Louisiana in the early 1820s, and came to the Atascosita District with his wife, children, and thirteen slaves about 1824.[47] The schedules of the United States Census of 1850 reveal that lower southerners continued to dominate the old Atascosita District, the land between the Sabine and Trinity, at mid-century. Nearly 70 percent of the immigrant population in 1850 had been born in South Carolina, Georgia, Florida, Alabama, Mississippi, and Louisiana.[48]

Many of the planters settled by Stephen F. Austin on the Coastal Prairie of his colony were also lower southerners. Austin adopted the policy of settling most slave-owning colonists from the Lower South on fertile alluvial lands along the large rivers in the Coastal Prairie, while shunting slaveless yeomen from the Upper South, who formed a larger part of the colony's original population, to the small tributary creeks of the back country interior of his colony. The manuscript schedules of the census of 1850 reveal that southerners from the coastal states made up 58 percent of the immigrant American rural population of the Coastal Prairie counties in the area of the old Austin Colony, and that Louisiana and Alabama were the two leading states of birth.[49]

While the overwhelming majority of Southeast Texas ranchers were Anglos, the ethnic minorities also participated (fig. 3.5). One member of the previously mentioned Ashworth clan, a "redbone" family of mixed white-black-Indian ancestry, owned far more cattle than anyone else in Jefferson County in 1850.[50] Only a few were Hispanic ranchers. "Joseph Coronow" (probably José Corona), a native of the "Viceroyalty of Mexico" and previous resident of Louisiana, was among the Atascosita District stockraisers in 1826. Corona, however, was apparently the only Hispanic rancher ever to reside east of the Colorado River in the Texas Coastal Prairie.[51] Curiously, the Spaniards never developed cattle ranches in these lush, inviting grasslands. A Spanish official reported only 3,000 people in all of Texas in 1820, excluding unconverted Indians and the Rio Grande population, and nearly all lived in only two settlements, San Antonio and Goliad. And even at Goliad, the inhabitants in 1821 had but "a few cattle." Stephen F. Austin, visiting the Coastal Prairie about 1820, found it completely empty of settlements.[52]

Several Spanish missions had become major ranching enterprises in the Coastal Bend section of the prairie corridor, in the South Texas diamond west of Guadalupe, in the 1700s. Nuestra Señora del Espiritu Santo de Zuñiga mission, which occupied several sites between modern Victoria and Goliad, claimed some 40,000 cattle about 1770, while nearby Nuestra Señora del Rosario had 30,000.[53] The secularization of the missions destroyed these enterprises long before Anglos approached the Coastal Prairie.

Had it not been for the colonization efforts of Martín de León, the nineteenth-century Hispanic ranching effort in the prairie corridor would have been altogether inconsequential. De León, a ranchero in the district of Nuevo Santander (now Tamaulipas), extended his operations into Texas as early as 1805, on the banks of the Aransas River. In 1823 he pioneered the Opelousas cattle trail to New Orleans, driving a herd

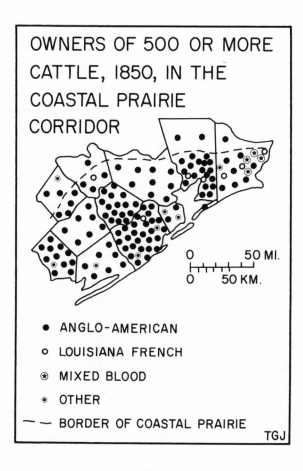

Fig. 3.5 By the middle of the nineteenth century, 137 herders owning 500 or more cattle lived in Southeast Texas. The majority, 86 percent, were Anglo-Americans; 5 percent were Louisiana French; and 3 percent were persons of mixed blood. No Spanish-surnamed ranchers were detected. Louisiana was by far the leading state of birth, accounting for 24 percent of the herders, followed by Kentucky (12 ½ percent), South Carolina (7 percent), Virginia (7 percent), and Georgia (6 percent). (Source: MS schedules of agriculture and free population, U.S. Census, 1850, for Austin, Brazoria, Colorado, Fort Bend, Galveston, Harris, Jackson, Jefferson, Liberty, Matagorda, and Wharton counties, Texas.)

from his Tamaulipas ranch across the Coastal Prairie to that destination. A year later, he led a group of Mexican colonists to the banks of the Guadalupe, west of Austin's Colony, in the Coastal Prairie, where the settlement of Victoria was established. De León and a number of fellow colonists soon operated large cattle ranches in the Victoria area. Following Hispanic custom, De León combined cattle and sheep on his Coastal Prairie range.[54]

Louisiana French cattlemen were more numerous than Hispanos in Southeast Texas, particularly east of the Trinity River. Certainly the most noteworthy of these was Taylor White, born Leblanc, who became the cattle king of Southeast Texas after immigrating from Louisiana in the late 1820s. Headquartered near Anahuac on the eastern shore of Galveston Bay, White owned herds ranging over much of present Chambers County and branded thousands of calves each year.[55] In spite of his example, the influx of French herders remained small until near mid-century. According to the tax lists of 1840, only three of the fifty persons reporting 100 or more cattle in counties east of the Trinity had French surnames, though quite possibly some had Anglicized their names, following White's example. By 1850, 19 percent of the large cattle owners of Jefferson County and 9 percent in adjacent Liberty County were French (fig. 3.5).[56] The immigration continued through most of the remainder of the century. A resident of Southeast Texas, recalling the 1870s, remembered that "the French people, the Guedrys, who came over from Louisiana and lived...on Batson Prairie,... brought cattle with them and after a few years...had a large number."[57] An index of the importance of these Louisiana French in helping shape the culture and economy of early Southeast Texas is perhaps provided by certain generic toponyms still in use there. Coastal Prairie inhabitants employ "island" as a generic term to mean a grove of trees and "cove" to describe an embayment of grassland into the adjacent woods. Both of these terms appear to be Anglicizations of common Cajun words and usages from the prairies of Southwest Louisiana.

The Irish, too, contributed to early Coastal Prairie cattle ranching, in their adopted homeland west of the Guadalupe River on the fringe of the South Texas diamond. "No town in

Texas possessed larger stocks of cattle" than Irish San Patricio on the Nueces River, where one settler owned "upwards of 1,300 head" and Thomas O'Connor of nearby Refugio County was adjudged to be the "most successful" cattleman in the region.[58] Beginning with a few head of cattle in 1837 or 1838, O'Connor, a Wexford immigrant, had become the unchallenged cattle baron of the Coastal Bend by the time of the Civil War. Nor was he alone, for by 1850 at least a third of the large-scale cattle raisers in Refugio County were Irish.[59] It would be tempting to attribute the rise of the Catholic Irish ranchers to their Celtic herding heritage. To do so, however, would be incorrect. Wexford, the source of many of the Texas Irish, was fertile farming country rather than cattle range. Moreover, the ranching practices of the Refugio and San Patricio Irish were patterned on those of the Mexicans and Coastal Prairie Anglos. As early as 1835, the Texas Irish were using the Spanish-derived word "ranch" to describe their activity.[60]

In sum, the cattlemen of the Texas Coastal Prairie were of diverse origins, but the overwhelming majority were Anglos and Louisiana French from the coastal fringe of the Lower South. East of the Colorado or Guadalupe rivers, nearly all ranchers were lower southerners. Anglos far outnumbered the French, even east of the Trinity, and the Carolina element was sizable.

Conclusion

It has been established (1) that large-scale open-range cattle ranching thrived in the Coastal Prairie of Southeast Texas in the period between 1820 and 1850; (2) that the large majority of persons engaged in this ranching were of lower-southern Anglo-American origin, from states farther east, where pine barrens cattle herding had long been practiced; (3) that, cartographically, the area of ranching in Southeast Texas appeared, by 1840, as simply the westernmost appendage of a belt of cattle herding stretching across the Lower South from Georgia and Florida to the fringes of the semiarid part of Texas; (4) that certain traits of Coastal Prairie ranching were distinctively lower southern in character; and (5) that there was no antecedent ranching by Latin Americans in Southeast Texas.

On the basis of these findings, I conclude, first, that cattle ranching was brought into Texas by lower southerners in the period 1820–40 and that this form of economy was initially established in the Coastal Prairie corridor of Southeast Texas, where it remained centered until about 1850. The presence in this area of certain ranching traits recognizable as uniquely lower southern, the presence of a population dominantly of lower-southern origin, the presence of a herder belt from Georgia to Texas, and the absence of antecedent Spanish-Mexican ranching, when viewed in conjunction, leave little justification for denying a major contribution by Anglo-American bearers of the Carolina tradition to the ranching of Southeast Texas. It was the area between the Sabine and the Colorado rather than the South Texas diamond that witnessed the first major Anglo-American cattle ranching on Texas soil.

Those who wish to regard the birthplace of western cattledom as that area where Anglo-American and Spanish-Mexican ranching traditions first merged should look, for origins, to these humid prairies of Southeast Texas and Southwest Louisiana and to the pine barrens from Mississippi through Florida, not to South Texas. Those, on the other hand, who prefer to emphasize the continuity of Anglo-American herding from the cowpens to the Great Plains should regard the Coastal Prairie as a key western segment of the major route of diffusion. From either viewpoint, the importance of the Coastal Prairie is great and the contribution of the lower southerner fundamental.

4
The Northeast Texas Prairies

THE THREE DECADES FROM 1820 TO 1850, which encompassed the occupation of the Coastal Prairie corridor by herders from the lower-southern pine barrens, also witnessed a settlement of Northeast Texas by certain other of Carolina's children, who introduced the cowpen culture there by way of the Upper South–Ohio Valley.[1] These colonists from the interior of North America implanted a purer Anglo herding tradition in Texas soil, one largely devoid of Hispanic and French influences. While less numerous and cattle-rich than their contemporary counterparts on the Coastal Prairie, these sons of highland southern coves and valleys made a significant contribution to the evolution of Great Plains ranching. Here, as in the southeast, a crucial link was forged in the westward diffusion of the Anglo herding tradition.

The Environment of Northeast Texas

The counties forming the focus of this chapter occupy a vegetational transition zone (fig. 4.1).[2] Even though the climate is a relatively uniform humid subtropical throughout this region, the nineteenth-century vegetation cover was quite varied. Dense pine and hardwood forests stood beside expanses of open blackland prairie; impenetrable thickets shared dominion with grassy oak openings. The pattern of forest and prairie formed an intricate mosaic, a complexity only hinted at in the accompanying map (fig. 4.1). To generalize, we can speak of another prairie corridor here, stretching from east to west across Northeast Texas, in which most of the early stockraising occurred.

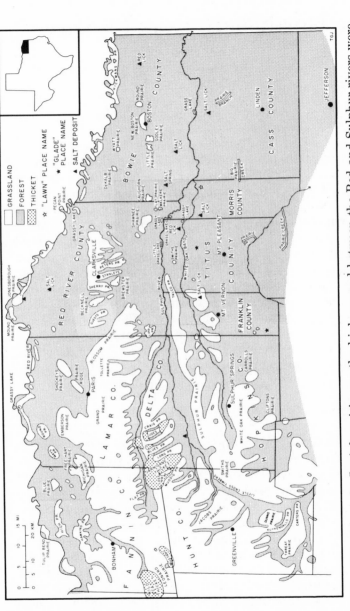

Fig. 4.1 The interfluvial prairies on the high ground between the Red and Sulphur rivers were collectively referred to as the Sulphur Fork Prairies. (Sources: U.S. Dept. of Agriculture soil surveys for various counties; U.S. Geological Survey topographic maps; numerous contemporary accounts by travelers and settlers; all available county and local histories; and original land survey field notes.)

The prairies of Northeast Texas belong in the "tall grass" category, but they were anything but uniform in characteristics, varying greatly in size, shape, soils, surface configuration, and plant growth when first encountered by Anglo-Americans. Some, particularly on the bottomland terraces of the Red River, were very nearly flat, while others were undulating or pocked with "hog-wallow" indentations six to twelve inches deep and ten to fifteen feet across. Prairie soils varied from heavy black waxy clays to light sands, with the so-called sand-flat prairies being more common in the eastern parts of the region.[3] The grass preferred by stockmen was locally known as wire grass, "a narrow leaf growing three or four feet in height" that was "considered very fattening for cattle." Good forage was also provided by calamus grass. Even within individual prairies, the character of the soil and vegetation was not spatially constant. Josiah Gregg, describing the Blossom Prairie as it appeared in 1841, observed that "most of the north of this prairie is of black soil covered with rosin weed—but a good deal of the South is of cold gray unproductive soil ... and covered with *wire grass*."[4]

Cattle could graze on these prairies for most of the year, then retreat in the short winter to the river and creek bottoms, rich in cane, ryegrass, and winter grass. Some winter forage could even be found in the hog-wallows, where grass reportedly remained green all year. The mild climate made unnecessary the transhumance typical of upper southern herders in the Appalachians and Ozarks. In some winters, the cattle did become "poor," but there were apparently no major die-offs. The only major winter hazard was river flooding, which occasionally caught cattle by surprise in the caney bottoms and drowned entire herds. In February 1843, for example, one stockraiser in Red River County lost 75 or 80 percent of his rather substantial cattle herd in this manner.[5]

Reflecting Anglo herder custom, the settlers fired the grasslands once or twice each year, in late winter and again in July, causing new green shoots to come forth. Burning no doubt helped maintain the prairies, because woodland has encroached on many grasslands in Northeast Texas in the decades since firing was outlawed.[6]

Here and there, both in bottomland and on interfluves, grew sizable thickets, consisting of a dense growth of dog-

wood and other brush, briars, vines, and trees (fig. 4.1). So
thick was the vegetation that bands of cattle rustlers and
other outlaws found secure hideouts here, and wild cattle
also sought refuge. The unwary visitor could become lost in
one of these thickets and wander about for days before
escaping.[7]

One problem faced by cattle raisers was the scarcity of
surface water in some prairies, especially during the long,
hot summers. Though one English visitor felt that there was
sufficient flowing water on the prairies to support cattle "for
the greater portion of the year," the American prairie veteran
Josiah Gregg pointed out the "almost absolute lack of constant springs" in the elongated interfluvial prairie between
the Red and Sulphur rivers.[8] As a consequence, cattle were at
times obliged to remain near waterholes in the bottomlands,
and the carrying capacity of the prairie range was thus
diminished. In rainy periods, the problem was often poor
drainage. The Blossom Prairie, for example, acquired "a lake
of considerable size" at such times.[9]

Salt was locally available. An observer in 1849 reported
that "saline impregnations appear in most parts of the country, and are of benefit to the large herds of wild and tame
cattle which roam over the immense prairies and woods."
According to another observer, "salt licks are very abundant."[10] Notable among these were Red Lick in Titus County
and Salt Well Slough in Red River County (fig. 4.1).

All things considered, the prairies of Northeast Texas
provided an excellent setting for open-range cattle raising.
Once the resident herds of bison, wild horses, and feral
longhorns were removed and wolfpacks reduced, the domestic livestock introduced by Anglo-American settlers inherited a superb range. In the years following, observers would
frequently comment on the fine condition of the range cattle
and the rarity of disease among them.[11]

The Anglo-American Occupance of Northeast Texas

Anglo-Americans began occupying Northeast Texas as
early as the period of Spanish rule, in 1814 and 1815.[12]
Known initially as the "Red River settlements," this scatter-

ing of backwoodsmen was until the mid-1830s administered by Miller County, Arkansas, since the location of the international boundary was uncertain. The population grew slowly but steadily, augmented by Anglos who were forcibly displaced from homes on the north bank of the Red River when that area was designated as the Indian Territory. In the first decade and a half, settlement clung largely to the bottomland terraces along the Red River, but in the early 1830s the occupation of the interfluvial grasslands, collectively known as the Sulphur Fork Prairies, began in earnest. By 1840, tax lists suggested a population of around 7,500, which rose to about 20,000 by 1850.[13] From the late 1830s to the Civil War, numerous sizable plantations were established on the terraces adjacent to the Red River, and the yeoman pioneers retreated southward.

In the main, the settlers of the Northeast Texas were derived from the Upper South. These backwoodsmen completely dominated the first twenty years of settlement, and even as late as 1850, upper southerners were the largest population origin group and Tennessee the leading state of birth in every county in the region. There were also sizable numbers of people from Arkansas, Missouri, and Kentucky.[14]

The Presence of Large Cattle Herds

Cattle were introduced into Northeast Texas by some of the earliest Anglo settlers. Perhaps the first accompanied a certain Nathaniel Robbins, who settled on the Pecan Point Prairie in 1817, bringing enough cattle, hogs, and horses that he could share with his neighbors.[15] By the early 1820s, the number of cattle in the Red River settlements was sufficient that small herds could be driven south to the ranges of the Austin Colony in south-central Texas. In 1825, a census of Miller County, Arkansas, which then included all the settlements in Northeast Texas, listed 55,000 cattle, 10,000 hogs, and 2,500 people, a cattle: population ratio 22: 1. Indicative of this abundance was a drive of about 100 cattle from the Jonesborough Prairie southward into the wooded region of East Texas in the early 1830s. A few years later, in 1836, an observer noted that the 200 or more families settled on the prairies between the Red and Sulphur rivers "appear to be an industrious ... people, possessing large herds of cattle and swine."[16]

More exact statistics concerning cattle holdings exist for the 1837–50 periods, in the form of tax lists and manuscript census schedules. These documents, though incomplete, reveal 148 different persons in Northeast Texas who owned 100 or more cattle at some time during that decade and a half.[17] Notable among them was the Kentuckian James E. Hopkins, who had 800 cattle bearing his "EH" brand ranging on the Sulphur Prairie in Hopkins County (fig. 4.1) by 1850, herds which increased to 1,600 by 1855.[18] Meredith Hart, who lived in Fannin County but kept most of his stock on the prairies of Hopkins County, was running 1,000 head of cattle with his "H" brand by 1850.[19] Both Hart and Hopkins had built up their herds over the period of a decade or more (table 4.1). Hart, the Missouri-born son of Ohioan John Hart, came to Northeast Texas from Arkansas as a boy in 1832 and already owned a herd of 20 cattle while still a lad of fifteen.[20]

So abundant had the cattle herds become by mid-century that a traveler in the prairies of Northeast Texas was moved to remark that "for miles in every direction there was nothing to be seen but the immense number of cattle feeding." Other observers wrote of "vast herds" and "large herds." Total numbers of cattle in the counties of Northeast Texas rose to 27,000 in 1845, 54,000 in 1850, and 82,000 in 1855.[21] While these figures are not nearly so impressive as the totals for counties along the Texas Gulf coast at the same period, they do document a thriving cattle business. We may conclude that cattle were present in Anglo settlements of Northeast Texas from 1817 onwards and that large herds were being developed at least as early as 1830.

The origins of the stockraisers owning a hundred or more cattle in Northeast Texas can be determined with some precision, based on the manuscript census schedules and on biographical sketches contained in various county and local histories (table 4.2). These data reveal an overwhelmingly upper-southern background for the stockmen. Tennessee was the leading state of birth, followed by Kentucky, and Missouri was the first-ranked state of residence prior to

TABLE 4.1
Development of Cattle Herds by Selected
Stockraisers in Northeast Texas

Year	James E. Hopkins, Red River & Hopkins Counties	Meredith Hart, Fannin & Hopkins Counties	Mansel W. Matthews, Red River & Hopkins Counties	Bartholomew Millhol- land, Lamar & Hopkins Counties	Mathias Click, Red River & Lamar Counties	Solomon Martha, & Daniel Waggoner, Red River & Hopkins Counties
1838	50	——	——	——	40	——
1840	50	20	0	——	75	0
1842	?	75	50	25	150	30
1844	?	175	?	50	150	50
1845	400	?	?	100	225	100
1846	400	500	90	125	150	100
1848	600	800	170	125	200	150
1849	600	900	250	250	180	240
1850	800	1000	306	212	208	412
1851	800	800	225	200	140	280
1853	1536	600	500	300	125	400
1854	1500	300	——	300	150	440

SOURCES: MS tax lists, in the Texas State Archives, Austin; MS agricultural schedules of the United States Census, 1850.

migration to Texas. Nearly one-fifth of the stockraisers claimed birth in the Carolinas, the colonial core area of the Anglo herding tradition. Typical was Solomon ("Sol") Waggoner, a native of South Carolina and former resident of Missouri and Lincoln County, Tennessee, who began herding cattle on the Blossom Prairie in Red River County shortly after 1840 (table 4.1).[22] William Becknell, owner of 215 cattle ranging the Red River County prairie which bore his name, came from the Boonslick country of Missouri, a notable early cattle herding region, and Eli Lindley, a Hopkins County stockraiser on Sulphur Prairie, had migrated from the Springfield area, also a center of the Missouri cattle industry (fig. 4.1).[23] James Latimer, who owned a large herd on the Sulphur Fork prairies east of Clarksville in Red River County, had previously resided in Carroll County, Tennessee, which had the highest cattle : population ratio of any Tennessee county in 1840.[24]

TABLE 4.2
ORIGINS OF STOCKRAISERS IN NORTHEAST TEXAS
BY STATE OF BIRTH AND REMOVAL

State or Territory	As Place of Birth of Stockraisers	As Place of Residence Prior to Removal to Texas
Tennessee	35%	23%
Kentucky	24	2
North Carolina	13	0
Virginia and West Virginia	11	0
South Carolina	5	0
Illinois	2	8
Indiana	2	4
Georgia	2	0
Maryland	1	0
Missouri	1	26
Alabama	1	6
Mississippi	1	9
Arkansas	0	15
Louisiana	0	2
Indian Territory	0	4
Other	1	2

SOURCES: MS Texas county tax lists, 1837–50, in the Texas State Archives, Austin; MS schedules of the Seventh United States Census, 1850, for Fannin, Hopkins, Hunt, Lamar, Red River, and Titus counties; and various county and local histories for the counties mentioned in note 2. Place of removal was generally determined by the "child ladder" method, employing the birthplace of children in the family.

NOTE: Stockraisers are defined here as persons owning 100 or more cattle at any time during the 1837–50 period. Of a total of 148 such persons, birthplace was ascertained for 97 (66 percent) and state of residence prior to removal to Texas for 53 (36 percent).

Very few of Northeast Texas's cattlemen came from the Deep South. Alabama, Georgia, Mississippi, and Louisiana combined accounted for only 4 percent of the births and 17 percent of the prior residences (table 4.2).

Open Range

There can be no question that the cattle herds in early Northeast Texas were running loose on the open range. One early reference, dating from 1830, tells of an "uncollected stock of cattle." Another, at mid-century, described how "cattle kept themselves within the home range." The second murder committed in Hopkins County, back in the 1840s, occurred because a settler had fenced in a waterhole previously used by open-range cattle. As late as 1880, the Fulbright family had thousands of cattle on open range in Red River County, as did the Edwardses in the river bottoms of adjacent Bowie County.[25]

Indeed, open range persisted in some marshy areas of Northeast Texas well into the twentieth century. About 1910, in the far northern reaches of Morris County, a region of Sulphur River swamps, "by common consent of the landowners, stock is still allowed to range." As late as 1942, open range existed "between the creeks" in Titus County, the strip of land between the Sulphur River and White Oak Bayou (fig. 4.1).[26]

Roundups and Penning

Periodic roundups and penning are inherent in the open-range system, and cowpens were in use from the early years of settlement. Court proceedings in 1835 mentioned "a cow pin enclosed with a rail fence," and similar descriptions exist for other parts of Northeast Texas.[27] The term "roundup" was apparently not used in this part of Texas. Even as late as the 1870s, "cow hunt" seems to have been the preferred designation.[28] Significantly, this had also been the case in the Carolinas.

Dogs were widely used in the cowhunting process, in keeping with Anglo tradition. These canines were the so-called leopard or Tennessee brindle dogs, and they are still bred, sold, and used in cattle management in Northeast Texas.[29]

Horses were apparently also used by the pioneer stockman of Northeast Texas, but no evidence of roping or other Hispanic horseback skills has been found. Meredith Hart, one of the most important cattle raisers of the region, kept between thirteen and twenty horses on his place, while James E. Hopkins owned sixteen horses at a time when his cattle numbered 1,600. By contrast, Mansel W. Matthews of Hopkins County owned forty horses and 250 cattle in 1849 and was obviously engaged partially in breeding and raising horses.[30]

The traditional Anglo technique of herd management by use of salt was also employed in Northeast Texas. A resident of Red River County, writing in 1850, described how "cattle are penned once a fortnight and salted, which is necessary to keep them gentle." The same practice was noted in Grayson County, immediately west of the study area, though stockmen there were apparently less regular in salting the cattle.[31]

Marking and Branding

As has been pointed out, the marking and branding of livestock was practiced by Anglo cattle raisers in colonial times on the eastern seaboard. In some cases in the East, stock were earmarked but not branded and the reverse was also true, particularly for horses. Brand and mark registration was required in all counties of Northeast Texas beginning in 1848, but many were in use long before that. Not all of these registries have survived to the present, but the pre-1850 records for Fannin, Hopkins, Lamar, and Red River counties are available and have been researched.[32] In these four counties alone, 156 brands and 242 earmarks were registered in the period from 1843 to 1850. The use of marks and brands in Northeast Texas reflected Anglo custom in several respects. Perhaps most notably, some 103 stockmen in the four-county survey registered only an earmark, with no brand (fig. 4.2). In the same sample, 139 registered both earmark and brand, and 16 only a brand. Also, the eighteenth-century South Carolina custom of branding horses with a simple letter was practiced in early Northeast Texas.[33]

Visitors to the rangelands of Northeast Texas often observed these ownership marks. "Each settler has his own mark upon his stock, which is known and respected by other settlers," noted Edward Smith in 1849. About that same time, a resident of Red River County concluded that "the cost of raising cattle amounts to nothing more than the time consumed in marking and branding."[34]

Still more important and revealing was a fundamental difference between Anglo and Hispano brand designs (fig.

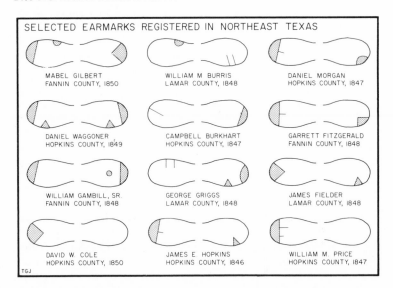

SELECTED EARMARKS REGISTERED IN NORTHEAST TEXAS

MABEL GILBERT
FANNIN COUNTY, 1850

WILLIAM M BURRIS
LAMAR COUNTY, 1848

DANIEL MORGAN
HOPKINS COUNTY, 1847

DANIEL WAGGONER
HOPKINS COUNTY, 1849

CAMPBELL BURKHART
HOPKINS COUNTY, 1847

GARRETT FITZGERALD
FANNIN COUNTY, 1848

WILLIAM GAMBILL, SR.
FANNIN COUNTY, 1848

GEORGE GRIGGS
LAMAR COUNTY, 1848

JAMES FIELDER
LAMAR COUNTY, 1848

DAVID W. COLE
HOPKINS COUNTY, 1850

JAMES E. HOPKINS
HOPKINS COUNTY, 1846

WILLIAM M. PRICE
HOPKINS COUNTY, 1847

TGJ

Fig. 4.2 The shaded portions were removed from the animal's ears, and additional slits were made in some cases, as shown. It would be interesting to compare these earmarks with some used in eighteenth-century South Carolina. (Sources: MS brand and mark registries, Fannin, Hopkins, and Lamar counties, at the courthouses in Bonham, Sulphur Springs, and Paris; see also Hortense W. Ward, "Ear Marks," pp. 106–16.

4.3). Anglos, both in the East and in Texas, normally chose block capital letters for brands, usually the initials of their surname and/or Christian name. Less frequently, they selected Arabic numerals as their brand designs. The Spaniards and Mexicans in Texas, by contrast, more often chose abstract designs rather than letters or numbers, frequently incorporating Moorish crescents and Indian-inspired figures into the design. The Hispanic-American styles were described by one observer as "crazy Mexican brands...with complicated crooked and curved lines and many curlicues." Northeast Texas cattle brands unmistakably reflect Anglo rather than Hispanic design tradition. Fully 80 percent of the brands in the four-county sample were simple upper-case block letters, and an additional 11 percent were Arabic numerals. By way of comparison, in a sample of forty-six brands registered by Spanish-surnamed ranchers in Texas

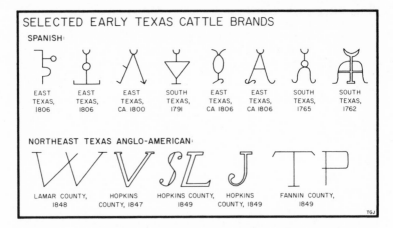

Fig. 4.3 Note the contrast between Spanish and Anglo styles. Some of the Spanish brands apparently contain Mexican Indian design influences. The Spanish brands shown for East Texas were used in the Nacogdoches area, south of the Anglo herding region in Northeast Texas. (Sources: MS brand and mark registries, Fannin, Hopkins, and Lamar counties, at the courthouses in Bonham, Sulphur Springs, and Paris; Gus L. Ford, ed., *Texas Cattle Brands*, pp. 1–2, 4–6; and Hortense W. Ward, "Indian Sign on the Spaniard's Cattle," pp. 94–105.

prior to 1836, less than half used letters, and even those were usually highly embellished. Only one was a numeral. Also absent from the Anglo brand lists of Northeast Texas were the "bar," "circle," "rocking," and other symbols which later became so common in West Texas.[35]

Markets

In the early years of settlement, markets for the cattle were inaccessible, due to the isolation of the Red River settlements. This no doubt retarded the development of large-scale cattle raising in the 1820s, as did depredations by wolf packs and Indians. About 1830, the first markets for livestock became available. The principal purchaser was the United States government, and the consumers were newly arrived Indians in the Oklahoma agencies and military personnel. As early as 1831, the Kentuckian Ben Milam, who was later to die in the Texas war of independence, was bidding to sell 20,000 to 50,000 pounds of beef to the United States government from his herds in the area. About the same time, Jesse Shelton, also a Kentuckian, and Elijah Clark on the Sulphur Fork prairies were furnishing beef by the hundred-thousands of pounds for the Indian agencies.[36] The Oklahoma market was short-lived, however, for the resettled Indians soon became self-sufficient in beef. Some cattle from Northeast Texas were sold in the Choctaw area as late as 1842, but the Indian market had peaked in the 1830s.[37]

As the Oklahoma market declined, the stockraisers of Northeast Texas began trailing cattle to Shreveport, founded at the head of navigation on the Red River in 1835. From there, cattle were shipped by river to New Orleans, the great livestock market of the Lower South. After the removal in the late 1830s of the huge logjam known as the "Red River Raft," some cattle were sent directly from Texan river ports to Louisiana.[38] In the 1840s, the town of Jefferson, located on a navigable tributary of the Red River in Marion County, southeast of the study area, became a major depot for Northeast Texas cattle (fig. 4.1). In the first six months of 1845, the customshouse east of Jefferson on the Republic of Texas –United States border recorded the export of 100,000 pounds of beef and 40,000 pounds of hides. Jefferson also acquired a meat-packing plant.[39]

By 1849, Edward Smith reported that "vast herds of steers are driven yearly to the southern market" from Northeast Texas. The fattened cattle, he said, "are purchased by dealers, and driven to Shreveport, whence they are shipped to New Orleans." Moreover, he explained, "the most profitable mode of selling is for one seller to have the charge of all the fat cattle of his neighbors, and to take them to New Orleans." A few years later, a resident of Hopkins County observed that "the surplus produce of our county is beef, pork, and mutton, all of which is walked to market."[40] At least one drive to the goldfields of California was made from Lamar County in 1850, and another herd from that county was taken to Little Rock.[41] Cattle were still being trailed across Northeast Texas in post-civil war times.

Another market for cattle was provided by the stream of migrants crossing the area on their way to points farther west. Several much-used emigrant roads crossed Northeast

Texas, and by the late 1840s stockraisers were selling small herds and individual animals to migrants.[42]

Even though trailing to market was common, many cattle in Northeast Texas were slaughtered locally for their hides. Numerous tanyards were operating in the oak woods of the area, and processed hides were among the region's major exports prior to about 1840.[43] The place name "Tanyard Bayou" is found today in Red River County, "Tanyard Creek" in Red River and Fannin counties, "Tanyard Branch" in Red River County, and "Tanbark Creek" in Fannin County. Early establishments included one called Flintham's Tanyard at Kiomatia in northwestern Red River County, another at the northern edge of the Blossom Prairie in Lamar County, three within a four-mile radius of Clarksville in Red River County by 1842, and an "immense" tanyard at Stephensboro in Red River County (fig. 4.1).[44] By 1849, an observer noted that "many tan yards are already established," and "the oak bark is very abundant, and can be obtained without cost."[45] By the 1840s, many of these yards were turning out manufactured leather goods. According to the 1860 census, there were twenty-one saddlery, harness, and other leather-working businesses in the counties of Northeast Texas.[46]

The price of cattle did not vary much during the 1820–50 period. The United States government was offering 2¢ per pound on the hoof in 1831, the exact price quoted in Red River County in December 1850.[47] In 1849, drovers purchased cattle for 2¢ or 3¢ per pound. An estate inventoried in 1830 contained a herd of cattle valued at about $2.25 per head. On tax declarations, most stockraisers in the 1840s valued their cattle at $4 to $6 per head, while full-grown animals were selling for $8 to $12 per head.[48] A steer worth $10 in Lamar County brought $45 at the New Orleans market in 1849, and the cost of river transport to the Crescent City was said to be $5 to $6 per head.[49]

Crop-Livestock Combinations

None of the stockraisers in early Northeast Texas devoted full attention to cattle. Swine were kept by virtually all cattle owners, following Carolina tradition, and frequently these droves of razorbacks were very large. James E. Hopkins of Hopkins County owned 800 cattle and 600 hogs in 1850. William Stone of neighboring Hunt County had 200 swine to go with his 500 cattle, and the Waggoner family of Hopkins County owned 100 swine and over 400 cattle.[50] The combination of cattle and hogs on the same open range stood in contrast to the Spanish-Mexican ranching system, in which pigs were not common. Many large-scale cattle raisers in Northeast Texas also kept at least small flocks of sheep. The previously mentioned James E. Hopkins owned 50 sheep, which produced 300 pounds of wool in 1850; and the Waggoners kept 350 head.[51] Jason Wilson, who lived in a section of southern Lamar that was later separated to become Delta County, was typical of the smaller stockraisers, and in 1848 he owned 100 cattle, 70 hogs, and 30 sheep.[52]

Every stockraiser had at least some acreage planted to crops. James E. Hopkins, who was typical of the large-scale stockmen, raised 500 bushels of corn, 600 bushels of oats, 20 bushels of rye, and 50 bushels of sweet potatoes in 1850. His Hopkins County neighbor Bartholomew Millholland, who owned 212 cattle and 150 swine, produced 100 bushels of corn and 40 bushels of oats. Many cattlemen also grew wheat.[53] These prairie dwellers were too far from market to ship their grain, so surplus was fed to their livestock.[54] Closer to the Red River and the Louisiana border, farmers often combined cotton raising with cattle herding.

But even though these overlappings existed, it is possible to discern Thünenian rings within Northeast Texas by mid-century. Closest to the Red River in the northeast and to the border in the southeast, the numbers of slaves and cotton plantations were greatest. Beyond this zone of relatively intensive plantation agriculture lay a belt, mainly in interior Fannin, Lamar, and Red River counties, where wheat and other cash grains were the principal farm crops. The southwesternmost areas, particularly Hopkins and Hunt counties, were the most remote from market and were dominated by open-range stock raising. Hopkins and Hunt together were by 1850 home to fully one-half of all stockmen in Northeast Texas who owned 200 or more cattle, in spite of the fact that these two counties were the least populous of the six. Cotton was a crop of no significance in Hopkins and Hunt, and very few slaves resided there.[55]

Cowhands

The black cowboy was not common in Northeast Texas, in keeping with the upper-southern yeoman tradition. No positive or negative correlation existed between slave ownership and cattle ownership. A standard statistical test of these two variables yielded a value very near zero.[56] In other words, the herds of cattle ranging the prairies were not simply the property of wealthy plantation owners resident in the river valleys. Some of the largest herds were owned by slaveless stockraisers; 38 percent of all persons who reported one hundred or more cattle in the 1837–50 period were slaveless. Included was Meredith Hart, owner of a thousand cattle. Another 12 percent of these cattlemen owned only one slave, and still another 30 percent owned between two and ten. Only 1 percent owned over fifty slaves. James E. Hopkins, the cattle "king" of Northeast Texas, had limited slaveholdings that ranged from four to eight in the 1840s. An observer in 1849 remarked that slaves were not suited to stock tending and that few were seen on the prairie ranges. An exception was Dan Waggoner of Hopkins County, founder of a legendary cattle empire, who purchased a black boy about twelve years of age to work as a herdsman in the early 1850s. The large majority of cowboys in Northeast Texas were Anglo-Americans of upper southern birth. Typical was S. G. Coyle from Osage County, Missouri, who was hired as a cowhand in 1846 in Hopkins County.[57]

Lack of Direct Hispanic Influence

Nor were the cowhands of Hispanic origin. In 1850, no person of Spanish surname or Mexican birth lived in the counties of Northeast Texas, and a year earlier, an English visitor to the region "did not find a Spaniard or Mexican amongst them."[58] This part of Texas contained the most purely old-stock American population found anywhere in the state by mid-century. Even as late as 1840, an eighty-five-mile-wide unpopulated zone separated the settlements of Northeast Texas from those on the Trinity River, and the district was administered as part of Arkansas until the mid-1830s.[59] One traveler in the region just south of the study area in 1849 did record seeing "two Mexicans boys" driving cattle to Shreveport, but they had apparently not come from Northeast Texas.[60]

Indeed, Hispanic influence of any type was apparently absent in the area even as late as mid-century. The region's vocabulary and place names provide additional evidence of this circumstance. The terms "ranch," "rancho," and "rancher," were not used. The cattlemen were called "stock-raisers" or "stock-rearers," and their landholdings "stock farms" or "grazing farms." In the census of 1850, cattle king James E. Hopkins was described as a "farmer & stockraser" by the marshal.[61] Other terms of Spanish origin, such as "lariat," "lasso," "wrangler," "vaquero," "dogie," "jerky," "chaps," "corral," "bronco," "remuda," and "rodeo," were likewise absent before 1850.

The first significant infusion of Hispanic influence into Northeast Texas came as a result of the Mexican War of 1846–48. Many men from this part of Texas went south to serve in the war, and some were no doubt influenced by what they saw on the ranches of South Texas and Mexico.

The period 1850–70 witnessed the spread of considerable Hispanic ranching influence into Northeast Texas. One indicator of this was the appearance of place names such as Saltillo in Hopkins County.[62] The word "ranch" spread with Spanish influence. It was being used by 1852 in Leon County, some one hundred miles south of the study area, and by 1860 in Denton County, forty miles to the west.[63] Subsequently, "Doak's Ranch" appeared in Red River County and "Wise Ranch" in Hopkins County. In 1860, according to the census marshal, a young Mexican-born herder named Ruiz had taken up residence in Fannin County, listing "vaccaro" (*vaquero*) as his profession, and two of his Anglo companions made a similar declaration.[64]

By the 1950s, vocabulary studies conducted in Northeast Texas revealed that "bronc," "corral," and "lariat" were known there.[65] Even so, only 2.5 percent of all persons interviewed used the word "corral" to mean an enclosure for cattle, as opposed to 53.5 percent who preferred "cowpen." A larger minority, 13.5 percent, used "corral" to mean a horse pen, but 70 percent gave the response "horse lot." Only 12 percent listed "dogie" for a motherless calf, and none of the interviewees knew the word "toro."[66]

The cattle breeds roaming the ranges of early Northeast Texas similarly revealed little Hispanic ancestry. Several Englishmen visiting the area in 1849 regarded the animals as "descendants of Durham stock imported into the States," including some from Missouri.[67] In all probability, these shorthorns were introduced in the 1840s and other breeds dominated earlier decades in Northeast Texas, but no early descriptions of the cattle have been found. A resident of Red River County referred to the local cattle simply as "native animals." These animals apparently varied considerably in appearance, for they were described by contemporary observers as being "exceedingly large," "small," "of every hue," and "a superior breed."[68] Some wild longhorns were in the area, but no attempt was made to capture and tame them. Instead, the Anglo practice was to shoot wild cattle.[69] Even so, some mixing between feral longhorns and the domestic stock surely occurred, though in the region west of the study area, in the Cross Timbers and north Texas prairies, the cattle raised in the later 1800s were not pure longhorns, but rather a mixture of Spanish stock and Anglo breeds derived in part from Northeast Texas.[70]

Nor is there mention prior to 1848 of any Spanish equipment such as the western saddle. The earliest reference to the horned saddle was in 1849, in the town of Jefferson, southeast of the area under study (fig. 4.1). There a British visitor described saddles which differed from his "by having a high projecting knob at the pummel." He noted that this saddle type had been introduced from Mexico and was used locally for hunting bison and wild horses.[71] There is no evidence that this western or Spanish saddle was being used by cowboys in Northeast Texas or that it was known at all in the region before 1848.

To these observations we must add the previously documented presence in Northeast Texas of such Anglo traits as the use of shepherd dogs and letter brands, range firing, and hog keeping. In sum, the evidence suggests that there was little or no Hispanic influence among the stockraisers of Northeast Texas prior to the end of the Mexican War. The nearest Spanish ranching area lay a hundred miles to the south, in the Nacogdoches area, and was separated from Northeast Texas until the 1840s by an unpopulated zone.[72]

While a direct Spanish-Mexican cultural input seems unlikely in view of the evidence presented, Hispanic influence may have been transmitted indirectly, though the pine barrens cattle complex of the Lower South, where Hispanic traits were incorporated very early. However, only one Anglo cattleman of note in Northeast Texas had proven ties to the pine barrens. He was Kendall Lewis, a native of Maryland who migrated to Hancock County, Georgia, as a child in about 1790, then fled as an outlaw to the Creek Indian nation in Alabama.[73] Lewis became a Creek citizen and married a woman from this tribe. A "white man turned Indian," Lewis came to Oklahoma with his adopted people in 1828 but was not allowed to have title to land there. In 1835 he moved on into Northeast Texas and settled a land grant near Prairie Branch, in what later became Titus County (fig. 4.1). There his cattle herds grew from 75 head in 1838 to 320 by 1844.[74] In 1846, Lewis moved back to Oklahoma. Though he may well have been a bearer of the Hispanic-influenced cattle culture complex of the Lower South, Lewis arrived in Northeast Texas after the herding economy there was already established and thriving. It is unlikely, therefore, that he exerted any shaping influence.

The Five Civilized Tribes, bearers of the pine barrens cattle tradition, established a thriving open-range economy in eastern Oklahoma, beginning about 1830, and they might conceivably have influenced events in Northeast Texas.[75] But as has been documented, the Northeast Texas cattle economy antedated that of the Oklahoma Indians, and in fact, as mentioned above, exported beef to the newly settled Indians in the 1830s.

Conclusion

An Anglo-American tradition of open-range cattle herding, probably derived from the Carolinas through the Upper South, was implanted in Northeast Texas in the 1820s by immigrants from upper southern states and was flourishing by the 1830s. A careful weighing of available evidence leads me to believe that these Anglo herders of Northeast Texas were the bearers of a herding tradition largely or entirely devoid of Hispanic influence before about 1848. Their pastoral system was largely unchanged from that of the Carolina hearth area. Of all the Anglo immigrants to Texas, theirs appears to have been the herding system least modified by Hispanic contacts.

Nor did this lifestyle vanish with the passing of the frontier. For thirty years or more after 1850, an increasingly Hispanicized open-range cattle-ranching economy continued to thrive in Northeast Texas, centered in the larger prairies. The large Wise Ranch on the White Oak Prairie in Hopkins County operated as late as 1898, and the prairies of northern Franklin County were "still used for grazing" as late as 1909 (fig. 4.1).[76] In general, however, open-range cattle raising was displaced from the Northeast Texas prairies between 1870 and 1890 by wheat and cotton farming, a displacement also aided by the spread of railroads and barbed wire.[77] Cattle ranching ultimately retreated to the marginal environments, which in Northeast Texas were the flood-prone bottomlands of the Red and Sulphur rivers. There such enterprises as Doak's Ranch in southern Red River County held on until the modern era, when fenced-range cattle ranching spread eastward across Texas to replace cotton. Thus, cattle ranching, rather than being merely a transitory frontier phase, maintained continuous existence in Northeast Texas from the 1820s to the present day.

5
The East Texas Piney Woods

THE TWO PRAIRIE CORRIDORS of eastern Texas that form the focus of chapters 3 and 4 are separated by a sizable tract of coniferous forest, known to its inhabitants as the Piney Woods. Stretching northward some two hundred miles from the northern edge of the Coastal Prairie to the margin of the Blackland Prairie, the East Texas Piney Woods cover all or most of twenty-seven counties (fig. 5.1). In this expansive woodland, Carolina immigrants fashioned yet another early-day cattle industry, forming one more diffusionary link between the eastern seaboard and the Great Plains.

The Environmental Setting

In several major respects early cattle herding in the Piney Woods differed from that in the bordering prairie corridors. The most obvious contrast lay in the character of the vegetational environment.

Actually, "Piney Woods" is somewhat of a misnomer, at least in describing the vegetational conditions of the area in the early nineteenth century. A visitor to East Texas today might find the name appropriate, since lumber companies have planted huge blocks of the region in commercial pine plantations, but the immigrant a century and a half or two centuries ago encountered a rather different environment. Pines shared dominion with a variety of hardwoods, small prairies were strewn like mothholes through the woodland, and among the trees grew a fine stand of grass, a product of countless centuries of Indian-set fires. Herds of bison and deer ranged through the East Texas Piney Woods.[1] "Early

103

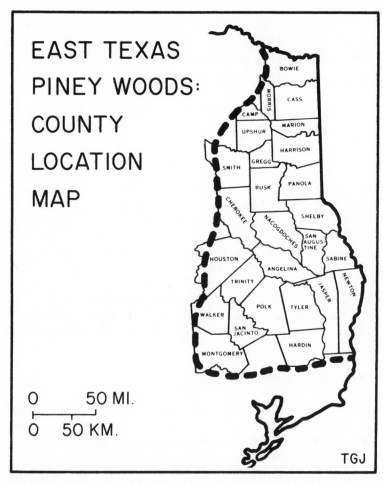

Fig. 5.1 The Piney Woods occupy an elongated north-south belt along the eastern boundary of Texas. Twenty-seven present-day counties lie wholly or largely within the Piney Woods.

settlers found the country much more open than it is today," wrote an East Texas county historian, for "on many a prairie, now timbered, grass grew from knee to waist high."[2] East Texas probably has more woodland today than it did in 1800. So altered is the vegetation that one must look to contemporary accounts and to surviving floral toponyms for evidence of what formerly existed (fig. 5.2).

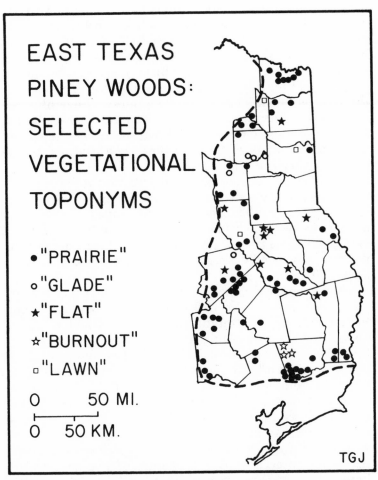

EAST TEXAS PINEY WOODS: SELECTED VEGETATIONAL TOPONYMS

- •"PRAIRIE"
- o"GLADE"
- ★"FLAT"
- ☆"BURNOUT"
- ◻"LAWN"

0   50 MI.

0   50 KM.

TGJ

Fig. 5.2 Grass was abundant in the nineteenth-century Piney Woods, sufficient to support sizable cattle herds. Place name elements such as "prairie," "glade," "flat," "burnout," and "lawn," dating from the 1800s, provide evidence. (Sources: U.S. Geological Survey quadrangle maps and Walter Prescott Webb and H. Bailey Carroll, eds., *The Handbook of Texas.*)

To be sure, parts of early East Texas bore a dense forest cover. Two visitors in 1835 described some areas as "thickly timbered" and "well timbered," remarking that Shelby County was "literally covered with oak of various kinds, black hickory, ash, dogwood . . . and occasionally intermixed with short-leaf pine." Jasper County had river bottom forests dominated by oaks, magnolias, beeches, and walnuts, while pine prevailed in the uplands, and the country north of Nacogdoches was an "almost unbroken forest" consisting of oaks in the valleys and a pine-hickory association on the interfluves. Pine ridges towered above oak-hickory valleys in the famous "Redlands" of Sabine County.[3] Generally, the admixture of hardwoods was greater in the northern half of the Piney Woods, where the sandy soils were also deeper and less acidic. Stands of longleaf pine were confined to the southern part of the woodland.

In a few places, notably the Big Thicket at the southern end of the Piney Woods, the forest was a tangle of vegetation. Describing the Big Thicket in 1835, one traveler declared it to be "the thickest woods I ever saw," counting "8 or 10 kinds of ever green undergrowth, privy, holly, 3 or 4 sorts of bay, wild peach tree, bay berry, &c, and so thick that you could not see a man 20 yards" away.[4]

More commonly, though, the forest had an open appearance. Just west of Nacogdoches in 1834, traveler Amos Parker saw "trees straight and tall, but standing so far apart, that a carriage might go almost any where among them. The grass grew beneath them, and we could see a great distance as we passed along." A decade later another wanderer, in Montgomery County, spoke of the "numberless 'pine barrens' that occur in this country," explaining that he meant "lands partaking of the forest and prairie." Similar were numerous "gentle swells, of red clayey soil, covered with oak, hickory, &c called oak openings."[5] Even as late as the 1920s, observers spoke of country of a "glady" nature, having "but a sparse growth of timber."[6] The place names "lawn," as in Woodlawn and Red Lawn, "glade," and "flat" survive here and there in East Texas as reminders of the former barrens and openings (fig. 5.2). Local residents also used the terms "flatwoods" and "post oak flats" to describe such vegetation.[7]

Also numerous were patches of open grasslands. Hundreds of small prairies greeted the first Piney Woods settlers, and the place name "prairie" occurs no fewer than fifty times in the region (fig. 5.2). Nineteenth-century travelers rarely failed to mention these prairies.[8] In Cherokee County, one transient in 1845 mentioned "several prairies of two or three miles in extent, which were covered with rank high grass and weeds," while another visitor in the same area described "pine Barrens interspersed with prairies, being bounded with long leaf pine."[9] These grasslands occurred both in river bottoms and on the interfluves, and generally were larger toward the western end of the Piney Woods.[10]

The East Texas settlers maintained the grassy openings, glades, and prairies by means of fire, duplicating an age-old Indian custom and traditional Carolina practice. A resident of the town of Nacogdoches complained in February 1841 that smoke from fires in the surrounding rural districts had filled the air for several days, and a traveler reported prairies burning in a nearby area in February five years earlier.[11] Anglos created several Big Thicket prairies through firing the woodlands, as is evidenced by the local use of the generic place name "burnout" (fig. 5.2).

Journeying on horseback along the Old Spanish Road, from Natchitoches, Louisiana, westward through the Piney Woods and on to distant San Antonio, a nineteenth-century traveler could experience most of the vegetational diversity of the East Texas woods. Amos Parker in 1834 entered Texas by this route. At the Sabine he found a strip of thick bottom forest, two or three miles wide on the Texas side, followed by an upland characterized by "oak openings," "pine plains," and an occasional "small prairie." West of Nacogdoches he encountered an open pine forest with abundant grass, "pine woods, oak woods, and small prairies," culminating in a large wet prairie near the banks of the Neches River. Upon crossing that river, he passed through "ten miles of pine woods, then prairies of a mile or so in extent, and post-oak openings."[12]

In effect, the Texas Piney Woods region, while somewhat inferior to the Coastal and Blackland prairies as a cattle range, was almost exactly what the pine barrens herders from the Lower South had known back east. It was as close an environmental twin to the coastal plain of South Carolina as could be found in Texas, a setting in which Carolina's deep southern children could easily feel at home.

Antecedent Hispanic Ranching

A second major difference between the Piney Woods and the
bordering prairie corridors was that there had been colonial
Hispanic cattle ranching in the woodlands. Unlikely as it
seems, colonial Spaniards chose to settle the forested portion
of East Texas, leaving the adjacent lush grasslands empty.
They originally came east of the Trinity, not as ranchers, but
as missionaries seeking large populations of sedentary farming Indians. The Spaniards found the largest numbers of
such prospective neophytes in the central Piney Woods and
concentrated missionary efforts there. They also came as
soldiers defending a far frontier, and the central Piney
Woods, directly opposite Natchitoches, was where they had
greatest cause to fear French intrusions.

Longhorn cattle were driven to the Piney Woods missions as early as the 1690s, but the local ranching economy
did not begin to thrive until the 1750s, by which time a
Hispanicized mixed-blood population had developed.[13] The
cattle industry suffered a setback in 1773 when Spanish
authorities, by then also in control of Louisiana, ordered
evacuation of the East Texas settlements.[14] Some colonists
returned a few years later, led by Antonio Gil Ibarvo
(Ybarbo), a 1729 native of the Piney Woods whose descendants live still today in the Nacogdoches area. While Ibarvo's
interests lay more in smuggling than cattle raising, he did
not neglect herding. Ibarvo's pre-1773 home had been at
Rancho Lobanillo in present Sabine County, and after
returning he settled at Rancho La Lucana, on the west bank
of Attoyac Bayou in Nacogdoches County.[15]

Spanish records list many cattle brands registered prior
to 1806 by the Ibarvos and other East Texas Hispanic families, including Cortinas, de la Garza, Gonzales, Sanches,
Flores, and Hernandes, and an official at Nacogdoches in
1804 reported that "almost all the inhabitants" of the district
worked at pastoral pursuits.[16] Louisiana provided the principal market. The eighteenth-century domain of these Hispanic ranchers is suggested by the present-day distribution
of creeks and other small tributary streams bearing Spanish
proper names (fig. 5.3).

Ranching by Hispanos in the Piney Woods gradually
declined after about 1810, though some brands were regis-

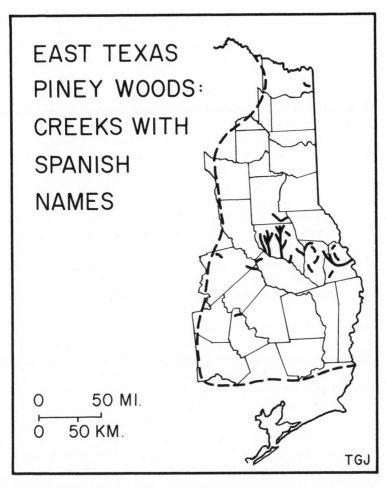

EAST TEXAS
PINEY WOODS:
CREEKS WITH
SPANISH
NAMES

0   50 MI.
0   50 KM.

TGJ

Fig. 5.3 The eighteenth- and early nineteenth-century range of
Hispanic cattle ranchers in East Texas is clearly revealed by the
distribution of surviving Spanish proper names for creeks. Their
activity centered in Nacogdoches, San Augustine, and Sabine counties. (Source: U.S. Geological Survey quadrangle maps).

tered by persons of Spanish surname as late as the 1820s and
1830s. By 1840 no Hispanic person in East Texas reported as
many as 100 cattle to the tax collector, the industry having
passed by then out of Mexican-American hands. The surviving East Texas Hispanos, numbering only about 300 by 1850,

lapsed into isolated subsistence farming or took menial posi-
tions in the town of Nacogdoches, overwhelmed by the
numerically superior Anglos.[17] There they remain today,
clustered around several rural Catholic churches and on
back streets of Nacogdoches.

To describe this pre-Anglo population of East Texas as
Hispanic is to mask the diverse backgrounds of the inhabitants. Caucasian, Indian, and African were all present in
Spanish East Texas, mixing in every conceivable way. Louisiana, the cattle market, also provided French, French half-
bloods, and blacks. Gil Ibarvo himself, the most influential
resident of the Piney Woods, was said to have been the off-
spring of an Andalusian father and a Negro mother.[18]
Eighteenth-century censuses of the Nacogdoches District
mention Spaniards, French, Irish, Italians, mestizos, mulattoes, and other racial mixtures called *lobos* and *coyotes*. In
1793, for example, Spaniards formed only one-fifth of the
civilian population in the district, while mestizos accounted
for over one-fourth and other persons of mixed blood for 28
percent.[19] Some of the blacks and mulattoes may have had
ancestral ties to the Carolinas, raising the possibility that
the ranching culture of Spanish East Texas was not purely
Hispanic, and the presence of small numbers of Louisiana
French further complicates the matter. Even so, by the beginning of the nineteenth century, the central Piney Woods
probably housed the purest Spanish ranching system to be
found anywhere along the lower-southern belt of pine barrens. The word *rancho* was widely used to describe stock
farms in the district between Nacogdoches and Natchitoches, even those owned by non-Hispanos, as late as the
1840s.[20]

Immigration from the East

Piney Woods cattle ranching was enriched in the nineteenth
century by immigrants from the eastern states, many of
whom were bearers of the Carolina or creolized pine barrens
herding system. In the vanguard of these immigrants were
small groups from the Civilized Tribes in the southeastern
United States, notably the Creeks, Choctaws, and Chero-

kees. First to arrive in East Texas, prior to 1810, were the Alabama-Coushatta Indians, classified as ethnic Creeks, who settled in the southern part of the Piney Woods, along the lower Neches and Trinity rivers.[21] By the early 1830s, Coushattas on the Trinity owned "good stocks of . . . cattle."[22]

Much more numerous were Cherokees, who began arriving about 1820 and concentrated in the western Piney Woods, around present Tyler and in the county which still today bears their tribal name.[23] Within a decade, Cherokee cattle herds had become sizable, and by 1833 their stock included more than 3,000 longhorns. Some Anglo immigrants purchased cattle from the Texas Cherokees in the middle 1830s.[24] Choctaws, though fewer in number than the Cherokees, probably also owned herds in East Texas. One focus of Choctaw settlement was Shelby County, where they formed 18 percent of the population in 1835, numbering 164.[25]

The years 1839 and 1840 witnessed the forcible expulsion of Cherokees and Choctaws from East Texas, ending their participation in Piney Woods ranching. Only the Alabamas and Coushattas remained, huddled in a small reservation in the Big Thicket, and their cattle industry was soon destroyed by Anglo rustlers.[26] It seems unlikely that these Indian immigrants played a significant role in the development of Texas ranching.

Close on the heels of the Civilized Tribes came Anglo immigrants, some accompanied by their African slaves and cattle herds. A few Anglos arrived in the Piney Woods of Texas as early as the 1790s, but the main influx came after 1820. The region drew upon both the Lower and Upper South for its settlers, since important immigrant roads from those two regions met at Nacogdoches. From the north came Trammel's Trace, a major pathway followed by Arkansans and Tennesseans into East Texas. Many lower southerners entered East Texas by way of an old Spanish road leading westward from Natchez, Mississippi, to Natchitoches, Louisiana, and on to Nacogdoches. A census in 1835 recorded over 4,000 white inhabitants in the Piney Woods, the large majority of them Anglos.[27] Also present were nearly 600 blacks. Tax lists for 1840 suggest a population of at least 17,000 whites and 4,500 blacks, and the census at mid-century revealed a total population of some 80,000, about one-third of which was black.[28] But in spite of this increase, many districts within the Piney Woods remained sparsely settled, with abundant open range for livestock. For example, Newton County in 1850 had only 1.79 inhabitants per square mile, and Angelina only 1.46.[29]

Anglo Herders

Many of the Anglo-American immigrants developed sizable herds of livestock in the Piney Woods. In the words of Fred Kniffen, East Texas "received considerable and steady impact from the piney-woods cattle traditions of the Anglo-American East."[30] Typical of this herder folk was J.N. Byler, born into the antebellum cattle culture of the area, who recalled in his later years that he "was raised in East Texas and worked cattle back in the piney woods and canebrakes of that region."[31]

The earliest Anglo cattlemen in the Piney Woods were William Barr and Peter Samuel Davenport, who settled in East Texas in the 1790s and developed a number of ranches, including one at Spanish Bluff, on the east side of the Trinity River in present Houston County. In 1810 Barr reported that he owned 780 cattle. Neither Barr nor Davenport, however, was a bearer of the Anglo herding tradition. The two had earlier resided in Pennsylvania and Spanish Louisiana, and Barr was an Ulsterman by birth. Early protégés of Barr and Davenport, such as John Durst and New Yorker Frost Thorn, also became notable East Texas cattlemen.[32] All of these early ranchers seem to have used the colonial Piney Woods Hispanic system as their model.

Beginning in the 1820s, immigration increased rapidly, and Anglos registered a number of cattle brands prior to 1840. The cattle industry began to grow rapidly about 1835, though the tax lists for 1840 reveal only 27 Anglos owning 100 or more cattle. In the ensuing decade, Piney Woods cattle ranching boomed, and by mid-century almost 300 Anglos reported 100 or more cattle.[33] Of those, 84 owned over 200, up from only 7 in 1840. The largest Piney Woods herd in 1850, totaling 1,012 head, belonged to former Louisianan Raleigh

Rogers of Montgomery County. A decade earlier, Rogers had owned 200 cattle. In 1850 he was closely followed by Sherrod Wright of Jasper County with 902 cattle and William D. Smith of Sabine with 820.

Spatially, the development of the Anglo cattle industry was unevenly distributed. Most large-scale cattle owners in 1840 and 1850 lived in the southern half of the Piney Woods, south of the Old Spanish Road (fig. 5.4). The ten southern counties of the Piney Woods, an area called Deep East Texas, housed 82 percent of the large herds in 1850, leaving only 18 percent in the ten northern counties. More exactly, the major herding area lay in the southwestern part of the Piney Woods, focused in lands bordering the Trinity River Valley. Counties there typically had five or six times as many cattle as people in 1850, while in the ten northern counties the ratio was usually less than two to one.[34]

Several factors may account for the concentration of cattle in the southern Piney Woods. A more typical pine barrens environment existed there. Longleaf pine was abundant in the southern part, soils were thinner and less fertile, and grass was perhaps more abundant. Deep East Texas lacked the superb "redlands" of the northern Piney Woods, a region sought as early as the 1830s by cotton planters.[35] Stretching from northern San Augustine and Nacogdoches counties up through Rusk and adjoining counties, the Redlands formed the prime cotton district of East Texas before the Civil War. The southern Piney Woods, with the exception of strips of plantations along the major streams, became a refuge for cowpen keepers.

Possibly, too, the greater importance of the southern counties lay in their proximity to the preeminent cattle industry in the Texas Coastal Prairie, described in chapter 3. But the major Piney Woods cattle concentration was isolated from the prairie by the intervening Big Thicket, where large-scale ranching never developed.

The origins of East Texas Anglo herders were diverse, but the major component came from states in the pine barrens belt of the coastal Lower South (table 5.1). More than six in ten of the large-scale cattlemen in 1850 had lived in one of the four nearest pine barrens states—Georgia, Alabama, Mississippi, and Lousiana—immediately prior to migrating

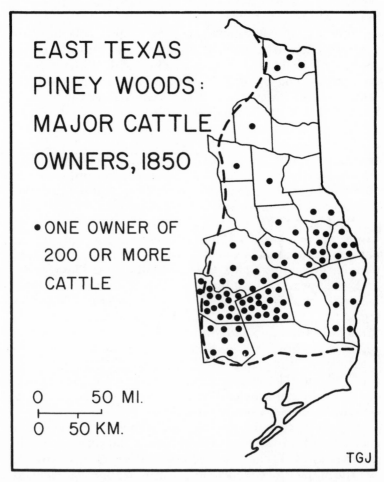

Fig. 5.4 Large-scale cattle ranching was concentrated by 1850 in the southern or southwestern part of the Piney Woods. All owners of 200 or more cattle were Anglo-Americans. Locations within counties are not specific. (Source: Seventh Census of the United States, 1850, MS agricultural schedules for the twenty Piney Woods counties.)

TABLE 5.1
ORIGINS OF OWNERS OF TWO HUNDRED OR MORE CATTLE,
EAST TEXAS PINEY WOODS, 1850

State	As Place of Birth of Stockraisers	As Place of Residence Prior to Removal to Texas
South Carolina	16%	0%
Tennessee	16	29
North Carolina	14	2½
Georgia	10	2½
Kentucky	9	0
Virginia	9	0
Mississippi	5	13
Louisiana	5	26
Alabama	4	21
Arkansas	2	2½
Missouri	0	0
Texas	1	——
Other	8	2½

SOURCE: Seventh Census of the United States, 1850, MS free population and agricultural schedules for Angelina, Bowie, Cass, Cherokee, Harrison, Houston, Jasper, Montgomery, Nacogdoches, Newton, Panola, Polk, Rusk, Sabine, San Augustine, Shelby, Smith, Tyler, Upshur, and Walker counties, Texas.

NOTE: Of a total of 84 persons owning 200 or more cattle, birthplace was ascertained for 77 (92 percent) and state of residence prior to migration to Texas for 38 (45 percent).

to Texas. Louisiana had been the previous home state of one-fourth of the cattlemen. Forty percent claimed birth in one of the chain of coastal states from South Carolina through Louisiana, and South Carolina alone had mothered more than one in every six. An additional 14 percent were natives of North Carolina, bringing the total for the Carolinas to 30 percent.

Perhaps typical of settlers following the pine barrens route to East Texas was the previously mentioned Sherrod Wright, a 1795 native of South Carolina or Georgia, who earned his first four cows and calves back east by serving as a substitute in the War of 1812. After being discharged, Wright married and moved west to the shores of Lake Pontchartrain in Louisiana, driving his small herd with him. He had become acquainted with the Pontchartrain region during his military service. In 1832 he migrated again, bringing

60 cattle to the Piney Woods of present Jasper County, Texas. By 1840 Wright's herd had increased to 100. Eventually, his cattle, ranging over 80,000 acres in Jasper and Newton counties, numbered 1,500.[36]

The Upper South was also represented. A quarter of the major cattle raisers claimed Tennessee or Kentucky birth, and Tennessee was the last previous residence of 29 percent. Typical was Emory Rains, an 1800 native of Warren County, Tennessee, who came to northeast Texas in 1826 and settled first in Lamar County, located in the Blackland Prairie corridor. From there, Rains moved to Shelby County in the Piney Woods, where the 1850 census listed him as owner of 402 cattle, a total exceeded in the county only by Kentuckian Jereboam Beauchamp's 431 Head.[37]

The Anglo cattle industry in the southern Piney Woods continued to thrive long after 1850. Turner Evans of Polk County herded 3,000 cattle as late as 1900, and the Renfros of Angelina County kept up to 2,000 head on ancestral family range in the 1880 to 1920 period.[38] The remarkable lifespan of Isaac P. Renfro, founder of the Angelina County cattle empire, suggests how a few generations of herders could connect twentieth century Texas to colonial Carolina. Born in Missouri in 1829, Renfro moved as a child to Texas about 1840 and resided there until his death at the age of ninety-nine in 1928.[39] Three lifespans like Renfro's would more than cover the period from South Carolina's beginnings to the modern era.

Open Range

From the early Spanish episode through very recent times, most of the Piney Woods has remained open range (figs. 5.5 and 5.6). In 1836, a German traveler remarked that cattle around Nacogdoches "graze freely in the surrounding woods," often straying "as far as twenty miles from the premises." Almost precisely a century later, in the middle 1930s, a United States Department of Agriculture scientist in Polk County reported that "large numbers of cattle...range at will over the timberlands," including cutover districts. As a result, the stock were neglected and semiferal. A visitor to

Fig. 5.5   Open-range cattle in the Piney Woods of Bowie County, Texas. This photo, dating from the early twentieth century, bore a hand-lettered inscription "product of N. E. Texas." The cattle appear to be of a mixed breed, with partial Hereford ancestry and some longhorn blood. (Source: Photo no. P-1442-16, in the archives of the Texarkana Historical Society Museum, used by permission of Katy Caver, curator.)

the Big Thicket in 1887 noted that "cattle feed on the rich cane abounding everywhere in the Thicket" and "become very wild in there," causing some herders to shoot them and take their hides instead of holding roundups. In 1935 Polk County cattle were said to range "in a half-wild condition over large areas and receive very little attention."[40]

Cowpens used during cattle hunts once dotted the southern half of the Texas Piney Woods. Reminders can be seen in such surviving place names as Cowpen Branch in Tyler County, Cowpen Creek in Angelina and again in Tyler County, and Herd Pen Creek in San Augustine County. No

Fig. 5.6 Open-range cattle of mixed British and longhorn ancestry, in the Northeast Texas Piney Woods, about 1916. Note the herder on horseback behind the cattle. (Source: Photo no. P-2097, in the archives of the Texarkana Historical Society Museum, used by permission of Katy Caver, curator.)

evidence suggests, however, that East Texans ever used "cowpen" in the Carolina meaning of "ranch." The typical Piney Woods stock pen was apparently enclosed by "staked and ridered" rail fences, but some had mere worm fences.[41]

Herd management rested in part on the use of dogs, variously referred to in the Piney Woods as "stock dogs," "cow dogs," "hog dogs," and "leopard dogs" (figs. 5.7, 5.8, and 5.9).[42] Herders recognized the unique value of these canines in woodland cattle raising. "He works through trailing cattle and subsequently baying or barking at them," wrote an admirer of one such animal, "until his master has time to hear the commotion and is on the scene," meanwhile so oppressing the cattle that they formed the classic bovine defense circle.[43] Other leopard dogs were trained to seize livestock by the lower lip, ear, or jowl.[44] East Texas stock dogs

Fig. 5.7 An East Texas "leopard dog," a type used in Piney Woods cattle herding from pioneer days to the present. The owner and breeder of this dog is Mr. V. C. ("Cowboy") Williams of rural Navasota in Grimes County, Texas, just west of the Piney Woods. (Photo 1976 by Jim Hurst of Houston, courtesy Mr. Williams and Mr. Hurst.)

are still used in managing herds, and a number of breeders raise them for sale to cattlemen (fig. 5.9). In 1974 the going East Texas price for a leopard dog was thirty-five dollars.[45]

Carolina's imprint on the cattle culture of the Texas Piney Woods also appeared in the use of whips to manage herds. A native and longtime resident of Newton County referred to this instrument as a "cowwhip," and implied they were common in the Piney Woods.[46]

Hispanic influence, possibly derived from the Spanish ranchers around Nacogdoches but more likely introduced from Louisiana, also appeared in the herd control techniques of the East Texas woodland cattlemen. Cowhands chased and roped cattle from horseback, in spite of the difficulties presented by the forested character of the land (fig. 5.6). The place name Horsepen Creek in Tyler County is suggestive of the importance of this technique. Even so, Hispanicization remained far from complete; riding boots and saddles often

Fig. 5.8 Another East Texas stock dog, not displaying the "leop-ard" markings but of the same general build. The dog was bred and raised by V.C. Williams of Grimes County. (Photo 1976 by Jim Hurst, courtesy Mr. Williams and Mr. Hurst.)

differed from western and Spanish types. A Newton County cowboy of the late nineteenth century, who also worked on a ranch in the Piney Woods of northern Liberty County, recalled that he did not own a western swell-forked saddle.[47]

Brands, Marks, and Cowhands

Both Spaniards and Anglos in the East Texas woodlands branded and marked their cattle.[48] But in spite of cultural contacts between the two groups, their respective brand design traditions remained largely intact (fig. 4.3). Of a sam-ple of twenty-six Piney Woods Spanish brands, 85 percent adhered to the Hispanic model of abstract designs and ornate, embellished letters. By contrast, 89 percent of the Anglo brands observed in the region consisted of simple block letters or, less commonly, unadorned Arabic numerals, in keeping with eastern seaboard tradition.[49]

Fig. 5.9 Mr. V. C. ("Cowboy") Williams of rural Navasota, Texas, holds leash on two of the East Texas stock dogs bred on his place in Grimes County. The picture reveals the blend of Anglo and Hispano herd control techniques so common in Texas, since Williams wears Spanish gear and his horse has a Mexican horned saddle. (Photo 1976 by Jim Hurst, courtesy Mr. Williams and Mr. Hurst.)

The evidence of the brand designs suggests that, in spite of the antecedent Spanish system, the Piney Woods Anglo cattlemen retained largely intact the distinctive style of herding they brought from the east. The Hispanic influence discernible among them was probably acquired in Mississippi and Louisiana rather than East Texas. Additional support for this probability comes from other quarters as well. The colonial Spanish ranching system in the region had severely declined by the 1820s, and no Spanish-surnamed persons owned large herds in 1840 or 1850.[50] Also, the focal point of Anglo ranching in the Piney Woods lay west and south of the older Spanish center (compare figs. 5.3 and 5.4).

Nor were the typical cowhands on Anglo ranches in the wooded region of East Texas of Hispanic origin. A great many, perhaps the majority, were Anglos. Such men are listed in the free population schedules of the 1850 census as "stock keepers" or "stock holders."[51] They differed little from the Carolina prototypes described in the previous century by Crèvecoeur. Without doubt many other antebellum cowboys in the region were blacks. The main cattle counties were 25 to 40 percent slave in population by 1850, and the two focal counties of the industry, Polk and Walker, both had black majorities by the time of the Civil War.[52] The planter-herder combination was common, and large numbers of cattle ranged the wooded portions of plantations even by 1840. Most of the large cattle owners also possessed slaves.[53]

Livestock Breeds and Combinations

Anglo herds in the Piney Woods were initially a mixture of British and Spanish-derived stock, but longhorn features probably prevailed from the very first and became more common as the century progressed.[54] Large cattle herds driven in by upper southerners in the 1830s probably consisted of British "scrub" stock, but they soon mixed with resident feral and domestic longhorns and with Spanish stock introduced from Louisiana and Mississippi.[55] Still, the end product a century later, in the 1930s, was recognized as an animal of "mixed breeding" (figs. 5.5 and 5.6).[56]

The Carolina custom of running both cattle and hogs on the same range was almost universal among woodland-dwelling Anglos in East Texas, and the "piney-wood rooter," a small, semiferal pig, occupied an important and traditional place in the regional diet.[57] The East Texas Hispanos, by contrast, raised few swine, in keeping with their Old World Iberian heritage. The pork-avoiding Moslem Moors had tarried long in ancestral Iberia, and the swine-supporting woodlands of Spain had largely vanished by medieval times. But by 1835, after only fifteen years of large-scale Anglo immigration to the Piney Woods, a Mexican government official placed the swine population of the Department of Nacogdoches at over 60,000.[58] In most Piney Woods counties, except those of the main cattle concentration in the southwestern part, hogs outnumbered bovines.[59]

Cattle Drives and Trails

As in early Spanish times, the principal markets for nineteenth-Century Piney Woods cattle lay in Louisiana and Mississippi, both in plantation districts and at river ports engaged in exporting tallow, hides, and barreled beef. Natchez, Natchitoches, and New Orleans were mentioned as markets for East Texas cattle by 1840, and the pattern persisted through the remainder of the century.[60] Henry C. Williams remembered that his father and uncle "drove a small herd of East Texas steers to Vicksburg" in 1865, after gathering them in Cass and adjoining counties of the northern Piney Woods, while Solomon Wright of Newton County recalled late nineteenth-century droving on the Beef Trail, which passed near his home. Regularly spaced along the trail were "beef stands," places where trail herds could be penned at night and drovers could find food and lodging.[61] Similar facilities, also called "stands," existed along drove roads in medieval Britain and eighteenth-century Carolina, suggesting a surviving British influence in the East Texas cattle industry.

Conclusion

The Piney Woods of East Texas, beginning in the middle eighteenth century, housed successive open-range cattle

industries operated by Hispanos, Indian immigrants from
the Southeast, and Anglo-Americans. These respective
industries overlapped little, either temporally or spatially.
The Hispanic activity, centered in present Nacogdoches, San
Augustine, and Sabine counties, flourished mainly between
1780 and 1820; while the Indians, concentrated in Cherokee
and Smith counties, northwest of Nacogdoches, were active
from the early 1820s to late 1830s. Anglo cattle herders,
assisted by their black slaves, rose to prominence in the
1840s, mainly in the southwestern Piney Woods, and continued an open-range system well into the twentieth century.

Derived largely from the coastal southern pine barrens
cattle tradition, the East Texas Anglo herders apparently
owed relatively little to the local antecedent Hispanic and
Amerindian ranching activity. Their cattle culture still bore
the unmistakable imprint of the Carolina cowpens and the
creole coast. Another foothold of the eastern seaboard herding complex was thus established on Texas soil, along the
eastern perimeter of what was to become, after the Civil War,
the Great Plains ranching empire.

6
East Meets West

THE THREE IMPLANTMENTS of Anglo cattle herding in eastern Texas between 1820 and 1850 were a prelude to events that transpired in the latter half of the century, and particularly in two crucial decades ending about 1870. The Coastal Prairie corridor, the southern Piney Woods, and the Blackland Prairie in the northeast witnessed the initial large-scale cattle ranching by Anglos on Texas soil, but in the final analysis these three regions served only as steppingstones along several diffusionary routes to the west, to the Great Plains, where southern Anglos would achieve their finest hour as a cattle-raising folk.

In 1850, most Anglo cattlemen still resided in the three East Texas core areas; by 1870 a great many ranged their herds in the west, within the southern and eastern margins of the Great Plains. Soon afterwards, beginning in the 1870s, they exploded westward and northward through much of the remainder of those expansive grasslands. East met west between 1850 and 1870 in Texas, with profound shaping results for the cattle-ranching industry beyond the hundredth meridian. The "manifest destiny" of Carolina's children on the open prairies of the west was realized.

Two Early Footholds in the Great Plains

The continued westward expansion by herders following Texas statehood in 1845 created, as early as 1860, the first two clusters of Anglo cattle ranching within the Great Plains (fig. 6.1).[1] One of these clusters lay in the Coastal Bend area, along and between the lower courses of the Guadalupe, San

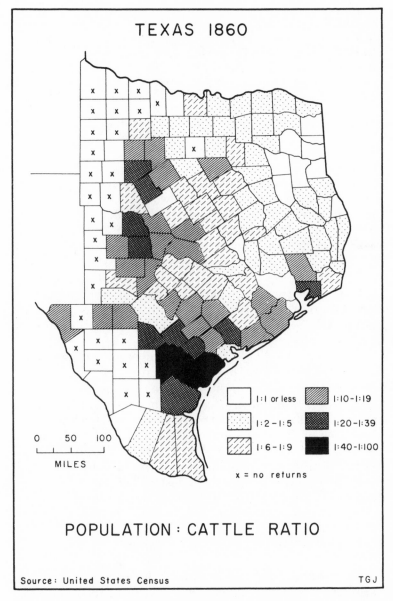

Fig. 6.1   By the eve of the Civil War, two cattle-ranching clusters had developed in Texas: the northeastern part of the "diamond" area and the Cross Timbers–Heart of Texas region.

Antonio, and Nueces rivers, a region that formed the north-eastern part of the South Texas "diamond" (fig. 3.2). In the process the Anglos overran, not for the first time in their spread westward from Carolina, a formerly important Hispanic ranching region. The Coastal Bend had been the scene of a thriving Spanish cattle industry, particularly in the 1700s, and some vestiges remained in the middle nineteenth century. The Anglos, like the Hispanos before them, found the prairies and brush country *chaparral* of the northeastern diamond well suited to cattle raising. The highest cattle-to-population ratios in Texas, over forty to one, were concentrated there by 1860, in Refugio, San Patricio, Bee, and Live Oak counties (fig. 6.1). By 1870, Anglos had expanded up the Nueces and San Antonio valleys, enlarging this South Texas ranching region to include, roughly, the northern half of the diamond area (fig. 6.2). In that year, the northern diamond housed fully one-third of the cattle population of Texas, a total of well over one million head.[2]

By contrast, the southern half of the diamond, which remained an Hispano stronghold, did not witness an increase in cattle ranching during these decades. Instead, the purest Mexican-American counties, those lining the Rio Grande, formed a sheep-ranching district. In the southern diamond as a whole, sheep outnumbered cattle two to one between 1850 and 1870, and in Webb County—the Laredo area—72,000 sheep shared the range with only 10,600 cattle in 1870.[3]

The second major new cattle-ranching cluster by 1860 lay on the central-western frontier of Texas, in a block of rolling to hilly counties drained by the middle courses of the Brazos and Colorado rivers, a region including a northern part known in the vernacular as the Cross Timbers and a southern section called the Heart of Texas (fig. 6.1). Belts of oak and cedar woodlands, interspersed with oak savannas and flanked by tall grass prairies, made this eastern margin of the Great Plains a fine setting for large-scale herding. Cultural geographer D.W. Meinig and historian R.N. Richardson designated the Cross Timbers–Heart of Texas as a "main source region" of the western cattle industry, noting that it produced "more notable cattlemen than any other region of equal size in America."[4] At the same time, the

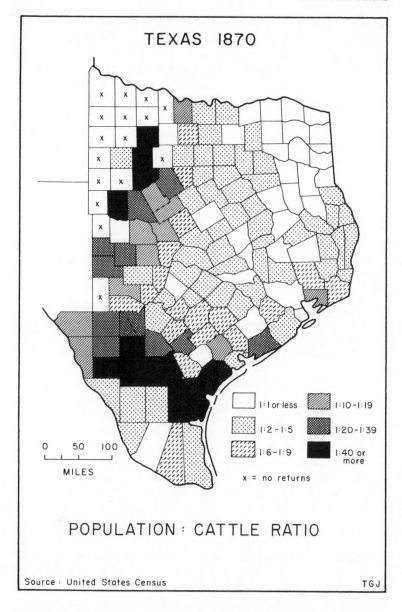

Fig. 6.2 The two Anglo cattle-ranching clusters within the margins of the Great Plains, just prior to a major migration of stockraisers into West Texas.

region formed one of the purest southern Anglo-American districts in Texas, lacking as it did any significant numbers of blacks, Hispanos, or European immigrants.[5]

During the 1860s, Comanche depredations retarded the growth of ranching in the Cross Timbers–Heart of Texas, but the industry remained intact and had spread slightly to the west by 1870 (fig. 6.2). The cattle population of the region in 1870 was considerably smaller than that of the northern diamond area, totaling only about 450,000 head, but the cattle : population ratio was ten to one. Erath County, centrally located in the region, was home to over 57,000 cattle in 1870, and adjacent Eastland County had 159 times more cattle than inhabitants.[6]

Wedged between the two principal cattle-ranching clusters by 1870 was a zone in the Texas Hill Country and Edwards Plateau where sheep were of major importance.[7] Never a major cattle region, the Hill Country–Edwards Plateau was settled in part by Germans, Poles, and Britishers, who were better acquainted with sheep raising.[8] Mexican shepherds were common. The introduction of Angora goats after about 1880 produced a combination sheep-goat-cattle-ranching economy that remains typical of the area still today.[9]

The two major cattle-ranching regions implanted within the southeastern margin of the Great Plains between 1850 and 1870 were created by cattlemen migrating from eastern Texas, from the three areas where Anglo herding had developed during the first half of the nineteenth century. The Coastal Prairie corridor played a key role in this westward thrust.

Diffusion from the Coastal Prairie of Southeast Texas

The creolized herding culture rooted in the Texas Coastal Prairie east of the Guadalupe or Lavaca rivers before 1845 subsequently made a significant contribution to the rise of ranching in the Great Plains. In the last decade and a half of the antebellum era, these lower southerners were largely responsible for developing the Coastal Bend ranching area in the South Texas diamond.

A few forerunners, the first bearers of the coastal southern cattle tradition to leave Southeast Texas and complete the century-old westward migration from the colonial cowpens to the Great Plains, entered the South Texas diamond even before 1845. After Texas statehood, this movement of Anglo-Texas herders along the Coastal Prairie corridor into the trans-Guadalupe area attained major proportions. The cattle population of the northern part of the South Texas diamond increased almost sevenfold between 1850 and 1860 (table 6.1).

One cattleman personally involved in the westward trek recalled that many ranchers who lived in the trans-Guadalupe country by 1856 had come with their stock from the humid Coastal Prairie of Southeast Texas. He specifically mentioned migrations by the Dobie and Cox families from the shores of Galveston Bay to the Nueces River country.[10] A resident of Refugio County, in the Coastal Bend, noted the movement of ranchers from "the extreme eastern part of Texas" to South Texas before 1860, and he also spoke of "large droves of cattle driven to the west from Middle and Eastern Texas and the western part of Louisiana."[11]

Other specific examples of migration provide additional support for the thesis that the Coastal Prairie corridor was the main source region of Anglo ranchers entering the Guadalupe, San Antonio, and Nueces river valleys and the remainder of the northern diamond (fig. 6.3). A cluster of ranching families, including the Kokernots, Littlefields, Wisemans, Welchs, and Barbers, migrated from the prairies of western Chambers and Liberty counties to the Guadalupe Valley of Gonzales County between 1848 and 1855, while their former neighbors the Maleys, Schulls, Dorsetts, and Dugats found new homes in Guadalupe and Bee counties.[12] The Coleman family moved from Liberty to San Patricio County in 1854, a migration paralleled by the McFaddins, who relocated hundreds of cattle from Jefferson County in Southeast Texas to the Refugio area in the Coastal Bend about the same time.[13]

When Anglo herders began entering the trans-Guadalupe country in the 1840s, they found a war-ravaged land from which most of the former Mexican ranchers had fled. Remaining behind were numerous longhorn cattle, as well as

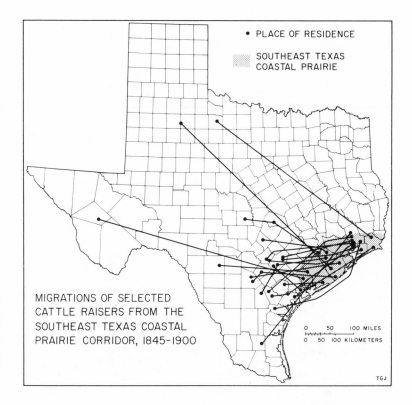

Fig. 6.3 The major goal of cattle raisers migrating from the Coastal Prairie of Southeast Texas was the northeastern part of the South Texas diamond, in the valleys of the Guadalupe, San Antonio, and Nueces rivers. All migrations which could be documented are shown. The families involved were as follows: Bell, Bryan, Coleman, Dorsett, Dugat, Fant, Gill, Jennings, Kokernot, Littlefield, McFaddin, McNeill, Maley, Mitchell, Morris, Polley, Rachal, Schull, Welch, Wiseman, and Word. Places of residence are not specific within counties, and routes of migration are stylized. Some migrations shown represent several families moving together. (Sources: Gus L. Ford, ed., *Texas Cattle Brands*, pp. 8–216; Kent Gardien, "Kokernot and His Tory," pp. 282, 292–93; J. Marvin Hunter, *The Trail Drivers of Texas*, pp. 397, 611–12; A. Ray Stephens, *The Taft Ranch*, p. 9; and Tad Moses, "Early Day Cattlemen," *The Cattleman* 34 [November 1947]: 88; [December 1947]: 28, 75; [February 1948]: 25, 66, 68.)

TABLE 6.1
The Westward Migration of Cattle Ranching in the Texas
Coastal Plain, 1850–60

Census Year	Coastal Prairie Corridor[a]			The Northern Diamond (Guadalupe–San Antonio–Nueces Valleys)[b]		
	Number of cattle	Number of cattle as a percentage of total Texas cattle	Population: cattle ratio	Number of cattle	Number of cattle as a percentage of total Texas cattle	Population: cattle ratio
1850	268,164	29	1:10	133,107	14	1:8
1860	408,704	12	1:8	882,514	25	1:15

SOURCES: *Seventh Census of the United States, 1850*, pp. 503–504, 514–15; *Eighth Census of the United States, 1860*, volume on population, pp. 484–86, and volume on agriculture, pp. 140,144, 148.

[a]The counties making up the Coastal Prairie corridor of Southeast Texas were, for 1850: Brazoria, Fort Bend, Galveston, Harris, Jackson, Jefferson, Liberty, Matagorda, and Wharton; for 1860, the same, plus Chambers and Orange.

[b]The counties in Guadalupe–San Antonio–Nueces valleys were, for 1850: Bexar, Calhoun, DeWitt, Goliad, Gonzales, Guadalupe, Lavaca, Medina, Refugio, San Patricio, and Victoria; for 1860, the same, plus Atascosa, Bee, Karnes, and Live Oak.

a relatively small population of *vaqueros*, some Irish-born ranchers, and a few Hispanic *rancheros*, such as the Navarro and de León families. The cattle industry of the Coastal Bend was all but dead. Even as late as 1850, relatively few ranchers owning over 100 cattle lived west and south of the Guadalupe River (table 6.1).[14] Between 1850, and 1860, Anglos from the Coastal Prairie corridor rebuilt the cattle industry of the trans-Guadalupe country, elevating it to a magnitude previously unknown. By the time of the Civil War, Coastal Prairie settlers had created the cattle-ranching focus in the Coastal Bend.

Even though many of its sons and daughters moved west after mid-century, the Coastal Prairie of Southeast Texas retained its status as a major ranching region. This continuing vitality was exemplified by Matagorda County, straddling the Colorado River at its junction with the Gulf. Matagorda's cattle population rose from 35,000 in 1850 to over 95,000 in 1870, and its cattle : population ratio soared from 16 : 1 to 28 : 1 in the same period. At the mouth of the Trinity River, Chambers County still had a 17 : 1 ratio of cattle to people in 1870.[15] Clearly, the concept of a transitory pastoral frontier is inappropriate for the Coastal Prairie corridor of Southeast Texas. Even to the present day, the humid prairies of the corridor retain a remnant of the economic venture that thrived there in the nineteenth century. Numerous ranches survive, stocked with herds of heat- and humidity-resistant breeds such as the Brahman. The Coastal Prairie persisted as a cattle area long enough to witness the twentieth-century eastward expansion of ranching, that backwash of the westward-moving wave of the nineteenth century which saw countless cotton fields from East Texas to Georgia turned into cattle pastures after 1930.

Even beyond the Guadalupe River, Anglo cattlemen in the South Texas diamond did not forget their traditional lower-southern markets. New Orleans remained their chief goal as late as the Civil War, and drives to Louisiana continued even in postbellum times.[16] The Crescent City's hold on the receding coastal cattle frontier strengthened with the advent of steamship cattle transport, and the port town of Indianola thrived as the major handler of Texas cattle shipped by sea to New Orleans.[17] Other cattle drives from the Guadalupe and San Antonio river valleys in the 1860s and

early 1870s reached Mobile, Natchez, Shreveport, and Wood-
ville in Mississippi.[18]

Diffusion from the Northeast Texas Prairies

The upper-southern cattle-raising tradition implanted in the
black prairies of Northeast Texas also spread westward after
about 1845 or 1850. While cattlemen from this region settled
widely through north-central and west Texas, it is clear that
their major thrust was directed at the Cross Timbers–Heart
of Texas cluster (fig. 6.4). The upper-southern herders from
the Blackland Prairie deserved a large part of the credit for
the rise of the central–west Texas frontier as a major focus of
ranching, for many cattle "barons" of the Cross Timbers–
Heart of Texas region got their start in the business in the
prairies of Northeast Texas. Both spatially and temporally,
the Cross Timbers–Heart of Texas was the successor to the
Blackland Prairie corridor as a major ranching region.

This succession, this inheritance from the northeast, can
perhaps best be illustrated by charting the migrations of
several leading personalities. Famous among these was
John Chisum, a native of Hardin (or possibly Hardeman)
County, Tennessee, who as a boy migrated to Northeast
Texas in the 1830s with his family.[19] His father, Claiborne
Chisum, settled in central Lamar County, built up sizable
landholdings, and soon had numerous cattle, hogs, and
sheep running on the Grand Prairie near the county seat of
Paris (fig. 4.1). John Chisum acquired his initial cattle-
raising experience on his father's place, and in 1850 he and
some other men drove a herd of cattle collected on the Grand
Prairie in western Lamar County to the goldfields of California (fig. 4.1). In the mid-1850s, Chisum moved west to Denton
County, where he established his own ranch on the prairies
near the edge of the Cross Timbers.

Equally prominent in the Texas ranching industry during the last half of the nineteenth century was Daniel Waggoner, a cattle baron of the first magnitude.[20] Dan, the son of
Solomon ("Sol") Waggoner, was born in 1828 in Lincoln
County, Tennessee, and as a boy took part in the family
migrations, first to Missouri and then to Northeast Texas.
Sol Waggoner settled initially on the Blossom Prairie in Red

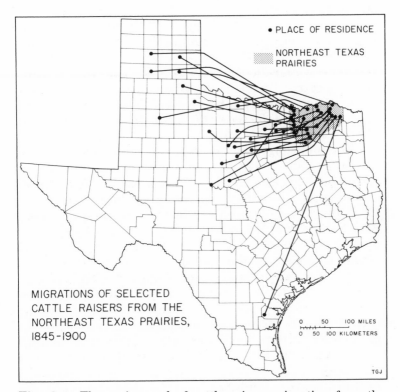

MIGRATIONS OF SELECTED
CATTLE RAISERS FROM THE
NORTHEAST TEXAS PRAIRIES,
1845-1900

Fig. 6.4 The major goal of cattle raisers migrating from the Northeast Texas Prairies was the Cross Timbers–Heart of Texas region, though some later migrants went directly to the Panhandle. All migrations which could be documented are shown. The families involved were as follows: Bivins, Black, Cartwright, Chisum, Clark, Clinton, Cox, Dalton, Douglas, Elder, Evans, Gilbert, Gunter, Igo, Loving, Montgomery, Oliver, Waggoner, and Wright. Places of residence are not specific within counties, and routes of migration are stylized. (Sources: Gus L. Ford, ed., *Texas Cattle Brands*, pp. 15–222; Lysius Gough, *Spur Jingles and Saddle Songs*, pp. 11, 13, 47, 67, 94; Walter P. Webb and H. Bailey Carroll, *The Handbook of Texas*, 1: 342–43, 688, and 2: 87, 850–51; J. Marvin Hunter, *The Trail Drivers of Texas*, pp. 523–24; B. B. Paddock, *A Twentieth Century History and Biographical Record of North and West Texas*, 1: 372.)

River County about 1839 and soon had cattle herds roaming the open range there (fig. 4.1). About 1848, the Waggoners moved down to Smith Prairie in Hopkins County, where Sol had received a land grant (fig. 4.1). By the next year Sol Waggoner was dead, and the family cattle business was taken over by his wife, Martha, and son Dan (table 4.1). Dan Waggoner's migration out of Northeast Texas with his cattle herds occurred about 1855, when he relocated in Wise County, in the Cross Timbers region. The famous Waggoner mansion can still be seen atop a hill on the east side of the Wise County seat, Decatur.

A similar migration pattern was followed by the noted cattleman Oliver Loving, born about 1812 in Hopkins County, Kentucky.[21] Loving came as an adult to Lamar County in Northeast Texas in the 1840s, then moved west to the Collin County prairies and later to the Cross Timbers of Palo Pinto County. Loving subsequently helped establish the famous Goodnight-Loving cattle trail, and a West Texas county is named for him.

Another well-known pioneer rancher was Mr. Mabel Gilbert, who, like Chisum, Waggoner, and Loving, came west from Northeast Texas.[22] A 1797 native of North Carolina, Gilbert migrated from Dickson County, Tennessee, to Fannin County in Northeast Texas in 1837, and by 1843 he had a cattle herd on the range several miles south of Bonham (fig. 4.1). In 1856 he moved west to Wichita County on the prairies west of the Cross Timbers.

A parallel migration brought Elijah and John Emberson from Lamar County in Northeast Texas in the early 1850s to the Pilot Point area of Denton County, at the border of the prairies and Cross Timbers.[23] Their father, John Emberson, Sr., had come from Arkansas, and earlier, Tennessee, to Lamar County in 1835, and he owned 100 cattle on Emberson Prairie by 1840 (fig. 4.1). The younger Embersons became noted early ranchers in Denton County.

The migration of Chisum, Waggoner, Loving, Gilbert, and the Embersons were typical of those of many Northeast Texas cattlemen (fig. 6.4). To trace the route of their movement is to illustrate the role of Northeast Texas and upper southerners in the development of the Cross Timbers–Heart of Texas ranching focus and, consequently, in the formation of the western cattle kingdom.

Westward from the Piney Woods

Upper southerners from Northeast Texas were not alone in developing the cattle industry in the Cross Timbers–Heart of Texas region. Herders who had previously resided in the Piney Woods, bearers of the creolized coastal southern cattle culture, joined them. The contribution of the East Texas Piney Woods to the west-central frontier is clearly revealed in the migration patterns of typical cattlemen (fig. 6.5), whose move to the Cross Timbers–Heart of Texas often occurred in two stages. West of the Piney Woods, in Central Texas, lay assorted fragments and belts of black prairie, and many East Texas woodland ranchers made an intermediate residential stopover in these grasslands before moving on to the central-western frontier.

Piney Woods herders began moving west in the early 1840s. Typical was John Durst, a 1797 Missouri native who had come to the Piney Woods by way of Louisiana in the early nineteenth century. Owner of 125 cattle in the woods of Nacogdoches County in 1840, Durst left East Texas three years later and purchased 2,000 acres in Leon County west of the Trinity. Included in his new ranch was part of the Leon Prairie, a small outlier of blackland, where over 400 of Durst's cattle ranged by 1850.[24]

Similarly, four of the six largest cattle owners in pine-clad Shelby County in the 1840s moved to the Blackland Prairie of Central Texas before 1860. Included were Jereboam Beauchamp, N. G. Hodges, and J. J. Hammond, who migrated with their herds of cattle to Navarro, a blackland county southeast of Dallas (fig. 6.5).[25] Later generations of the Beauchamps moved farther west to the Cross Timbers and the Texas Panhandle.[26] Emory Rains relocated from Shelby to the blackland county which today bears his name in the 1850s.[27]

The two-stage migration to the Cross Timbers by way of the Blackland Prairie, as well as the coastal southern background of many Piney Woods cattlemen, is beautifully illustrated by the lives of George Webb Slaughter and his eldest son, Christopher Columbus ("Lum") Slaughter.[28] Born in the pine barrens of southern Mississippi in 1811, George migrated as a boy and young man to Louisiana in 1825 and to Sabine County, Texas, in 1830. Preaching and small-scale

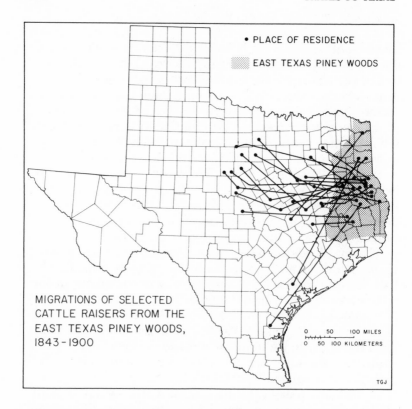

Fig. 6.5   The major goal of cattle raisers migrating from the East
Texas Piney Woods was the Cross Timbers–Heart of Texas region
in the central part of the state. Many made a residential stopover in
the Blackland Prairie of Central Texas. All migrations which could
be documented are shown. The families involved were as follows:
Beauchamp, Burks, Coggin, Dial, Durst, Evans, Hammond,
Hodges, Latham, Merchant, Nash, Rains, Reynolds, Rose, Shipp,
Slaughter, Smith, Whitcomb, Williams, Wilson, Windham, and
Wyers. Places of residence are not specific within counties, and
routes of migration are stylized. Some migrations shown represent
several families moving together. (Sources: Gus L. Ford, ed., *Texas
Cattle Brands*, pp. 8–223; J. Marvin Hunter, *The Trail Drivers of
Texas*, p. 949; Walter P. Webb and H. Bailey Carroll, *The Handbook
of Texas*, 1: 527 and 2: 432,618; Tad Moses, "Early Day Cattlemen,"
The Cattleman 34 [January 1948]: p. 40; Andrew Davis, "Folk Life
in Early Texas," p. 326; Roy Grimes, *Three Hundred Years in Victoria County*, p. 421).

cattle raising along the divide between the Sabine River and the Patroon Bayou occupied most of his time in the new Texas home. Lum, born in Sabine County in 1837, learned when still only twelve years old to work his father's stock, and by age fifteen he had purchased 70 cattle from an uncle. In that same year, 1852, the Slaughters moved west with their herds to a new home in Freestone County, on the margin of the Central Texas Blackland Prairie. Discontented with the quality of the range there, the Slaughters in 1856 migrated again, to the hills of Palo Pinto County in the rapidly developing Cross Timbers–Heart of Texas ranching region. By 1860 they owned over 800 cattle on the Palo Pinto range. These they trailed to Shreveport and other eastern markets, but in 1870 the Slaughters drove 3,000 head to the Kansas railroads. In time, Lum Slaughter acquired land-holdings of one million acres, in three huge ranches, and became the largest taxpayer in all of Texas. The Slaughters' cattle-herding experience thus bridged from the pine barrens of the Deep South to the Great Plains.

Continuing Diffusion after 1870

Many Anglos paused only briefly in South Texas and the Cross Timbers–Heart of Texas areas before continuing their migration. From these two clearly defined bases in the margins of the Great Plains, they spread rapidly westward and northward after 1870. In the wake of the decimation of the Plains Indians and the bison herds, Anglo herders, continuing the thrust that had long before brought their genealogical and cultural ancestors out of Carolina, surged through much of the Great Plains.

In this expansion, cattlemen from the two regions followed different paths westward. The primary goal of ranchers emigrating from South Texas was the trans-Pecos country, including the Davis Mountains and Big Bend (fig. 6.6).[29] These inheritors of the coastal cattle tradition rarely ventured north of the thirty-second parallel, clinging instead to counties on or near the Mexican border. In South Texas and the Coastal Prairie, many of them had become accustomed to using Mexican *vaqueros*, a dependence which may

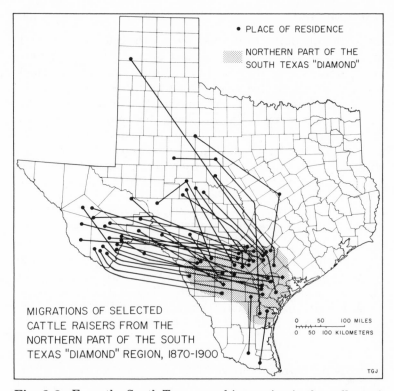

Fig. 6.6 From the South Texas ranching region in the valleys of the Guadalupe, San Antonio, and Nueces rivers, cattlemen spread mainly west, into the trans-Pecos country, including the Big Bend area and the Davis Mountains. Few migrated north of the 32° parallel of latitude. Overall, South Texas was far less important than the Cross Timbers–Heart of Texas as a source of western ranchers (see fig. 6.6). All migrations which could be documented are shown. The families involved were as follows: Bluntzer, Bourland, Bryan, Buttrill, Byler, Childress, Crosson, Dull, Gill, Haley, Harris, Kokernot, Lackey, Littlefield, Lowe, McCutcheon, McIntyre, Mansfield, Mitchell, Morris, Neighbors, Newton, Pulliam, Quebedeaux, Rabb, Reininger, Serna, Shanklin, Shoemake, Stillwell, Townsend, Walton, and Wilson. Places of residence are not specific within counties, and routes of migration are stylized. (Sources: Gus L. Ford, ed., *Texas Cattle Brands*, pp. 18–212; Tad Moses, "Early Day Cattlemen," *The Cattleman*, 34, [November 1947]: 96; [December 1947]: 28, 72, 75, 76; [January 1948]: 40, 60; and [February 1948]: 66; Walter P. Webb and H. Bailey Carroll, *The Handbook of Texas*, 2: 66; Eldon S. Branda, ed., *The Handbook of Texas*, 3: 484 and Clifford B. Casey, *Mirages, Mysteries, and Reality: Brewster County, Texas*, pp. 154, 353, 383, 390, 393, 399, 401, 404, 408, 418, 422.)

help explain their migration pattern. In semiarid Southwest Texas, near the border, they could continue to ranch in the manner they had known in the valleys of the Guadalupe, San Antonio and Nueces rivers. Theirs remained a far southern, creolized herding culture, and they were not major participants in the spread of ranching through the Great Plains.

Instead, the Cross Timbers–Heart of Texas cattlemen provided the main westward and northward movement after 1870 (fig. 6.7). The spread of ranching into the Texas South Plains and Panhandle was largely their work, as was a major thrust up the Concho Valley, across a low divide to the Pecos River, and northward along that stream into eastern New Mexico.[30] Many soon expanded their ranching operations into states north of Texas, carrying the Anglo herding system through the Great Plains. Some of the families and personalities involved in this migration from central Texas have been mentioned earlier. John Chisum helped pioneer the Concho Valley route to New Mexico; Dan Waggoner expanded his huge operation into the Red River Valley at the base of the Texas Panhandle; and Lum Slaughter acquired ranch lands in the South Plains, bordering New Mexico.[31] West Texas, in very considerable measure, was colonized from East and Central Texas, a pattern initially established by cattlemen from the Cross Timbers–Heart of Texas. More than that, these sons of the Piney Woods and Upper South were chiefly responsible for bringing Carolina to the Great Plains.

Anglo Herding Traits in the West

As Anglo cattle herders spread westward after mid-century, they did not forsake the Carolina heritage. Rather, they introduced elements of their cattle tradition, passing on to descendants in the west many ancestral herding traits from the southeastern seaboard (fig. 6.8). They remained, in goodly measure, Carolina's children.

One typically Anglo custom imported to the west was the use of herder dogs. Tilden, the county seat of McMullen in the South Texas diamond, was called Dog Town in the 1870s, due to the local ranchers' habit of using packs of dogs to round up

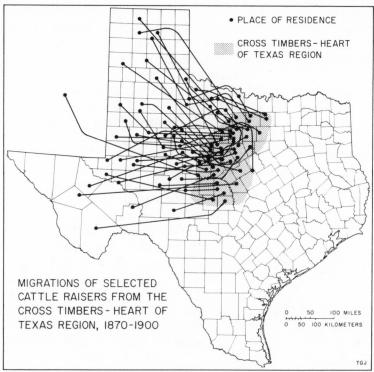

● PLACE OF RESIDENCE

CROSS TIMBERS – HEART
OF TEXAS REGION

MIGRATIONS OF SELECTED
CATTLE RAISERS FROM THE
CROSS TIMBERS – HEART OF
TEXAS REGION, 1870–1900

0   50   100 MILES
0   50   100 KILOMETERS

TGJ

Fig. 6.7 From the Cross Timbers–Heart of Texas region, cattle
ranchers spread after 1870 to occupy the South Plains and Pan-
handle. A comparison of figs. 6.6 and 6.7 reveals clearly that the
Cross Timbers–Heart of Texas was the most important source of
Anglo-Texan ranchers in the occupance of the southern Great
Plains. All migrations which could be documented are shown. The
families involved were as follows: Allen, Askey, Beauchamp,
Brownfield, Brunson, Burnett, Chisum, Cochran, Cowden, Cox,
Driver, Elder, Elkins, Estes, Evans, Forbis, Funk, Goodnight,
Halsell, Henderson, Hitson, Johnson, Koonsman, Mann, Means,
Merchant, Page, Patterson, Richardson, Robertson, Slaughter,
Soules, Taylor, Tharp, Waggoner, Weatherby, Wood, Wright, Wylie,
and Young. Places of residence are not specific within counties, and
routes of migration are stylized. (Sources: Gus L. Ford, ed., *Texas
Cattle Brands*, pp. 14-222; Walter P. Webb and H. Bailey Carroll,
The Handbook of Texas, 1: 253-54, and 2: 618; Tad Moses, "Early
Day Cattlemen," *The Cattleman* 34 [November 1947]: 98; [January
1948]: 39, 66;[February 1948]: 62, 66; [December 1947]: 28; and
Clifford B. Casey, *Mirages, Mysteries, and Reality: Brewster
County, Texas*, p. 394.)

cattle in the surrounding brush country. Even the Mexican *vaqueros* on the famous King Ranch in South Texas had herder dogs by the 1940s, using them to find cattle that strayed into brush thickets. To the north, also, in the Cross Timbers–Heart of Texas ranching region, leopard dogs were common.[32] Their use declined to the west, on the open grasslands, and relatively few major ranches in West Texas kept such canines. One late nineteenth-century rancher in the Texas Panhandle did own a pack of seventy-five "greyhounds," but their job was to protect his cattle from wolves and coyotes rather than to herd stock. These hounds lived in a low, elongated "mush house," and the man in charge of them was called a "mush-pot wrangler."[33]

Black cowboys made a more effective transition to the west (fig. 6.8). Famous Cross Timbers cattlemen such as Dan Waggoner and Oliver Loving used black cowhands before and after the Civil War. On his Wichita County ranch in 1880, Waggoner employed thirty-one Anglos, one black, and one Mexican as cowboys.[34] Even in the South Texas diamond, where *vaquero* labor was common, black cowboys were occasionally found. For example, C. C. Cox, a rancher in Live Oak County in the Coastal Bend area, used Negro help in the late 1850s. Blacks accompanied the Anglo rancher migration to West Texas, where sixty-eight of them worked as cowboys by 1880 (fig. 6.9; Table 6.2). While these blacks made up only 4 percent of the cowboy work force, a far lower proportion than claimed by some historians, their presence in West Texas is undeniable.[35] Some worked for the huge XIT Ranch on the Texas High Plains. Eventually, a few blacks even became ranch owners in West Texas, and Negro cowhands continued to find employment on ranches there into the present century.

Some Anglo herding vocabulary also reached the west intact. A good example is the word "pen," widely used through West and South Texas from postbellum times to the present (fig. 6.8). At Lytle Gap, near Abilene in West Texas, an early rancher "built pens ... on Elm Creek at the gap for penning purposes in returning cattle."[36] Modern maps of the western part of the state reveal place names such as Rock Pen Creek in Irion County, Pen Branch in King County, and Tascosa Stock Pens in Oldham County. Even in Hispanic South Texas, one finds Cantinas Pens in Hidalgo County

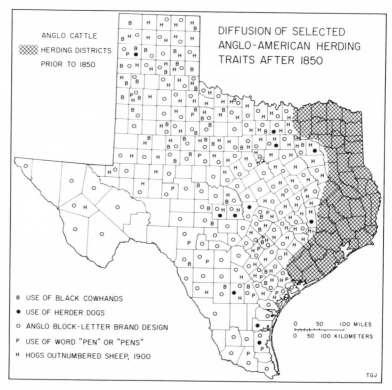

Fig. 6.8 Anglo traits were most evident in the Pannandle-South Plains area, settled by herders from the Cross Timbers–Heart of Texas region. (Sources: Gus L. Ford, ed., *Texas Cattle Brands*, pp. 7–210; sources cited in notes 32, 33, 34, 35; *Twelfth Census of the U.S., 1900*, 5: 481–85; Ernest R. Archambeau, "The First Federal Census in the Panhandle, 1880," pp. 48, 49, 64, 71, 131; W. H. Jackson and S. A. Long, *The Texas Stock Directory*; J. Marvin Hunter, *The Trail Drivers of Texas*, pp. 115, 340, 403, 481, 656, 839; Bailey C. Hanes, *Bill Pickett, Bulldogger*, pp. 17, 20; various topographic quadrangle maps published by the U.S. Geological Survey; various county histories; and the MS population schedules of the 1880 census.)

and Mifflin Pens on the King Ranch. The Carolina term "cowhunt" also survived the long journey to the Great Plains.[37]

Typical Anglo brand designs, consisting of unadorned block letters and Arabic numerals, spread widely through

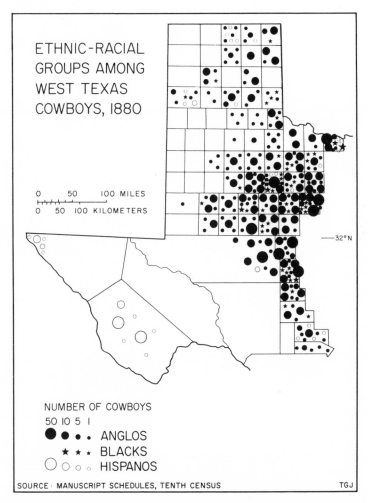

ETHNIC-RACIAL
GROUPS AMONG
WEST TEXAS
COWBOYS, 1880

0   50   100 MILES
0   50   100 KILOMETERS

—32°N

NUMBER OF COWBOYS
50 10 5 1
● ● • ∙ ANGLOS
★ ★ ⋆ BLACKS
◯ ○ ∘ ∘ HISPANOS

SOURCE : MANUSCRIPT SCHEDULES, TENTH CENSUS   TGJ

Fig. 6.9 All persons who were working cattle are included, but
ranch owners are excluded. Census marshals variously described
such men as "cowboy," "cattle herder," "works cattle," "cattle
hand," "cattle boss," "cattle driver," "cow herder," and the like.
Care was taken to exclude all persons employed as sheep herders,
goat herders, swine herders, horse raisers, cooks, and common
laborers. If the marshal listed profession simply as "herder" or
"stock herder," the presence of cattle on the ranch in question was
ascertained as a prerequisite for including the person. In some
counties, such as Pecos and Crockett, the marshals' entries concerning profession were inadequate to permit any person to be included.
The few European-born cowboys detected were excluded from the
map.

TABLE 6.2
ETHNIC-RACIAL GROUPS AMONG WEST TEXAS COWBOYS, 1880

Group	North of 32° Latitude[a]		South of 32° Latitude[b]		West Texas Total	
	Number	As percentage of total	Number	As percentage of total	Number	As percentage of total
Anglos	966	93	387	72	1,383	86
Blacks	56	5	12	2	68	4
Hispanos	21	2	141	26	162	10

SOURCES: Manuscript schedules of the Tenth Census of the United States, 1880.

NOTE: Figures include all persons demonstrably working cattle. See also Fig. 6.9.

[a] Counties included: Armstrong, Baylor, Borden, Briscoe, Carson, Childress, Collingsworth, Cottle, Crosby, Dawson, Deaf Smith, Dickens, Donley, Fisher, Floyd, Gaines, Garza, Gray, Hall, Hansford, Hardeman, Hartley, Haskell, Hemphill, Howard, Hutchinson, Jones, Kent, King, Knox, Lipscomb, Lubbock, Lynn, Martin, Mitchell, Motley, Nolan, Ochiltree, Oldham, Potter, Randall, Roberts, Scurry, Shackelford, Stonewall, Swisher, Taylor, Throckmorton, Wheeler, Wichita, and Wilbarger.

[b] Counties included: Bandera, Concho, Crockett, Edwards, El Paso, Kerr, Kimble, Menard, Pecos, Presidio, Runnels, and Tom Green.

West Texas and became the most common type there (fig. 6.8).[38] Even when embellished with "bars," "rockers," "circles," or similar design features, the basic part of the brand normally remained a simple letter and/or number. A colonial South Carolinian would have found nothing remarkable about most West Texas brands. Indeed, a number of these brands came west, unaltered, from the southern states to find a place in the ranch country of late nineteenth-century Texas. For example, the "T2" brand, originated in 1803 by the Thompson family of Clarke County, in the pine barrens of South Alabama, was still in use eighty years later by Thompson descendants in Dimmit County, located in the South Texas diamond.[39] James H. Banta first used his "JIM" brand in Henry County, in the Ozark Plateau ranching country of Missouri, and when he migrated to the frontier of North Texas, he continued it. The Elkins family brought their "RE" brand from the cattle country of Illinois to the Cross Timbers–Heart of Texas region in the early 1850s.[40]

Typically Anglo, too, was the custom of giving brands a popular name, such as "lazy J" for a letter *J* placed sideways or "four sixes" for the 6666 brand. Spanish brands, by contrast, rarely had names. When pressed for a name, Hispanics will sometimes refer to particular brands simply as "fierro viejo," "the old iron."[41] In Texas, the nameless Spanish brands, characterized by abstract designs or Mexican-Indian marks, never spread northward through the Great Plains, remaining confined with few exceptions, to the South Texas diamond and the Piney Woods (fig. 6.10).[42] Even there, Anglo-type brands were prevalent by 1865.[43]

Hispanic-derived longhorns, according to the commonly accepted account, provided the livestock for the early cattle industry of West Texas and the Great Plains. Only later, after the advent of barbed wire, were improved breeds introduced to displace the longhorn, goes the traditional argument. My evidence suggests, on the contrary, that West Texas cattle were not pureblood longhorns in the pre-fence era and that bloodlines derived from the Anglo-American East were always present. Dan Waggoner's experience in the Cross Timbers region is illustrative. As was described earlier, Waggoner began as a cattle raiser in the Blackland Prairie corridor of Northeast Texas, then moved his herds to

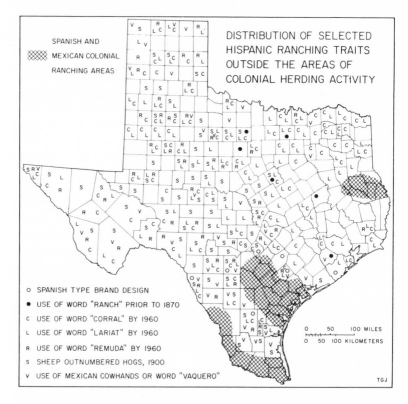

Fig. 6.10 Certain Hispanic traits, mainly skills and terminology related to horsemanship, spread into the Great Plains, while others never diffused significantly out of South Texas. (Sources: Elmer B. Atwood, *The Regional Vocabulary of Texas*, pp. 132, 137, 149, 150, 152, 161; Gus L. Ford, ed., *Texas Cattle Brands*, pp. 1-210; U.S. censuses, 1850–80, MS population and agricultural schedules; *Twelfth Census of the U.S., 1900*, 5: 481–85; Fred A. Tarpley, "A Word Atlas of Northeast Texas," pp. 175, 177; D. Port Smythe, "D. Port Smythe's Journey Across Early Texas," p. 3; James B. Barry, "The Diary of James Buckner Barry," p. 158; various county histories; and the MS population schedules of the 1880 census.)

the Cross Timbers of Wise County in the 1850s. About 1865 he became aware of a "slow change in appearance" in his cattle from one year to the next. Seeking the cause of this change, Waggoner finally located a single feral longhorn bull among his stock. This bull fought and defeated Waggoner's smaller bulls, presumably of British origin, and collected a sizable entourage of cows. Supposedly, Waggoner's uninvited longhorn was the first of his breed to appear as far north as Wise County.[44] Thus, on the very eve of the surge by Anglo ranchers onto the Great Plains, one of the legendary cattle kings noticed the first appearance of longhorn traits in his herd. It seems very likely that other cattle introduced to the Cross Timbers from Northeast Texas, such as the herd brought from Fannin to Palo Pinto County about 1858, were also dominantly British.[45]

Nor were the cattle trailed west from the Piney Woods of unmixed Hispanic ancestry—and the East Texas area remained a major source of western cattle throughout the nineteenth century. In the 1880s cattlemen from West Texas came to the southern Piney Woods looking for herd replacements, and one East Texas resident recalled that "every once in a while somebody would go along the big road" in front of his house, "with a small herd of cattle, drifting them west to grass and prairie country."[46]

Further diluting the longhorn parentage of early West Texas herds were cattle introduced directly from eastern states. One early rancher in the Cross Timbers had come from Alabama with some nonlonghorn stock, and Lum Slaughter, the cattle baron of Palo Pinto County in the Cross Timbers, imported shorthorn bulls from Kentucky as early as 1871 to improve his herd.[47] It may well be true that Texas ranchers sent their purer longhorn animals north to stock the Great Plains ranges between 1870 and 1890, keeping the superior, part-British cattle to restock their own ranges. In this way, Texas cattle could have gotten the reputation in the north of being longhorns, even though the actual makeup of the herds reflected a mixture of Spanish and British stock. At any rate, the claim that pure longhorn cattle prevailed on the West Texas ranges between 1870 and 1890 deserves to be challenged. Not even the crucial Coastal Prairie corridor, the southernmost of the Anglo routes westward, was stocked with pure longhorns.

Livestock combinations also affirm that Anglo influence penetrated the Great Plains. The traditional cattle-hog association remained intact, particularly in the Cross Timbers–Heart of Texas region, where Anglo herders kept roughly one-fourth as many swine as cattle.[48] Two narrow,

north-south belts of oak forest—the Cross Timbers—
provided excellent range for hogs there, while the adjacent
prairies served as cattle range. Indeed, the attractiveness of
the Cross Timbers–Heart of Texas region to Anglo herders
may have rested as much on the mast-filled woods as on the
lush grasslands. In the westward movement of Anglo-Texan
ranchers, the Cross Timbers–Heart of Texas region was the
last district where large numbers of cattle and hogs could
conveniently be combined on the open range.

Anglos in the northern half of the South Texas diamond
had less success in continuing the traditional cattle-hog
association. In 1870, swine were only a tenth as numerous as
cattle there, partly because woodlands were not abundant.
The few counties containing tracts of oak forest, such as
Guadalupe, Gonzales, Lavaca, Wilson, and Atascosa, had
swine populations far above average for the region.[49]

As Anglo cattlemen spread westward from the two frontier bases onto the grasslands of the Great Plains, swine
ceased to be a major ranch animal. Even so, small numbers
of hogs were owned by Anglo ranchers in the grassy Panhandle–South Plains area, where swine often outnumbered
sheep (fig. 6.8).[50] Typically, the West Texas ranchers kept
their hogs penned rather than on the open range, in numbers
sufficient only to provide pork for the ranch population.[51]

Anglo influence can also be detected in certain elements
of West Texas cowboy folklife. Traditional music provides a
good example in the "bury-me-not" theme, which displays
both British and Hispanic influences.[52] A more detailed
analysis of Great Plains cowboy folk culture and its antecedents is much needed, but no comprehensive study presently
exists.

Hispanic Traits in the West

Carolina, then, was abundantly represented in the Great
Plains cattle industry. But so, too, was Latin America. Western ranching vocabulary abounded with Spanish loanwords
such as "corral," "ranch" "remuda," "morral," "lariat,"
"bronc," and "pinto," and various other aspects of nonmate-
rial and material herding culture on the Great Plains
reflected Hispanic influence (fig. 6.10). Traditionally, the

South Texas diamond has been designated as the primary scene of Hispanicization.

It is not my intent to deny the Hispanos a role in the evolution of Great Plains ranching. Rather, the argument presented here and reinforced by findings presented in the preceding four chapters is (1) that the role of the South Texas diamond as an arena of Hispanicization has been greatly overemphasized and (2) that the case for Hispanic influence in the Great Plains has been consistently overstated.

Absorption of Spanish herding traits by lower southern Anglos began in the late eighteenth century, far to the east along the creole coast. As was documented in chapters 2 and 3, Hispanicization began in earnest in southern Louisiana and the Natchez area of Mississippi, and the process continued in the Coastal Prairie corridor of Southeast Texas, where Anglos employed Mexican herders and used lariats by 1830. Census marshals working the Coastal Prairie counties of Southeast Texas in 1850 found additional evidence that Hispanicization was well advanced there. They listed the profession of a Fort Bend County Anglo as "owner of ranch," while in nearby Jackson County one of the nine Mexican-American inhabitants declared himself to be a "becero" (*vaquero*).[53] The creolized herding culture carried west of the Guadalupe River by Anglos after 1845 or 1850 probably differed only in minor respects from the remnant Hispanic system already rooted there.

Moreover, the Mexican rancheros of the South Texas diamond had very nearly disappeared before 1850. In the Guadalupe, San Antonio, and Nueces river valleys—the crucial Coastal Bend area in the northeastern part of the diamond—only 10 persons of Spanish surname owned 100 or more cattle at mid-century, and the total number of resident Hispanic "herdsmen" was but 181, of whom 92 lived south of the Nueces River.[54] In the most purely Mexican portion of South Texas—the Rio Grande Valley between Laredo and the Gulf—only 12 Spanish-surnamed persons owned as many as 100 cattle in 1850, and this southern part of the diamond remained inconsequential as a cattle-ranching region. Moreover, banditry, lasting from the 1850s through the middle 1870s, made cattle ranching in the district between the Nueces River and the Rio Grande next to impossible for Hispanos and Anglos alike.[55]

A culture in rapid decline, such as that of the South
Texas Hispanic rancheros between 1840 and 1880, is unlikely to exert much shaping influence on a vital, expanding
neighbor culture. It is therefore more appropriate to regard
the cattle industry that thrived in the northern part of the
diamond area by 1860 and 1870 as mainly an Anglo-
American achievement, as a successor of the creolized lower-
southern herder culture. The diamond was the westernmost
in a succession of arenas where coastal Anglos met Hispanos, and not demonstrably the most important.

The overemphasis on South Texas as a scene of Hispanicization has, in turn, led to an incorrect view of that region
as the "cradle" of the Texas and Great Plains cattle industry.[56] In fact, a better argument can be made for the South
Texas diamond as a cradle of Texas sheep ranching. The
combination of sheep and cattle on the same range, a combination in which sheep not infrequently exceeded cattle in
importance, was typical of Hispanic-American ranching. In
the southern half of the South Texas diamond, exactly such a
situation existed in the middle nineteenth century, as was
suggested earlier.[57] One result, perhaps, was that some
Anglo ranchers in the northern half of the diamond, by 1870,
combined cattle and sheep raising. Sheep outnumbered
swine almost two to one in the northern diamond, a major
departure from coastal southern Anglo tradition.[58] Perhaps
the sheep-ranching industry which developed in the
Edwards Plateau region by 1880 can be traced to this experience gained in the South Texas diamond.

The principal Hispanic-American contribution to western cattle ranching lay in horsemanship and related paraphernalia and vocabulary. Anglos thereby acquired equestrian techniques well suited to open grassland country. Most
likely, this acquisition began far to the east, perhaps even in
Florida and South Georgia, and was largely completed in the
Coastal Prairie of southern Louisiana and Southeast Texas.
When Anglo and Hispano ranchers met again in the trans-
Guadalupe country, both were mounted herdsmen.

Not only has South Texas been falsely designated as the
cradle of the western cattle kingdom and overrated as a scene
of Hispanicization, but also (and perhaps consequently) the
extent of Spanish influence in the Great Plains ranching

industry has been overestimated. The incorrect assumption that Anglos were neophytes who adopted intact the Hispanic herding system has led scholars of that school of thought to look for a Mexican behind every sagebrush. A good example of such overstatement is Sandra Myres's claim that the *mesta*, an Hispanic stockraisers' guild traceable to medieval Spain, was the forerunner of such Anglo cattlemen's organizations as the Panhandle Stockmen's Association, established in 1880, and the Texas and Southwestern Cattle Raisers Association, founded in the Cross Timbers area in 1877.[59] This extravagant claim has no documented factual basis. The Cross Timbers–Heart of Texas was the less Hispanicized of the two major cattle-ranching districts of Texas by 1870, and yet it produced the first Anglo stockmen's organization. It is more logical to seek the origin of such associations in the traditional communalism of the Anglo frontier, the same communalism that produced claim clubs, house raisings, wagon trains, and home-guard militia.[60]

Similarly, Professor Myres has maintained that western cattle brands were derived from Hispanic prototypes.[61] To do so, she has had to overlook the pronounced differences in style pointed out in chapter 4 and the proven importation of Anglo brands from eastern states.

Still, as suggested earlier, Hispanic influence existed in the Great Plains, most notably in horsemanship (fig. 6.10). Agents and routes of diffusion must be found to account for the presence of these Spanish traits. Since Anglos ranching in the South Texas diamond were more thoroughly Hispanicized than any others, as a result of their long experience on the creole coast, they would seem to provide the key. Closer inspection, however, reveals several apparent problems with this diffusion model. First, a number of Hispanic traits failed to spread northward from the diamond area. Among these was the "Mexican plan" of herding, adopted by some Anglos in the Nueces Valley of South Texas in the 1850s. It involved a roundup or *rodeo* "once a week or oftener," instead of only once or twice each year, as was the Anglo custom.[62]

Nor did large-scale sheep raising or the use of Mexican *vaqueros* spread notably north of the thirty-second parallel. Only 2 percent of the cowhands employed north of that parallel in 1880 were Hispanos (table 6.2) (fig. 6.9). In fact, when

Anglo ranchers in the Texas Panhandle were confronted by Hispano sheepmen from another source—New Mexico—in the late 1870s and early 1880s, Anglo-Texas ranchers stuck by their cattle and rejected the opportunity to give sheep a major place in their range operation. The Panhandle's Hispano *pastores*, who numbered 358 in 1880, had recently arrived from New Mexico. Though they accounted in that year for 22 percent of the Panhandle's total population—70 percent in the four western border counties—the Hispanos were quickly shunted out and their sheep replaced by Anglo cattle. They left behind only some place names.[63]

Another problem with accepting South Texas Anglos as a major source of Hispanic traits lies in their migration routes. As we have seen, their principal path in the latter part of the nineteenth century led westward to the trans-Pecos country, not north into the Great Plains proper (fig. 6.6). Relocation diffusion in the form of migration from South Texas cannot explain the spread of Hispanic traits, since migration routes ran at right angles to the presumed direction of trait diffusion.

This apparent problem is resolved by a consideration of marketing routes. After the Civil War, South Texas Anglo cattlemen broke their longstanding allegiance to New Orleans as a market and began trailing herds northward to Missouri and Kansas, following the earlier example of ranchers in northern and central Texas. The principal cattle trails serving South Texas led directly north, through the Cross Timbers–Heart of Texas region (fig. 6.11). Hispanic horsemanship skills, with the related items of material culture and vocabulary as well as the word "ranch," appear to have diffused northward along the cattle trails and to have been implanted in the Cross Timbers–Heart of Texas. Another potent force in the northward diffusion of Hispanic herding traits was the Mexican War of 1846-48, in which numerous Texans from the northern and central portions of the state saw action in the south. These contacts with South Texas were renewed during the Civil War, when the blockade of Texan ports forced a variety of goods to be shipped out through Mexican ports. So, while migration routes ran east to west, important north-south avenues of communication were opened by two wars and a new marketing pattern.

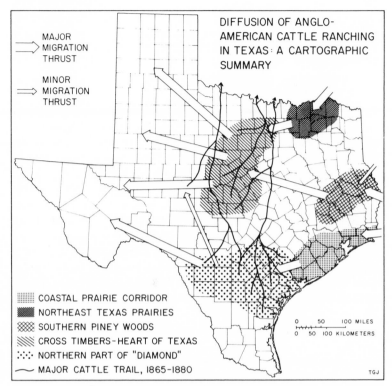

Fig. 6.11 The major postbellum cattle trails ran at right angles to the direction of migration, encouraging south-to-north cultural diffusion.

These avenues brought selected Hispanic traits and huge numbers of longhorn cattle north without noticeably influencing migration. Principally in this manner, the techniques of the creole coast cowmen reached the Great Plains.

Conclusion

Great Plains cattle ranching in the open-range era during the latter part of the nineteenth century contained an important Anglo-American component, a component that derived ultimately from seventeenth-century South Carolina. A spatial and temporal continuity between the colonial South

Atlantic seaboard and western Texas has been demon-
strated. Great Plains open-range cattle ranchers belonged in
part among South Carolina children, both genealogically and
culturally.

Geographer Donald Meinig enumerated "about twenty"
nuclei of colonization on the Atlantic coast of North America
in which distinct local cultures developed, later to spread
westward and contribute to the shaping of the United
States.[64] Boston and its environs, for example, gave us the
Puritan work ethic; the Delaware Valley provided the log
cabin and family-operated farm; the Chesapeake Tidewater
was the source of the plantation. Among the twenty, too, was
Charleston and its hinterland, though its importance has
generally been underestimated. Henceforth, colonial South
Carolina, whose legacy reached the grassy expanses of the
Great Plains, should be regarded as a cultural hearth of great
significance to the evolution and understanding of both the
South and the West. It should take its rightful place along-
side the other major colonial nuclei as one of the major
shapers of American culture and institutions.

What, then, remains to be said concerning the six
schools of thought outlined in chapter 1 which propose to
explain cattle ranching in terms of ethnicity, physical environment, frontier stages, and market accessibility models?
The answer, in the case of West Texas and the Great Plains,
seems to be that all six provide part of the explanation but
none suffices alone. The processes of origin were complex.

In ethnic terms, western ranching reflects a unique mixture of groups, a blending of British, African, Hispanic, and
probably also French, German, and Amerindian influences.
The crucial early mixing occurred in one confined locality,
lowland South Carolina, the southern fringe of the English
colonial empire in North America, where a favorable juxta-
position of Britons and West Africans occurred. Westward
along the creole coast of the Lower South, as far as the
Nueces Valley of Texas, vigorous ethnic blending continued
for two centuries.

Environmentally, a subtropical belt of pine barrens better suited to grazing than cultivation provided a hospitable,
though certainly not determinant, physical setting for the
incubation of Carolina cattle herding. The same pine

barrens, together with canebrakes, small prairies, and grassland corridors, offered suitable pathways to the west. Ultimately, ranching reached the greatest stretch of grassland on the North American continent, an environment that encouraged expansion of herding on a scale previously unknown.

Frontier conditions, most notably a shortage of labor, contributed to the rise of ranching in South Carolina, but large-scale cattle herding was not typical of other English colonial frontiers in America. Often, but not always, in the areas where it was implanted, ranching was confined to a pioneer stage and disappeared with the passing of the Anglo frontier. While helpful in certain instances, the concept of cattle herding as an occupance stage is not universally applicable in the westward diffusion to the Great Plains.

A desire to participate in the market of the Thünenian World City, coupled with the difficulty of access typical of frontier areas, helps explain the viability of an extensive form of land-use such as livestock ranching. The market, emanating initially from western Europe through the West Indian plantations, was essential to the rise and spread of open-range herding. But in the final analysis, the market model cannot explain the precise character of a frontier economy.

In sum, western ranching was the product of ethnic creolization occuring in a frontier setting and a suitable physical environment, under favorable market conditions. Had any one of these elements—culture, contact, remoteness, environment, or market—been fundamentally different, western ranching would also have been different, or quite possibly would not have come to exist at all. Indeed, when one element—remoteness—was broken down by railroads and the industrial age around the turn of the present century, traditional open-range cattle ranching quickly disappeared. Carolina's reign on the western grasslands was short, limited to the brief, pleasant interlude between the arrival of the first cattlemen and the coming of the machine age.

Notes

Chapter 1

1. The nucleus of this chapter first appeared as an article: Terry G. Jordan, "The Origin and Distribution of Open-Range Cattle Ranching," *Social Science Quarterly* 53 (1972): 105-21.

2. Paul Vidal de la Blache, "Les genres de vie dans la géographie humaine," *Annales de Géographie* 20 (1911): 193-212, 289-304; Max Sorre, "La notion de genre de vie et sa valeur actuelle," *Annales de Géographie* 57 (1948): 97-108, 193-204.

3. Frederick Jackson Turner, "The Significance of the Frontier in American History," *Annual Report of the American Historical Association for the Year 1893*, p. 208.

4. Henry E. Fritz, "The Cattlemen's Frontier in the Trans-Mississippi West: An Annotated Bibliography," *Arizona and the West* 14 (1972): 45-70, 169-90. Among the works by geographers are: Kenneth D. Israel, "The Cattle Industry of Mississippi, Its Origin and Changes Through Time Up to 1850" (Ph.D. diss., University of Southern Mississippi, 1970); Fred Kniffen, "The Western Cattle Complex: Notes on Differentiation and Diffusion," *Western Folklore* 12 (1953): 179-85; Terry G. Jordan, "The Origin of Anglo-American Cattle Ranching in Texas: A Documentation of Diffusion From the Lower South," *Economic Geography* 45 (1969): 63-87; idem, "Texan Influence in Nineteenth-Century Arizona Cattle Ranching," *Journal of the West* 14 (1975): 15-17; Lauren C. Post, "The Old Cattle Industry of Southwestern Louisiana," *McNeese Review* 9 (1957): 43-55; Gary S. Dunbar, "Colonial Carolina Cowpens," *Agricultural History* 35 (1961): 125-30; Eugene J. Wilhelm, "Animal Drives—A Case Study in Historical Geography," *Journal of Geography* 66 (1967): 327-334; and Terry G. Jordan, "Early Northeast Texas and the Evolution of Western Ranching," *Annals, Association of American Geographers* 67: (1977), 66-87. See also: J. E. Spencer and Ronald J. Horvath, "How Does An Agricultural Region Originate?" *Annals, Association of American Geographers* 53 (1963): 74-92. Recent works by historians include: Forrest McDonald and Grady McWhiney, "The Antebellum Southern

Herdsman: A Reinterpretation," *Joural of Southern History* 41 (1975): 147–66; David Wheeler, "The Beef Cattle Industry in the United States: Colonial Origins," *Panhandle-Plains Historical Review* 46 (1973): 54–67; Sandra L. Myres, "The Ranching Frontier: Spanish Institutional Backgrounds of the Plains Cattle Industry," in *Essays on the American West,* ed. Harold M. Hollingsworth and Sandra L. Myres, pp. 19–39; Francis L. Fugate, "Origins of the Range Cattle Era in South Texas," *Agricultural History* 35 (1961): 155–58; and John D. W. Guice, "Cattle Raisers of the Old Southwest: A Reinterpretation," *Western Historical Quarterly* 8 (1977): 167–87.

    5. "The Reign of King Hog: New Perspectives on the Antebellum Southern Livestock Industry," a session at the New Orleans meeting of the Organization of American Historians, April 1979; participating were John H. Moore, Forrest McDonald, Grady McWhiney, James W. Whitaker, John D. W. Guice, William N. Parker, and Terry G. Jordan.

    6. Lewis C. Gray, *History of Agriculture in the Southern United States,* p. 19.

    7. Pierre Deffontaines, *Contribution à la Géographie pastorale de l'Amérique latine,* pp. 25–26.

    8. Jordan, "Origin and Distribution of Open-Range Cattle Ranching," pp. 105–11.

    9. Turner, "Significance of the Frontier in American History," p. 208.

    10. Frederick Jackson Turner, *The Frontier in American History,* p. 16.

    11. W. K. Hancock, "Evolution of the Settlers' Frontier, Southern Africa," chap. 1 in *Survey of British Commonwealth Affairs,* vol. 2 pt. 2, p. 20.

    12. N. C. Pollock and Swanzie Agnew, *An Historical Geography of South Africa,* pp. 45–46, 56–68.

    13. Hancock, "Evolution of the Settlers' Frontier," p. 22; W. K. Hancock, "Perspective View," chap. 1 in *Survey of British Commonwealth Affairs,* vol. 2 pt. 1, p. 12.

    14. K. W. Robinson, "Population and Land Use in The Sydney District: 1788–1820," *New Zealand Geographer* 9 (1953): 155.

    15. T. M. Perry, *Australia's First Frontier: The Spread of Settlement in New South Wales, 1788–1829,* pp. 26–27, 33, 132.

    16. Hancock, "Perspective View," p. 5.

    17. See, for example, Jeff Carter, *In the Tracks of the Cattle.*

    18. H. C. Allen, *Bush and Backwoods: A Comparison of the Frontier in Australia and the United States,* pp. 75, 79. See also Paul F. Sharp, "Three Frontiers: Some Comparative Studies of Canadian, American, and Australian Settlement," *Pacific Historical Review* 24 (1955): 369–77.

19. The sources on Latin-American cattle ranching are numerous. See, for example, Deffontaines, *Contribution à Géographie pastorale de l'Amérique latine*; Leo Waibel, "Die Viehzuchtgebiete der südlichen Halbkugel," *Geographische Zeitschrift* 28 (1922): 54–74; Herbert Wilhelmy, "Die Weidewirtschaft im heissen Tiefland Nordkolumbiens," *Geographische Rundschau* 6 (1954): 41–54; William M. Denevan, "Cattle Ranching in the Mojos Savannas of Northeastern Bolivia," *Yearbook, Association of Pacific Coast Geographers* 25 (1963): 37–44; G. Langdon White, "Cattle Raising: A Way of Life in the Venezuelan Llanos," *Scientific Monthly* 83 (1956): 122–29; Carl Johannessen, "Savannas of Interior Honduras," *Ibero-Americana* 46 (1963): 36–47; Donald D. Brand, "The Early History of the Range Cattle Industry in Northern Mexico," *Agricultural History* 35 (1961): 132–39; John Thompson, "Production, Marketing, and Consumption of Cattle in El Salvador," *Professional Geographer* 13, 5 (Sept. 1961): 18–22; C. Gary Lobb, "The Historical Geography of the Cattle Regions along Brazil's Southern Frontier" (Ph.D. diss., University of California, Berkeley, 1970); O. Quelle, "Die kontinentalen Viehstrassen Südamerikas," *Petermanns Geographische Mitteilungen* 80 (1934): 114–17; and Richard J. Morrisey, "The Northward Expansion of Cattle Ranching in New Spain, 1550–1600," *Agricultural History* 25 (1951): 115–21.

20. Sandra L. Myres, "The Spanish Cattle Kingdom in the Province of Texas," *Texana* 4 (1966): 233–46; Odie B. Faulk, "Ranching in Spanish Texas," *Hispanic American Historical Review* 45 (1965): 257–66; Charles Arnade, "Cattle Raising in Spanish Florida, 1513–1763," *Agricultural History* 35 (1961): 116–24; L. T. Burcham, "Cattle and Range Forage in California: 1770–1880," *Agricultural History* 35 (1961): 140–49; Sandra L. Myres, *The Ranch in Spanish Texas, 1691–1800*; J. J. Wagoner, *History of the Cattle Industry in Southern Arizona, 1540–1940*; Richard J. Morrisey, "The Early Range Cattle Industry in Arizona," *Agricultural History* 24 (1950): 151–56; and Charles Ramsdell, "Espiritu Santo: An Early Texas Cattle Ranch," *Texas Geographic Magazine* 13, No. 1 (1949): 21–25.

21. Denevan, "Cattle Ranching in the Mojos Savannas," pp. 43–44; Johannessen, "Savannas of Interior Honduras," pp. 40–41.

22. Frank L. Owsley, *Plain Folk of the Old South*, pp. 24–27. For another statement of the frontier stage thesis, see Frank L. Owsley, "The Pattern of Migration and Settlement on the Southern Frontier," *Journal of Southern History* 11 (1945): 147–76.

23. McDonald and McWhiney, "Antebellum Southern Herdsman," p. 152.

24. Edmund Spenser, "A View of the State of Ireland," p. 35, in James Ware, *Two Histories of Ireland*.

25. Charles J. Bishko, "The Peninsular Background of Latin American Cattle Ranching," *Hispanic American Historical Review* 32 (1952): 515.

26. Post, "The Old Cattle Industry," p. 45.

27. E. Estyn Evans, "Culture and Land Use in the Old West of North America," *Heidelberger Studien zur Kulturgeographie* 15 (1966): 72-80.

28. McDonald and McWhiney, "Antebellum Southern Herdsman," pp. 156-59, 166.

29. A. R. B. Haldane, *The Drove Roads of Scotland.*

30. Xavier de Planhol, "Le Chien de Berger: Développement et Signification Géographique d'une Technique Pastorale," *Bulletin de l'Association de Géographes Français* no. 370 (1969), pp. 355-68; E. Estyn Evans, *The Personality of Ireland: Habitat, Heritage and History*, pp. 11-12.

31. B. Hofmeister, "Wesen und Erscheinungsformen der Transhumance," *Erdkunde* 15 (1961): 121-35; Phillippe Arbos, "The Geography of the Pastoral Life: Illustrated with European Examples," *Geographical Review* 13 (1923): 559-75; Robert Aitken, "Routes of Transhumance on the Spanish Meseta," *Geographical Journal* 106 (1945): 59-69; George Kish, "Transhumance in Southern Italy," *Michigan Academy of Sciences, Arts and Letters, Papers* 39 (1953): 301-7; André Fribourg, "La transhumance en Espagne," *Annales de Géographie* 19 (1910): 231-44; E. Müller, "Die Herdenwanderungen im Mittelmeergebiet," *Petermanns Geographische Mitteilungen* 84 (1938): 364-70; Elwyn Davies, "The Pattern of Transhumance in Europe," *Geography* 26 (1941): 155-68; Th. Lefebvre, "La transhumance dans les Basses-Pyrénées", *Annales de Géographie* 37 (1928): 35-60; Ian M. Matley, "Transhumance in Bosnia and Herzegovina," *Geographical Review* 58 (1968): 231-61.

32. E. Estyn Evans, *Irish Folk Ways*, pp. 34-37.

33. Deffontaines, *Contribution à la géographie pastorale,* pp. 65-79; F. A. Daus, "Transhumación de montaña en Neuquen," *Gaea* 8 (1948): 383-426; L. H. Halverson, "The Great Karroo of South Africa," *Journal of Geography* 29 (1930): 290.

34. Bishko, "Peninsular Background," pp. 493-95, 498, 506, 508-9.

35. Michel-Guillaume St. Jean de Crèvecoeur, *Journey into Northern Pennsylvania and the State of New York*, pp. 333-35.

36. Terry G. Jordan and Gilbert J. Jordan, *Ernst and Lisette Jordan: German Pioneers in Texas*, pp. 49-50.

37. Harry J. Carman, ed., *American Husbandry*, pp. 119-20, 240-41, 249-50, 254-55, 343.

38. [James Glen], *A Description of South Carolina*, p. 68.

39. Charles Hooton, *St. Louis' Isle, or Texiana*, p. 66.

40. Gisela Fiedler, "Kulturgeographische Untersuchungen in der Sierra de Gredos, Spanien," *Würzburger Geographische Arbeiten*, no. 33 (1970), pp. 115, 118–21.

41. Homer, *Odyssey*, book 12, lines 127–40.

42. Bishko, "Peninsular Background," p. 492.

43. Peter H. Wood, " 'It Was a Negro Taught Them,' a New Look at African Labor in Early South Carolina," *Journal of Asian and African Studies* 9 (1974): 168–69. See also: Peter H. Wood, *Black Majority*, pp. 30–32.

44. Wood, "Negro Taught Them," p. 169.

45. Ibid., p. 170.

46. Philip Durham and Everett L. Jones, *The Negro Cowboys*.

47. Wood, *Black Majority,* pp. 31–32; Julian Mason, "The Etymology of 'Buckaroo,' " *American Speech* 35 (1960): 51, 52, 53.

48. H. Boesch, "Nomadismus, Transhumanz und Alpwirtschaft," *Die Alpen* 6 (1951): 202–7.

49. Hancock, "Perspective View," p. 13; for another statement of the environmentalist view, see Bernd Andreae, *Betriebsformen in der Landwirtschaft*, pp. 181–94.

50. Walter Prescott Webb, *The Great Plains*, pp. 10–45, 205–69.

51. J. Frank Dobie, *The Longhorns*, pp. 29–30.

52. Fugate, "Origins of the Range Cattle Era," p. 157.

53. Webb, *Great Plains*, p. 208.

54. See, for example: Walter M. Kollmorgen, "The Woodsman's Assaults on the Domain of the Cattleman," *Annals, Association of American Geographers* 59 (1969): 215–217; Richard J. Morrisey, "The Shaping of Two Frontiers," *Américas*, 3, no. 1 (January 1951), p. 5. See also various works by Herbert E. Bolton, as, for example, *Bolton and The Spanish Borderlands*, p. 60.

55. Myres, "The Ranching Frontier," pp. 19–39.

56. Johann Heinrich von Thünen, *Von Thünen's Isolated State*.

57. Michael Chisholm, *Rural Settlement and Land Use*; Edgar S. Dunn, Jr., *The Location of Agricultural Production*; Richard Peet, "Von Thünen Theory and the Dynamics of Agricultural Expansion," *Explorations in Economic History* 8 (1970–71): 181–201; idem, "The Spatial Expansion of Commercial Agriculture in the Nineteenth Century: A von Thünen Explanation," *Economic Geography* 45 (1969): 283–301.

58. Ronald J. Horvath, "Von Thünen's Isolated State and the Area around Addis Ababa, Ethiopia," *Annals, Association of American Geographers* 59 (1969): 323.

59. Ursula Ewald, "The von Thünen Principle and Agricultural Zonation in Colonial Mexico," *Journal of Historical Geography* 3 (1977): 123.

60. Richard Peet, "Influences of the British Market on Agriculture and Related Economic Development in Europe Before 1860," *Transactions, Institute of British Geographers* no. 56 (1972): p. 2.

61. Ibid., p. 9.

62. See: Lauren C. Post, "The Upgrading of Beef Cattle on the Great Plains," *California Geographer* 2 (1961): 23-30.

63. James A. Wilson, "Cattlemen, Packers, and Government: Retreating Individualism on the Texas Range," *Southwestern Historical Quarterly* 74 (1971): 525-34.

64. Virginia K. Fry, "Reindeer Ranching in Northern Russia," *Professional Geographer* 23 (1971): 146-51.

Chapter 2

1. Jacob Claus, "Detailed Information and Account for those who are Inclined to America and are Interested in Settling in the Province of Pennsylvania," *Pennsylvania Magazine of History and Biography* 49 (1925): 126; Harry J. Carman, ed. *American Husbandry*, pp. 120, 241; Peter H. Wood, "'It Was a Negro Taught Them,' A New Look at African Labor in Early South Carolina," *Journal of Asian and African Studies* 9 (1974): 168; H. Roy Merrens, ed. *The Colonial South Carolina Scene: Contemporary Views, 1697-1774*, p. 186, quoting James Glen.

2. Carman, *American Husbandry*, p. 343.

3. Gary S. Dunbar, *Historical Geography of the North Carolina Outer Banks*, pp. 16, 120.

4. [James Glen], *A Description of South Carolina*, p. 68; Carman, *American Husbandry*, p. 119; Merrens, *Colonial South Carolina*, p. 186, quoting James Glen.

5. Johann Martin Bolzius, "Johann Martin Bolzius Answers a Questionnaire on Carolina and Georgia," ed. and trans. Klaus G. Loewald, Beverly Starika, and Paul S. Taylor, *William and Mary Quarterly*, 3d ser., no. 14 (1957), p. 233; Carman, *American Husbandry*, pp. 249-50, 254-55.

6. *Archives of Maryland (Proceedings of the Council of Maryland, 1636-1667)*, 3: 295.

7. Peter H. Wood, *Black Majority*, p. 332.

8. Walter Clark, comp. and ed. *The State Records of North Carolina*, 23: 165.

9. A. S. Salley, Jr., *The History of Orangeburg County, South Carolina*, p. 171; Wood, *Black Majority*, p. 29; idem "It Was A Negro Taught Them," p. 167-70.

10. Glen, *Description of South Carolina*, p. 68. Similar South Carolina figures were reported by James Freeman in 1712; see Merrens, *Colonial South Carolina*, p. 48.

11. [George Milligen-Johnston], *A Short Description of the Province of South Carolina... Written in the Year 1763*, p. 28.

12. Carman, *American Husbandry*, pp. 119, 240-41, 343.

13. William Logan, "William Logan's Journal of a Journey to Georgia, 1745," *Pennsylvania Magazine of History and Biography* 36 (1912): 15; Phil Gersmehl, "Factors Leading to Mountaintop Grazing in the Southern Appalachians," *Southeastern Geographer* 10 (1970): 68; Gary S. Dunbar, "Colonial Carolina Cowpens," *Agricultural History* 35 (1961): 128; idem, *North Carolina Outer Banks*, p. 31; *Archives of Maryland*, 3: 295; Merrens, *Colonial South Carolina*, p. 180, quoting James Glen.

14. John L. Cotter and J. Paul Hudson, *New Discoveries at Jamestown: Site of the First Successful English Settlement in America*, pp. 87, 89; Wood, "It Was A Negro Taught Them," p. 173.

15. William G. DeBrahm, *DeBrahm's Report of the General Survey in the Southern District of North America*, p. 96.

16. Eugene J. Wilhelm, Jr., "Animal Drives in the Southern Highlands," *Mountain Life & Work* 42 (Summer 1966): 8; Dunbar, "Colonial Carolina Cowpens," p. 129.

17. Lewis C. Gray, *History of Agriculture in the Southern United States*, p. 147; Ralph T. Whitelaw, *Virginia's Eastern Shore: A History of Northampton and Accomack Counties*, 2:1040; *Archives of Maryland*, 3:295; William L. Saunders, *The Colonial Records of North Carolina*, 1:385.

18. Wood, *Black Majority*, pp. 174, 177; Dunbar, "Colonial Carolina Cowpens," p. 126.

19. Dunbar, "Colonial Carolina Cowpens," p. 126; Merrens, *Colonial South Carolina*, pp. 119, 180, 186, quoting James Glen and "A Young Gentleman."

20. Merrens, *Colonial South Carolina*, p. 120, quoting "A Young Gentleman."

21. Allen D. Candler, ed. and comp., *The Colonial Records of Georgia*, 4:314, 2:502; Clark, *State Records of North Carolina*, 23:57; *DeBrahm's Report*, pp. 95-96; Dunbar, "Colonial Carolina Cowpens," p. 126; Merrens, *Colonial South Carolina*, p. 186, quoting James Glen. A "pinder" is defined as "a poundkeeper, as of a manor" in *Webster's New International Dictionary of the English Language*, Second Edition, Unabridged (Springfield, Mass.: G. & C. Merriam, 1955), p. 1866.

22. Michel-Guillaume St. Jean de Crèvecoeur, *Crèvecoeur's Eighteenth-Century Travels in Pennsylvania & New York*, p. 152; Candler, *Colonial Records of Georgia*, 4:161; *DeBrahm's Report*, pp. 180-86; Wilhelm, "Animal Drives in the Southern Highlands," p. 8.

23. Wood, *Black Majority*, pp. 105-6; idem, "It was a Negro Taught Them," p. 169.

24. *South-Carolina and American General Gazette*, 18 February 1779, as quoted in Dunbar, "Colonial Carolina Cowpens," p. 126; Merrens, *Colonial South Carolina*, p. 161.

25. Wood, "It Was a Negro Taught Them," p. 169.

26. Clark, *State Records of North Carolina*, 23:167.

27. E. Estyn Evans, *The Personality of Ireland: Habitat, Heritage and History*, pp. 11-12; Xavier de Planhol, "Le Chien de Berger: Développement et Signification Géographique d'une Technique Pastorale," *Bulletin de l'Association de Géographes Français*, no. 370 (1969:) pp. 355-68.

28. A. R. B. Haldane, *The Drove Roads of Scotland*, pp. 26-27 and picture following p. 166.

29. Bailey C. Hanes, *Bill Pickett, Bulldogger: The Biography of a Black Cowboy*, p. 4.

30. Frederic Remington, "Cracker Cowboys of Florida," *Harper's New Monthly Magazine* 91 (1895): 344 (quote); J. W. LeBon, Jr., "The Catahoula Hog Dog: A Folk Breed," *Pioneer America* 3, no. 2 (July 1971): 35, 38-44; idem, "The Catahoula Hog Dog: A Cultural Trait of the Upland South" (M. A. thesis, Louisiana State University, Baton Rouge, 1970).

31. W. Theodore Mealor, Jr., and Merle C. Prunty, "Open-Range Ranching in Southern Florida," *Annals, Association of American Geographers* 66 (1976): 363; George H. Dacy, *Four Centuries of Florida Ranching*, pp. 68-69.

32. Hanes, *Bill Pickett, Bulldogger*, pp. 11, 15, 18.

33. Haldane, *Drove Roads of Scotland*, picture following p. 166; Michel-Guillaume St. Jean de Crèvecoeur, *Journey into Northern Pennsylvania and the State of New York*, p. 337; Candler, *Colonial Records of Georgia*, 4:314; Dunbar, "Colonial Carolina Cowpens," p. 126; Merrens, *Colonial South Carolina*, p. 49, quoting James Freeman.

34. Crèvecoeur, *Journey into Northern Pennsylvania*, p. 336; Crèvecoeur, *Eighteenth-Century Travels*, p. 146—see also Charles W. Towne and Edward N. Wentworth, *Cattle and Men*, p. 145; Crèvecoeur, *Eighteenth-Century Travels*, pp. 146-53.

35. Wilhelm, "Animal Drives in the Southern Highlands," p. 7; Dunbar, "Colonial Carolina Cowpens," p. 130; Gilbert J. Jordan, *Yesterday in the Texas Hill Country*, pp. 64, 66.

36. Remington, "Cracker Cowboys of Florida," p. 345.

37. Wilhelm, "Animal Drives in the Southern Highlands," p. 8; Carman, *American Husbandry*, p. 343; Gersmehl, "Factors Leading to Mountaintop Grazing," p. 67; Crèvecoeur, *Eighteenth-Century Travels*, pp. 153, 151; Carl O. Sauer, *The Geography of the Ozark Highland of Missouri*, Geographic Society of Chicago, Bulletin no. 7, 1920, p. 161; E. Cotton Mather, "Five Major Ranch Types

of the Central Great Plains," *Annals, Association of American Geographers* 46 (1956): 262; idem, "The Production and Marketing of Wyoming Beef Cattle," *Economic Geography* 26 (1950): 81–93; Robert E. Williams, "Cattle in the Southeastern United States, or the Original Wild West," *Corral Dust* 10, no. 2 (1965): 5; Dunbar, *North Carolina Outer Banks*, p. 31.

38. Wilhelm, "Animal Drives in the Southern Highlands, p. 8; Crèvecoeur, *Eighteenth-Century Travels*, p. 152; see also Eugene J. Wilhelm, "Animal Drives—A Case Study in Historical Geography," *Journal of Geography* 66 (1967): 327–34.

39. Wilhelm, "Animal Drives in the Southern Highlands," p. 10.

40. Edmund C. Burnett, "Hog Raising and Hog Driving in the Region of the French Broad River," *Agricultural History* 20 (1946): 87–88.

41. Porte Crayon (pseudonym for David Hunter Strother), "Virginia Illustrated," *Harper's New Monthly Magazine* 10 (Feb. 1855): 302. See also Wilhelm, "Animal Drives in the Southern Highlands," pp. 10–11.

42. John P. Egmont, *The Journal of the Earl of Egmont*, p. 106; Gersmehl, "Factors Leading to Mountaintop Grazing," p. 71.

43. Crèvecoeur, *Journey into Northern Pennsylvania*, p. 342.

44. H. Roy Merrens, *Colonial North Carolina in the Eighteenth Century*, p. 137.

45. Wood, *Black Majority*, pp. 29–30.

46. Dunbar, "Colonial Carolina Cowpens," p. 126.

47. Dunbar, "Colonial Carolina Cowpens," p. 127; Wilhelm, "Animal Drives in the Southern Highlands," p. 7; Towne and Wentworth, *Cattle and Men*, p. 147; Wood, "It Was a Negro Taught Them," p. 169; Wilhelm, "Animal Drives in the Southern Highlands," p. 10.

48. Cornelius C. Cox, "Reminiscences of C. C. Cox," *Texas State Historical Association, Quarterly* 6 (1902–1903): 208–9.

49. Dunbar, "Colonial Carolina Cowpens," pp. 125–29; Towne and Wentworth, *Cattle and Men*, pp. 141–42.

50. Glen, *Description of South Carolina*, p. 68; Merrens, *Colonial South Carolina*, pp. 47, 180–81, quoting James Freeman and James Glen.

51. Merrens, *Colonial South Carolina*, p. 119, quoting "A Young Gentleman"—the same observer noted "Captain Bellinger's cow-pen" near or on a savanna owned by the captain; ibid., p. 92, quoting Mark Catesby; ibid., p. 49, quoting James Freeman.

52. Wood, "It Was A Negro Taught Them," p. 168; idem, *Black Majority*, pp. 29–30, 55; *DeBrahm's Report*, map following p. 98.

53. Evelyn M. Frazier and William E. Fripp, "Names in Colleton County," *Names in South Carolina* 12 (Winter 1965): 11–12;

Merrens, *Colonial South Carolina*, p. 69, quoting Francis Yonge; Wood, *Black Majority*, p. 31; Dunbar, "Colonial Carolina Cowpens,"pp. 128-29.

54. Wood, *Black Majority*, p. 32; Merrens, *Colonial South Carolina*, p. 69, quoting Francis Yonge; ibid., p. 43, quoting James Freeman; ibid., pp. 33, 43, quoting "A Report of the Governor and Council, 1708" and James Freeman.

55. Wesley N. Laing, "Cattle in Early Virginia" (Ph.D. diss., University of Virginia, Charlottesville, 1954), pp. 129-39, 224-25; Dunbar, "Colonial Carolina Cowpens," p. 125; Merrens, *Colonial South Carolina*, p. 250.

56. Merrens, *Colonial South Carolina*, pp. 119-20, quoting "A Young Gentleman."

57. Charles Arnade, "Cattle Raising in Spanish Florida, 1513-1763," *Agricultural History* 35 (1961): 116-24.

58. Dunbar, "Colonial Carolina Cowpens," p. 128; Wilhelm, "Animal Drives in the Southern Highlands,"p. 10.

59. Merrens, *Colonial South Carolina*, p. 181, quoting James Glen—see also "Johann Martin Bolzius Answers a Questionnaire," 15 (1958): 242, 248, 252; Clark, *State Records of North Carolina*, 23: 676; Charles Woodmason, *The Carolina Backcountry on the Eve of the Revolution*, p. 214.

60. *Compendium of the Enumeration of the Inhabitants and Statistics of the United States as Obtained at the Department of State, from the Returns of the Sixth Census*, p. 191.

61. J. D. B. DeBow, *Statistical View of the United States . . . Being a Compendium of the Seventh Census*, p. 117.

62. John D. W. Guice, "Cattle Raisers of the Old Southwest: A Reinterpretation," *Western Historical Quarterly* 8 (1977): 167-87; Kenneth D. Israel, "The Cattle Industry of Mississippi, Its Origin and Its Changes Through Time Up to 1850" (Ph.D. diss., University of Southern Mississippi, Hattiesburg, 1970); Frank L. Owsley, *Plain Folk of the Old South*, p. 26; Gray, *History of Agriculture*, pp. 833-34; John H. Moore, *Agriculture in Ante-Bellum Mississippi*, p. 62; Thomas C. Croker, Jr., "The Longleaf Pine Story." *Journal of Forest History* 23 (1979): 32, 35.

63. Candler, *Colonial Records of Georgia*, 1:389.

64. Merrens, *Colonial South Carolina*, p. 119, quoting "A Young Gentleman"; Candler, *Colonial Records of Georgia*, 4:160-61; ibid., pp. 314-15; ibid., 2:502, 520, 6:173; Merrens, *Colonial South Carolina*, p. 120, quoting "A Young Gentleman."

65. *DeBrahm's Report*, pp. 95, 96, 142.

66. Carman, *American Husbandry*, p. 343.

67. *DeBrahm's Report*, pp. 180-86, 212; William T. Mealor, Jr., "The Open Range Ranch in South Florida and Its Contemporary

Successors" (Ph.D. diss., University of Georgia, Athens, 1972); Dacy, *Four Centuries of Florida Ranching*; Mealor and Prunty, "Open-Range Ranching in Southern Florida," pp. 360–63, 368; Remington, "Cracker Cowboys of Florida," pp. 339–45.

68. Sam B. Hilliard, *Hog Meat and Hoecake: Food Supply in the Old South, 1840–1860*, pp. 116–22.

69. DeBow, *Compendium of the Seventh Census*, p. 117; Hilliard, *Hog Meat and Hoecake*, p. 117.

70. Fred B. Kniffen, *Louisiana: Its Land and People*, pp. 129, 130, 156.

71. Gilbert Imlay, *A Topographical Description of the Western Territory of North America*, pp. 434, 440.

72. Lauren C. Post, "The Old Cattle Industry of Southwestern Louisiana," *McNeese Review* 9 (1957): 43–55; Guice, "Cattle Raisers of the Old Southwest," p. 173; Gray, *History of Agriculture*, p. 80, 159.

73. Lauren C. Post, *Cajun Sketches from the Prairies of Southwest Louisiana*, pp. 50, 59; Guice, "Cattle Raisers of the Old Southwest," p. 176.

74. Thomas Nuttall, *A Journal of Travels into the Arkansa Territory, During the Year 1819*, p. 78; Crèvecoeur, *Journey into Northern Pennsylvania*, p. 458.

75. *Compendium ... of the Sixth Census*, pp. 94, 323.

76. Imlay, *Topographical Description*, p. 422.

77. Ibid., p. 447, quoting Thomas Hutchins; Israel, "Cattle Industry of Mississippi," pp. 31, 107; Guice, "Cattle Raisers of the Old Southwest," pp. 175–76; Mealor and Prunty, "Open-Range Ranching in Southern Florida," pp. 364–65.

78. Fred B. Kniffen, "The Western Cattle Complex: Notes on Differentiation and Diffusion," *Western Folklore* 12 (1953): 179; Fred B. Kniffen, "A Spanish (?) Spinner in Louisiana," *Southern Folklore Quarterly* 13 (December 1949): 194–99; Post, *Cajun Sketches*, pp. 50-53.

79. Merrens, *Colonial South Carolina*, p. 120, quoting "A Young Gentleman"; Candler, *Colonial Records of Georgia*, 7:626— for more on Cowkeeper, see K. W. Porter, "The Founder of the 'Seminole Nation': Secoffee or Cowkeeper," *Florida Historical Quarterly* 27 (1949): 362–84, and K. W. Porter, "The Cowkeeper Dynasty of the Seminole Nation," *Florida Historical Quarterly* 30 (1952): 341–49; William Bartram, *The Travels of William Bartram*, pp. 163–67.

80. Benjamin Hawkins, "A Sketch of the Creek Country in the Years 1798 and 1799," in *Creek Indian History*, Georgia Historical Society, Collections and Transactions 3, pt. 1 (1938): 45–46; Post, *Cajun Sketches*, pp. 50, 59; Paul C. Henlein, *Cattle Kingdom in the Ohio Valley, 1783–1860*, p. 14; Gary C. Goodwin, *Cherokees in Tran-*

sition: A Study of Changing Culture and Environment Prior to 1775, pp. 134-35; Michael F. Doran, "Antebellum Cattle Herding in the Indian Territory," *Geographical Review* 66 (1976): 48-58.

81. J. L. Dillard, "The Lingua Franca in the American Southwest," *Revista Interamericana Review* 3 (1973): 285-88.

82. Such a family were the Ashworths. See Andrew F. Muir, "The Free Negro in Jefferson and Orange Counties, Texas," *Journal of Negro History* 35 (1950): 185-91.

83. Mealor and Prunty, "Open-Range Ranching in Southern Florida," pp. 363-65; Israel, "Cattle Industry of Mississippi," pp. 81, 84; Guice, "Cattle Raisers of the Old Southwest," pp. 182-85.

84. Mealor and Prunty, "Open-Range Ranching in Southern Florida," p. 365; Guice, "Cattle Raisers of the Old Southwest," p. 177.

85. Goodwin, *Cherokees in Transition*, p. 135.

86. Crèvecoeur, *Journey into Northern Pennsylvania*, p. 337; idem, *Eighteenth-Century Travels*, p. 153.

87. Clark, *State Records of North Carolina*, 23:59.

88. Saunders, *Colonial Records of North Carolina*, 4:53; Clark, *State Records of North Carolina*, 23:167, 676; Merrens, *Colonial North Carolina*, pp. 138, 140; Dunbar, *North Carolina Outer Banks*, pp. 18, 31; Carman, *American Husbandry*, pp. 240-41.

89. Saunders, *Colonial Records of North Carolina*, 5:322; Clark, *State Records of North Carolina*, 23:676; Merrens, *Colonial North Carolina*, pp. 136-37.

90. Wilhelm, "Animal Drives in the Southern Highlands," p. 10; Goodwin, *Cherokees in Transition*, p. 134; Gersmehl, "Factors Leading to Mountaintop Grazing," p. 68; James W. Whitaker, "Cattle Raising and Trade in Western North Carolina, 1820-1860: A Micro-Study" (Paper read at the annual meeting of the Organization of American Historians, New Orleans, 14 April 1979), MS copy in possession of T. G. J.

91. DeBow, *Compendium of the Seventh Census*, p. 117; Imlay, *Topographical Description*, p. 518.

92. Henlein, *Cattle Kingdom in the Ohio Valley*, pp. 4, 7, 14; David L. Wheeler, "The Beef Cattle Industry in the Old Northwest, 1803-1860," *Panhandle-Plains Historical Review* 47 (1974): 31-32; Carl O. Sauer, *Geography of the Pennyroyal*, p. 137.

93. Imlay, *Topographical Description*, pp. 175, 346, 358; Sauer, *Geography of the Pennyroyal*, p. 138; *Compendium... of the Sixth Census*, pp. 74, 263.

94. Henlein, *Cattle Kingdom in the Ohio Valley*, pp. 5, 12-13, 15; R. L. Jones, "The Beef Cattle Industry in Ohio Prior to the Civil War," *Ohio Historical Quarterly* 64 (1955): 168-94; Paul C. Henlein, "Cattle Driving from the Ohio Country, 1800-1850," *Agricultural*

History 28 (1954): 83-95.

95. Henlein, *Cattle Kingdom in the Ohio Valley*, pp. 18, 19; Wheeler, "Beef Cattle Industry in the Old Northwest," pp. 33, 41, 44; Paul W. Gates, "Hoosier Cattle Kings," *Indiana Magazine of History* 44 (1948): 1-24; *Compendium... of the Sixth Census*, pp. 86, 299.

96. Henlein, *Cattle Kingdom in the Ohio Valley*, pp. 9, 169; Sauer, *Geography of the Ozark Highland*, pp. 121-22, 141.

97. Paul C. Henlein, "Shifting Range-Feeder Patterns in the Ohio Valley Before 1860," *Agricultural History* 31 (1957): 1-12; Wilhelm, "Animal Drives in the Southern Highlands," p. 10; F. A. Michaux, *Travels to the West of the Mountains, in the States of Ohio, Kentucky, and Tennessea*, pp. 190-91. For good accounts of the rise of feeding, see James W. Whitaker, *Feedlot Empire: Beef Cattle Feeding in Illinois and Iowa, 1840-1900*, and Allan G. Bogue, *From Prairie to Corn Belt.*

98. DeBow, *Compendium of the Seventh Census*, p. 117; William C. Holden, *A Ranching Saga: The Lives of William Electious Halsell and Ewing Halsell*, 1:4-11; Seventh Census of the United States, 1850, MS free population schedule, Guadalupe County, Texas, household no. 138; Michaux, *Travels to the West*, p. 189.

99. Michaux, *Travels to the West*, pp. 191-92; Henlein, *Cattle Kingdom in the Ohio Valley*, pp. 17, 19, 69, 102-4, 119.

100. Henlein, *Cattle Kingdom in the Ohio Valley*, pp. 4, 5, 17; Sauer, *Geography of the Ozark Highland*, p. 161.

101. Imlay, *Topographical Description*, p. 501; Wheeler, "Beef Cattle Industry in the Old Northwest," pp. 37-38.

102. Henlein, *Cattle Kingdom in the Ohio Valley*, p. 21.

103. Ibid., pp. 14, 21, 30-38, 176.

Chapter 3

1. The nucleus of this chapter is my article, "The Origin of Anglo-American Cattle Ranching in Texas: A Documentation of Diffusion from the Lower South," *Economic Geography* 45 (1969): 63-87.

2. Francis Moore, Jr., *Map and Description of Texas, Containing Sketches of its History, Geology, Geography and Statistics*, p. 9; *A Visit to Texas: Being the Journal of a Traveller Through Those Parts Most Interesting to American Settlers*, pp. 40-41, 185-86; Gideon Lincecum, "Journal of Licecum's Travels in Texas, 1835," ed. A. L. Bradford and T. N. Campbell, *Southwestern Historical Quarterly* 53 (1949-50): 187.

3. Eugene C. Barker, ed., *The Austin Papers*, vol. 1, *Annual Report of the American Historical Association for the Year 1919*, vol. 2, pt. 1, p. 809; William Bollaert, *William Bollaert's Texas*, pp. 74-75; *Visit to Texas*, pp. 14, 88, 177; Ralph S. Jackson, *Home on the Double Bayou: Memories of an East Texas Ranch,* p. 107.

4. *Visit To Texas*, pp. 33, 36, 78, 86, 192; Lincecum, "Journal," p. 188; Bollaert, *Texas*, p. 108; Thomas A. Morris, *Miscellany: Consisting of Essays, Biographical Sketches, and Notes of Travel*, p. 343; Mary Austin Holley, *Texas* pp. 16, 49, 50; Moore, *Map and Description of Texas*, p. 6; Mary Austin Holley, *Texas: Observations, Historical, Geographical and Descriptive, in a Series of Letters*, p. 61; Amos A. Parker, *Trip to the West and Texas*, pp. 180-81.

5. *Texas Almanac and State Industrial Guide 1966-1967*, pp. 116-21; Glenn T. Trewartha, *An Introduction to Climate*, p. 235.

6. William Kennedy, *Texas: The Rise, Progress, and Prospects of the Republic of Texas*, p. 97; Francis C. Sheridan, *Galveston Island, Or, A Few Months Off the Coast of Texas*, p. 14; *Visit to Texas*, pp. 33, 43, 193; Holley, *Texas* (1836), pp. 50-61; Andrew F. Muir, ed., *Texas in 1837: An Anonymous, Contemporary Narrative*, p. 67.

7. The best secondary source on Austin's Colony is Eugene C. Barker, *The Life of Stephen F. Austin.*

8. For the census of 1826, see part 2 of the "Appendix to Empresario Contracts," in vol. 54 of the MS Spanish and Mexican Records, General Land Office of Texas, Austin, pp. 8-17. The 1831 census, a MS entitled "Censo y Estadistica, Estado de Coahuila y Texas, Departamto. de Bexar, Villa de San Felipe de Austin, Año de 1831," is in the Nacogdoches Archive at the Texas State Archives, Austin.

9. *Seventh Census of the United States, 1850*, pp. 503-4, totals for Brazoria, Fort Bend, Galveston, Harris, Jackson, Matagorda, and Wharton counties.

10. Mary M. Osburn, ed., "The Atascosita Census of 1826," *Texana* 1 (1963): 299-321; Juan N. Almonte, "Statistical Report on Texas," *Southwestern Historical Quarterly* 28 (1925): 206; *Seventh Census, 1850*, pp. 503-4.

11. Andrew F. Muir, "The Free Negro in Jefferson and Orange Counties, Texas," *Journal of Negro History* 35 (1950): 185-91.

12. A. B. J. Hammett, *The Empresario Don Martin De Leon*; William H. Oberste, *Texas Irish Empresarios and Their Colonies.*

13. It should be noted that some studies have been made in which cattle ranching in the Coastal Prairie is mentioned. See Max C. Odom, "A History of the Cattle Industry in East Texas" (M.A. thesis, Univ. of Texas, 1958), pp. 14-33; Joe F. Combs, "Cattle

Ranching in the Coastal Area One of the Oldest Industries to Claim Attention of Texans," *Coastal Cattleman* 2, no. 1 (May 1936): 3, 9; Ruth G. Francis, "The Coastal Cow Country—The Saga of James Taylor White, First," *ibid.* 6, no. 7 (September 1940): 21–23; and "The First Cattle Ranch in Texas," *Frontier Times* 13 (1936): 304–8.

14. For specific examples, see Mary C. Rabb, *Travels and Adventures in Texas in the 1820's*, pp. 1–2, and J. H. Kuykendall, ed., "Reminiscences of Early Texans," *Texas State Historical Association, Quarterly* 7 (1903–1904): 29–30; Tad Moses, "Development of the Cattle Business in Texas," *Texas Almanac and State Industrial Guide, 1949–1950* (Dallas: A. H. Belo, 1949), p. 257; *Galveston Daily News*, 11 April 1878, as cited in J. Frank Dobie, *The Longhorns*, p. 30.

15. Barker, *Austin Papers* (vol. 1, 1919): vol. 2, pt. 1, p. 863, vol. 2, pt.2, p. 1427; MS Austin Colony census of 1826, in part 2 of the "Appendix to Empresario Contracts," in vol. 54 of the MS Spanish and Mexican records of the General Land Office of Texas, Austin, p. 17; MS "Censo y Estadistica, Estado de Coahuila y Texas, Departamto. de Bexar, Villa de San Felipe de Austin, Año de 1830" and the same for "Año de 1831," Texas State Archives, Austin.

16. *Visit to Texas*, pp. 42, 43, 47, 69; Muir, *Texas in 1837*, pp. 31, 60, 65, 66, 120.

17. Osburn, "Atascosita Census," pp. 305–21; *Visit to Texas*, pp. 84, 91; David Woodman, Jr., *Guide to Texas Emigrants*, pp. 63, 166; Joshua James and Alexander McCrae, *A Journal of a Tour in Texas,* p. 13; Almonte, "Statistical Report on Texas," pp. 201, 215; Melinda Rankin, *Texas in 1850*, p. 91.

18. Through laws passed in 1838 and 1840, the Republic of Texas levied a tax of ten cents per head on all cattle over twenty-five in number belonging to any person. See H. P. N. Gammel, ed., *Laws of Texas*, 1:1514; 2:190. The manuscript tax lists for all but five of the thirty-two counties of Texas in 1840 are preserved at the State Archives at Austin. They were published under a very misleading title; see Gifford E. White, ed., *The 1840 Census of the Republic of Texas*.

19. MS tax lists, Republic of Texas, 1840 and 1845, State Archives, Austin. See also *Journals of the Senate of the First Legislature of the State of Texas*, pp. 64, 68–69.

20. *Seventh Census of the U. S., 1850*, pp. 503–4, 514–15. Brazoria, Fort Bend, Galveston, Harris, Jackson, Jefferson, Liberty, Matagorda, and Wharton counties were used to represent the Coastal Prairie.

21. Francis R. Lubbock, *Six Decades in Texas or Memoirs*, pp. 122, 125, 139.

22. *Seventh Census of the U.S., 1850*, pp. 503–4, population

figures for Brazoria, Fort Bend, Galveston, Harris, Jackson, Jefferson, Liberty, Matagorda, and Wharton counties. The areas of the counties in square miles were obtained from Jacob DeCordova, *Texas: Her Resources and Her Public Men*, p. 104.

23. *Visit to Texas*, pp. 23, 38–39; Moore, *Map and Description*, p. 9; Lubbock, *Six Decades in Texas*, pp. 126; 130–31; S. A. Wright, as quoted in Francis E. Abernethy, ed., *Tales from the Big Thicket*, p. 120; Jackson, *Home on the Double Bayou*, p. 24.

24. "Stock-Raising," *Texas Almanac for 1861*, pp. 149–50.

25. Jackson, *Home on the Double Bayou*, p. 24; "Stock-Raising," *Texas Almanac for 1861*, pp. 149, 150; Moore, *Map and Description*, p. 9.

26. Moore, *Map and Description*, p. 9; *Visit to Texas*, pp. 43, 118–19; Woodman, *Guide to Texas Emigrants*, pp. 34, 182.

27. Mrs. Dilue Harris, "Reminiscences of Mrs. Dilue Harris," *Texas State Historical Association, Quarterly* 4 (1900–1901): 100; Cornelius C. Cox, "Reminiscences of C. C. Cox," ibid. 6 (1902–1903): 128; Lubbock, *Six Decades in Texas*, pp. 126–29, 139; Bollaert, *Texas*, pp. 249–50; Charles Hooton, *St. Louis' Isle, or Texiana*, p. 66; Muir, *Texas in 1837*, p. 66–67.

28. *Visit to Texas*, pp. 91–92, 249; Parker, *Trip to the West*, p. 147; Woodman, *Guide to Texas Emigrants*, pp. 34, 63, 181. Other references to early cattle drives to Louisiana and Mississippi include the *Telegraph and Texas Register* (Columbia, Texas), issue of 31 October 1835; Kennedy, *Texas* (1925), p. 136; Bollaert, *Texas*, pp. 249–50; and Almonte, "Statistical Report," p. 201.

29. R. B. Blake, "Beef Trail," *The Handbook of Texas*, 1:138; Woodman, *Guide to Texas Emigrants*, p. 62.

30. J. C. Clopper, "J. C. Clopper's Journal and Book of Memoranda for 1828," *Texas State Historical Association, Quarterly* 13 (1909–10): 60–62, 77; *Texas in 1840, or the Emigrant's Guide to the New Republic*, p. 51.

31. [Frederick B. Page], *Prairiedom: Rambles and Scrambles in Texas or New Estrémadura*, p. 85; Lubbock, *Six Decades in Texas*, p. 138; Hooton, *St. Louis' Isle*, p. 122.

32. James E. Winston, "Notes on Commercial Relations between New Orleans and Texan Ports, 1838–1839," *Southwestern Historical Quarterly* 34 (1930–31): 104; "Reminiscences of Mrs. Dilue Harris," p. 122.

33. Sheridan, *Galveston Island*, p. 14.

34. Barker, *Austin Papers* (vol. 1, 1919): vol. 2, pt. 1, p. 705.

35. Benjamin Lundy, *The Life, Travels and Opinions of Benjamin Lundy, Including His Journeys to Texas and Mexico*, p. 38; *Visit to Texas*, p. 43; Muir, *Texas in 1837*, p. 118; Bollaert, *Texas*, p. 287; José E. de la Peña, *With Santa Anna in Texas: A Personal Narrative of the Revolution*, p. 118.

36. Arthur Ikin, *Texas: Its History, Topography, Agriculture, Commerce, and General Statistics*, p. 49; Kennedy, *Texas* (1925), p. 133; Lauren C. Post, "The Old Cattle Industry of Southwestern Louisiana," *McNeese Review* 9 (1957): 45, 46, 49; Dobie, *The Longhorns*, p. 31.

37. Walter P. Webb, *The Great Plains*, p. 207.

38. *Visit to Texas*, pp. 43-44, 118-19; Lubbock, *Six Decades in Texas*, pp. 128, 137; Ikin, *Texas*, p. 49; "Stock-Raising," *Texas Almanac for 1861*, p. 150.

39. MS Texas tax lists, 1840, for Brazoria, Fort Bend, Galveston, Harris, Jefferson, and Liberty counties, Texas State Archives; José María Sánchez, "A Trip to Texas in 1828," *Southwestern Historical Quarterly* 29 (1926): 274. See also Lundy, *Life, Travels and Opinions*, p. 38, and *Visit to Texas*, p. 39.

40. See, for example, Cox, "Reminiscences," p. 128; Lubbock, *Six Decades in Texas*, pp. 136-37; Philip Durham and Everett L. Jones, *The Negro Cowboys*.

41. "Stock-Raising," *Texas Almanac for 1861*, pp. 149, 150.

42. Holley, *Texas* (1836), pp. 127-28; Holley, *Observations*, p. 138; Mrs. Matilda C. F. Houstoun, *Texas and the Gulf of Mexico; or Yachting in the New World*, 2: 119-20; Seventh Census of the United States, 1850, MS population schedules for Brazoria, Fort Bend, Galveston, Harris, Jackson, Jefferson, Liberty, Matagorda, and Wharton counties, Texas.

43. Seventh Census of the U. S., MS agricultural schedules, for Brazoria County, Texas; Sánchez, "Trip to Texas," p. 274; *Visit to Texas*, pp. 39, 91, 118.

44. Seventh Census of the U. S., MS agricultural schedules for Jefferson and Liberty counties, Texas; MS Texas tax lists, 1840, for the Coastal Prairie counties (see note 39).

45. Seventh Census of the U. S., MS agricultural schedules, Jefferson Co., Texas; Lubbock, *Six Decades in Texas*, p. 126; *Visit to Texas*, p. 36.

46. Osburn, "Atascosita Census," pp. 305-21.

47. Ibid., p. 313.

48. Seventh Census of the U. S., MS population schedules, for Jefferson and Liberty counties, Texas.

49. Barker, *Austin Papers* (vol. I, 1919): vol. 2, pt. 1, p. 717; Seventh Census of the U.S., MS population schedules for Brazoria, Fort Bend, Galveston, Harris, Jackson, Matagorda, and Wharton counties, Texas. The "coastal states" referred to are those of the Lower South plus North Carolina and Virginia.

50. Muir, "The Free Negro in Jefferson and Orange Counties," p. 194.

51. Osburn, "Atascosita Census," pp. 305-21; MS Texas tax lists, 1840; Seventh Census of the U.S., MS population schedules.

52. Stephen F. Austin, "Journal on his First Trip to Texas," *Texas State Historical Association, Quarterly* 7 (1903-1904): 286-307 (quote from p. 298).

53. Roy Grimes, ed., *Three Hundred Years in Victoria County*, p. 366.

54. Mrs. Thomas O'Connor, "Martín De León" and "De León's Colony." *The Handbook of Texas*, 1:484-85; Hammett, *Empresario Don Martin De Leon*, pp. 7, 25; J. H. Kuykendall, "Reminiscences of Early Texans," *Texas State Historical Association, Quarterly* 6 (1902-1903): 253; Daniel Shipman, *Frontier Life...Fifty-eight Years in Texas*, p. 42.

55. *Visit to Texas*, pp. 118-21; Francis, "Coastal Cow Country—Saga of James Taylor White," pp. 21-23.

56. MS Texas tax lists, 1840, for Jefferson and Liberty counties; Seventh census of the U.S., MS population schedules for Jefferson and Liberty counties, Texas.

57. Abernethy, *Tales from the Big Thicket*, p. 67.

58. Oberste, *Texas Irish Empresarios*, pp. 226-27; "Stock-Raising," *Texas Almanac for 1861*, p. 152; Hobart Huson, *Refugio: A Comprehensive History*, 1:263; 429-30, and vol. 2, chap. 43.

59. Margaret R. Warburton, "A History of the O'Connor Ranch, 1834-1939" (M.A. thesis, Catholic University of America, Washington, D.C., 1939); "Stock-Raising," *Texas Almanac for 1861*, p. 152; Seventh census of the U.S., MS population and agricultural schedules, for Refugio County, Texas.

60. Oberste, *Texas Irish Empresarios*, p. 172.

Chapter 4

1. This chapter first appeared, in slightly different form, as "Early Northeast Texas and the Evolution of Western Ranching," *Annals, Association of American Geographers* 67 (1977): 66-87.

2. The counties are: Delta, Fannin, Franklin, Hopkins, Hunt, Lamar, Red River, and Titus. Of these, only six existed in 1850; Delta and Franklin were created in the 1870s.

3. E. H. Templin and R. M. Marshall, *Soil Survey of Hunt County, Texas*, p. 13; A. E. Kocher and W. S. Lyman, *Soil Survey of Franklin County, Texas*, p. 19.

4. Edward Smith, *Account of a Journey through North-Eastern Texas, Undertaken in 1849*, p. 26; John Barrow, *Facts Relating to North-Eastern Texas, Condensed from Notes Made During A Tour*, p. 13; Josiah Gregg, *Diary & Letters of Josiah Gregg, Southwestern Enterprises 1840-1847*, p. 86.

5. Franklin H. Clark, as quoted, in *Report of the Commis-*

sioner of Patents for the Year 1850. Part II. Agriculture, p. 189; Smith, *Account of a Journey*, pp. 26, 127; Barrow, *Facts Relating to North-Eastern Texas*, p. 56; *Northern Standard* (Clarksville, Texas) vol. 1, no. 22 (4 February 1843), p. 2.

    6. Smith, *Account of a Journey*, p. 26; Traylor Russell, *History of Titus County, Texas*, 2:119.

    7. Ikie Gray Patteson, *Loose Leaves: A History of Delta County, Texas*, pp. 37, 48, 177.

    8. Gregg, *Diary & Letters of Josiah Gregg*, p. 82; Barrow, *Facts Relating to North-Eastern Texas*, p. 12.

    9. Andrew Davis, "Folk Life in Early Texas: The Autobiography of Andrew Davis," ed. R. L. Jones, *Southwestern Historical Quarterly* 43 (1939–40): 328.

    10. Barrow, *Facts Relating to North-Eastern Texas*, p. 10; Smith, *Account of a Journey*, p. 36.

    11. William Banta and J. W. Caldwell, Jr., *Twenty-Seven Years on the Texas Frontier*, p. 112; Davis, "Folk Life in Early Texas," pp. 327, 332–33; Smith, *Account of a Journey*, pp. 26, 28, 48; Barrow, *Facts Relating to North-Eastern Texas*, pp. 13, 56.

    12. The best general source on Anglo settlements is Rex W. Strickland, "Anglo-American Activities in Northeast Texas, 1803–1845" (Ph.D. diss., University of Texas, Austin, 1937).

    13. MS Texas tax lists for Red River and Fannin counties, 1840, Texas State Archives, Austin; *Seventh Census of the United States, 1850*, pp. 503–4, figures for Fannin, Hopkins, Hunt, Lamar, Red River, and Titus counties. The 1840 total was calculated by multiplying the number of taxpayers times four plus the number of slaves reported.

    14. Seventh Census of the United States, 1850, MS population schedules for Fannin, Hopkins, Hunt, Lamar, Red River, and Titus counties, Texas; Strickland, "Anglo-American Activities;" Terry G. Jordan, "Population Origins in Texas, 1850," *Geographical Review* 59 (1969): 87, 90.

    15. Strickland, "Anglo-American Activities," p. 76.

    16. William B. DeWees, *Letters from an Early Settler of Texas*, p. 25; Mary C. Rabb, *Travels and Adventures in Texas in the 1820's*, pp. 1–2; MS "A Census of Miller County, Arkansas, July 10, 1825," taken by Claiborne Wright, County Assessor, in the Bureau of Rolls, Office of the Secretary of State, as quoted in Strickland, "Anglo-American Activities," p. 135; Davis, "Folk Life in Early Texas," p. 323; *Executive Document, 25th Congress, 2nd Session, Document 351, Serial 332*, pp. 769–70, as quoted in John D. Osburn, "A History of Present Red River County Area through 1845" (M.A. thesis, Southern Methodist University, 1954), p. 57.

17. MS Texas tax lists for Fannin, Hopkins, Hunt, Lamar, Red River, and Titus counties, 1837–50; Seventh Census of the U.S., MS agricultural schedules for the same counties.

18. MS Texas tax lists for Hopkins County, 1850 and 1855; Seventh Census of the U.S., MS agricultural and population schedules for Hopkins County; MS register of brands and marks, Hopkins County, Texas, in the county courthouse, Sulphur Springs.

19. MS Texas tax lists for Fannin and Hopkins counties, 1850; Seventh Census of the U.S., MS agricultural and population schedules for the same counties; MS register of brands and marks, Hopkins County.

20. Floy Crandall Hodge, *A History of Fannin County, Featuring Pioneer Families*, p. 188; MS Texas tax lists for Fannin County, 1840.

21. William E. Sawyer, "A Young Man Comes to Texas in 1852," *Texana* 7 (1969): 18; Smith, *Account of a Journey*, p. 29; Barrow, *Facts Relating to North-Eastern Texas*, p. 15; *Journals of the Senate of the First Legislature of the State of Texas*, pp. 68–69; *Texas Almanac for 1857*, pp. 69–70; *Seventh Census of the U.S. 1850*, pp. 514–15, figures for Fannin, Hopkins, Hunt, Lamar, Red River, and Titus counties.

22. MS biographical information on Solomon Waggoner, provided by H. A. McCarty, manager of the Waggoner Estate, 3942 Paradise, Vernon, Texas, 1978. For more detail on the Waggoner genealogy, see William C. Holden, *A Ranching Saga* 1: 29.

23. Rex W. Strickland, "William Becknell," *The Handbook of Texas*, 1:134; MS tax lists of Red River County, Texas, 1845; Seventh Census of the U.S., 1850, MS schedules of agriculture, Hopkins County, Texas; E. B. Fleming, *Early History of Hopkins County, Texas*, 119–22.

24. Strickland, "Anglo-American Activities," p. 208; Seventh Census of the U.S., MS schedules of agriculture, Red River County, Texas; and *Compendium of the Enumeration of the Inhabitants and Statistics of the United States, as Obtained at the Department of State, from the Returns of the Sixth Census*, pp. 70, 251. Carroll County reported 12,362 people and 47,163 cattle.

25. MS "Estate of Claybourn Wright, Dec[eased], Sept. 9, 1830," published in Pat B. Clark, *The History of Clarksville and Old Red River County*, p. 99; Smith, *Account of a Journey*, p. 131; Fleming, *Early History of Hopkins County*, pp. 56–7; Gus L. Ford, ed., *Texas Cattle Brands: A Catalog of the Texas Centennial Exposition Exhibit, 1936*, pp. 10, 65.

26. E. B. Watson and Risden T. Allen, *Soil Survey of Morris County, Texas*, p. 12; Russell, *History of Titus County*, 1: 147.

27. MS court documents, published in Clark, *History of Clarksville*, pp. 93-94; Patteson, *Loose Leaves,* p. 88.

28. Lysius Gough, *Spur Jingles and Saddle Songs: Rhymes and Miscellany of Cow Camp and Cattle Trails in the Early Eighties*, p. 7.

29. Jack Freeman, "Dogs Handy in Roundup," *Dallas Morning News* (Dallas, Texas), Saturday, 12 April 1975, p. 32A; "Denton County's Shepherd Dogs," in Ed F. Bates, *History and Reminiscences of Denton County* (Denton: McNitzsky, 1918), pp. 399-400. On the present-day sale of such dogs in Northeast Texas, see Frank X. Tolbert, "Tolbert's Texas," *Dallas Morning News* (Dallas, Texas), 10 August 1974, p. 19A, and Randy Eli Grothe, "106 Dogs, A Man and A Bear," *Dallas Morning News*, 26 March 1977, p. 36E.

30. MS Texas tax lists for Hopkins County, 1846-55.

31. Clark, *Report of the Commissioner*, p. 189; John Brooke, as quoted in *Report of the Commissioner of Patents for the Year 1855. Part 2. Agriculture*, p. 26.

32. MS register of brands and marks, Fannin, Hopkins, and Lamar counties, in the courthouses at Bonham, Sulphur Springs, and Paris; "Stock Brands and Markings," compiled for Red River County by J. E. Matlock, in the MS collection "History of Grazing in Texas," Historical Records Survey, Work Projects Administration, 1939, pp. 2-21, Box 2R332, University of Texas Archives, Austin. See also Ford, *Texas Cattle Brands*, pp. 10, 15.

33. A. S. Salley, Jr., *The History of Orangeburg County, South Carolina*, p. 218, and Wright estate inventory, quoted in Clark, *History of Clarksville*, p. 102.

34. Smith, *Account of a Journey*, p. 127; Clark, *Report of the Commissioner*, p. 189.

35. Lauren C. Post, *Cajun Sketches from the Prairies of Southwest Lousiana*, p. 53 (quotation); Ford, *Texas Cattle Brands*, pp. 1-6. See also the sources cited in note 32.

36. John M. Dor, letter to Col. B. R. Milam, dated 14 May 1831, published in *Yanaguana Society Publications, Volume V: Texas Letters* (San Antonio: Yanaguana Society, 1940), pp. 56-57; "Indian Removals," *Senate Documents*, 25th Congress, 1st Session, no. 512, 1, pp. 949-55, quoted in Strickland, "Anglo-American Activities," p. 238; Alexander W. Neville, *The History of Lamar County*, p. 233.

37. Norman A. Graebner, "History of Cattle Ranching in Eastern Oklahoma," *Chronicles of Oklahoma* 21 (1943): 300-11; Michael F. Doran, "Antebellum Cattle Herding in the Indian Territory," *Geographical Review* 66 (1976): 48-58; Strickland, "Anglo-American Activities," p. 378.

38. Barrow, *Facts Relating to North-Eastern Texas*, p. 39; Max

C. Odom, "A History of the Cattle Industry in East Texas" (M.A. thesis, University of Texas, Austin, 1958), p. 38; Clark, *Report of the Commissioner*, p. 189.

39. Wayne R. White, "The Historical Geography of Marion County, Texas 1830-1890: An Example from the Era of Steamboat Navigation on Inland Waters" (M.A. thesis, University of Texas, Austin, 1964), pp. 52-53; Odom, "History of the Cattle Industry," p. 39.

40. Smith, *Account of a Journey*, pp. 29, 33; Robert Hargrave, letter written in 1852, published in Gladys St. Clair, *A History of Hopkins County, Texas*, p. 22.

41. Neville, *History of Lamar County*, p. 190; Minnie T. Harper and George D. Harper, *Old Ranches*, p. 61.

42. Mary James Eubank, "A Journal of Our Trip to Texas, October 6, 1853," ed. W. C. Nunn, *Texana* 10 (1972): 39.

43. Corrinne E. Crow, "Settlement Patterns and Subsequent Social Development of Red River County, 1814-1849" (M.A. thesis, East Texas State University, 1972), p. 58.

44. *Northern Standard*, vol. 1, no. 4, (10 September 1842), p. 2, and vol. 5, no. 52 (22 April, 1848), p. 4; Walter P. Webb and H. Bailey Carroll, eds., *The Handbook of Texas*, 1: 963; Clark; *History of Clarksville*, pp. 241-42.

45. Smith, *Account of a Journey*, p. 94.

46. *Manufactures of the United States in 1860, Compiled from the Original Returns of the Eighth Census*, pp. 581-90.

47. Dor letter, *Yanaguana Society Publications*, p. 56; Clark, *Report of the Commissioner*, p. 189.

48. Smith, *Account of a Journey*, p. 33; Clark, *History of Clarksville*, p. 102; MS Texas tax lists for Red River and Fannin counties, 1846, 1848; Clark, *Report of the Commissioner*, p. 189.

49. Clark, *Report of the Commissioner*, p. 189; Smith, *Account of A Journey*, pp. 33-34.

50. Seventh Census of the U.S., MS agricultural schedules for Hopkins and Hunt counties, Texas.

51. Seventh Census of the U.S., MS agricultural schedules for Hopkins and Hunt counties, Texas.

52. MS Texas tax lists for Lamar County, 1848.

53. Seventh Census of the U.S., MS agricultural schedules for Hopkins County, Texas.

54. Barrow, *Facts Relating to North-Eastern Texas*, p. 13.

55. This paragraph is based on the Seventh Census of the U.S., MS agricultural and population schedules, and *Seventh Census of the United States, 1850*, pp. 503-4, 514-20.

56. A standard multi-variate test was applied to all persons owning fifty or more cattle at any time during the 1837-50 period, as reported in county tax lists ($n = 301$). The coefficient of correlation

(Pearson) was 0.08, indicating that there was no significant statistical correlation between the number of cattle owned and the number of slaves owned.

57. MS Texas tax lists for the six counties of Northeast Texas, 1837–50; Seventh Census of the U.S., MS population schedules for the six counties of Northeast Texas; MS Texas tax lists for Fannin County 1842–54, for Hopkins County 1846–54; MS Texas tax lists for Red River County 1837–55, for Lamar County 1841–55; Smith, *Account of A Journey*, pp. 84–85; Holden, *A Ranching Saga*, 1: 27; Fleming, *Early History of Hopkins County*, p. 87.

58. Smith, *Account of A Journey*, p. 63; Seventh Census of the U.S., MS population schedules for the counties of Northeast Texas.

59. George W. Bonnell, *Topographical Description of Texas*, p. 25.

60. Barrow, *Facts Relating to North-Eastern Texas*, p. 56.

61. *Northern Standard*, vol. 3, no. 50 (11 March 1846), p. 2; Barrow, *Facts Relating to North-Eastern Texas*, p. 13; Smith, *Account of A Journey*, p. 84; Seventh Census of the U.S., MS agricultural schedules for Hopkins County, p. 323.

62. Carla Smith Shields, "Spanish Influences on East Texas Place Names and Vocabulary" (M.A. thesis, East Texas State University, 1966), pp. 11–41.

63. D. Port Smythe, "D. Port Smythe's Journey Across Early Texas," *Texas Geographic Magazine* 6 (Fall 1942): 3; Eighth Census of the United States, 1860, MS free population schedules for Denton County, p. 88 (mentions "Valetta Ranch").

64. Eighth Census of the U.S., MS free population schedules for Fannin County, p. 28.

65. Elmer Bagby Atwood, *The Regional Vocabulary of Texas*, pp. 150, 158, 161; Fred A. Tarpley, "A Word Atlas of Northeast Texas" (Ph. D. diss., Louisiana State University, 1960).

66. Tarpley, "A Word Atlas," pp. 175, 177, 216, 225.

67. Barrow, *Facts Relating to North-Eastern Texas*, p. 56; Smith, *Account of A Journey*, pp. 28, 127.

68. Clark, *Report of the Commissioner*, p. 189; Barrow, *Facts Relating to North-Eastern Texas*, p. 15; Smith, *Account of A Journey*, p. 28; Frederick Marryat, *Narrative of the Travels and Adventures of Monsieur Violet*, 3:3.

69. Patteson, *Loose Leaves*, p. 32.

70. Rupert N. Richardson, *The Frontier of Northwest Texas, 1846 to 1876*, p. 150.

71. Barrow, *Facts Relating to North-Eastern Texas*, p. 35.

72. Odom, "History of the Cattle Industry," pp. 9–12; Adolphus Sterne, *Hurrah for Texas! The Dairy of Adolphus Sterne 1838–1851*, p. 66.

73. Traylor Russell, "Kendall Lewis," *Texana* 9 (1971): 17–32.

74. MS Texas tax lists for Red River County, 1838-44.

75. Doran, "Antebellum Cattle Herding in the Indian Territory;" Graebner, "History of Cattle Ranching in Eastern Oklahoma."

76. Webb and Carroll, *Handbook of Texas*, 1: 207; Kocher and Lyman, *Soil Survey of Franklin County*, p. 14.

77. E. H. Templin et al., *Soil Survey of Fannin County, Texas*, p. 13.

Chapter 5

1. Erhard Rostlund, "The Geographic Range of the Historic Bison in the Southeast," *Annals, Association of American Geographers* 50 (1960): 395-407.

2. Hattie Roach, *The Hills of Cherokee*, p. 38.

3. Joshua James and Alexander McCrae, *A Journal of A Tour in Texas*, pp. 5, 13; Jacob DeCordova, *Texas: Her Resources and Her Public Men*, p. 279; and William B. DeWees, *Letters from an Early Settler of Texas*, pp. 22-23; Thomas A. Morris, *Miscellany: Consisting of Essays, Biographical Sketches, and Notes of Travel*, p. 325.

4. Gideon Lincecum, "Journal of Lincecum's Travels in Texas, 1835," *Southwestern Historical Quarterly* 53 (1949-50): 185.

5. Amos A. Parker, *Trip to the West and Texas*, pp. 118, 120, 122; William Bollaert, *William Bollaert's Texas*, pp. 266-67—for other descriptions of pine barrens, see Lincecum, "Journal of Lincecum's Travels," p. 184; William Kennedy, *Texas: The Rise, Progress, and Prospects of the Republic of Texas*, pp. 137-38; and William A. McClintock, "Journal of a Trip through Texas and Northern Mexico in 1846-1847," *Southwestern Historical Quarterly* 34 (1930-31): 23.

6. L. R. Schoenmann et al., *Soil Survey of Bowie County, Texas*, p. 37.

7. Walter P. Webb and H. Bailey Carroll, eds., *The Handbook of Texas*, 2:931.

8. Gustav Dresel, *Houston Journal: Adventures in North America and Texas, 1837-1841*, pp. 62, 66; Benjamin Lundy, *The Life, Travels and Opinions of Benjamin Lundy, Including his Journeys to Texas and Mexico*, p. 119; Francis Moore, Jr., *Map and Description of Texas, Containing Sketches of its History, Geology, Geography and Statistics*, pp. 82, 84-85, 115, 117, 124; James W. Parker, *The Rachel Plummer Narrative*, p. 51; Stephen F. Austin, "Journal on His First Trip to Texas," *Texas State Historical Association, Quarterly*, 7 (1903-1904): 291, 292; McClintock, "Journal of a Trip," p. 25; Kennedy, *Texas*, pp. 139, 140, 143.

9. [Frederic B. Page], *Prairiedom: Rambles and Scrambles in Texas or New Estrémadura*, p. 63; Lincecum, "Journal of Lincecum's Travels," p. 184.

10. Lundy, *Life, Travels and Opinions*, pp. 118-19.

11. Adolphus Sterne, *Hurrah for Texas! The Dairy of Adolphus Sterne 1838-1851*, p. 30; William F. Gray, *From Virginia to Texas, 1835: Dairy of Col. Wm. F. Gray*, p. 102. See also Solomon A. Wright, *My Rambles as East Texas Cowboy, Hunter, Fisherman, Tie-Cutter*, p. 77.

12. Parker, *Trip to the West*, pp. 118, 120, 122, 123, 125.

13. Sandra L. Myres, "The Spanish Cattle Kingdom in the Province of Texas," *Texana* 4 (1966): 235.

14. Herbert E. Bolton, "The Spanish Abandonment and Re-Occupation of East Texas, 1773-1779," *Texas State Historical Association, Quarterly* 9 (1905): 67-137.

15. R. B. Blake, "Gil Antonio Ibarvo," *Handbook of Texas*, 1: 873; Max C. Odom, "A History of the Cattle Industry in East Texas" (M.A. thesis, University of Texas, Austin, 1958), pp. 9-12.

16. Gus L. Ford, ed., *Texas Cattle Brands: A Catalog of the Texas Centennial Exposition Exhibit, 1936*, pp. 2-6; Odie B. Faulk, "Ranching in Spanish Texas," *Hispanic American Historical Review* 45 (1965): 262-63.

17. Ford, *Texas Cattle Brands*, pp. 2-6; MS Texas tax lists for Harrison, Houston, Jasper, Montgomery, Nacogdoches, Sabine, San Augustine, and Shelby counties, 1840, in the Texas State Archives, Austin; Seventh Census of the United States, 1850, MS free population schedules for Angelina, Cherokee, Nacogdoches, and San Augustine counties, Texas.

18. Blake, "Gil Antonio Ibarvo," p. 873; Bolton, "Spanish Abandonment and Re-Occupation," p. 84.

19. MS census of the town and district of Nacogdoches, 1793, in part 6 of the Béxar Archives, at the University of Texas Archives, Austin.

20. Josiah Gregg, *Dairy and Letters of Josiah Gregg, Southwestern Enterprises 1840-1847*, p. 90; Sterne, *Hurrah for Texas!*, p. 66.

21. For general sources on the Creek Indians in Texas, see P. V. Malone, *Sam Houston's Indians—The Alabama-Coushetti;* Ruth Peebles, "The Westward Migration of the Alabama and Coushatta Indians," (M.A. thesis, Sam Houston State University, Huntsville, Texas, 1968); Harriet Smither, "The Alabama Indians of Texas," *Southwestern Historical Quarterly* 36 (1932): 83-108; and Gilbert M. Culbertson, "The Creek Indians in East Texas" *East Texas Historical Journal* 14 (Fall 1976): 20-25.

22. Mary Austin Holley, *Texas: Observations, Historical, Geo-*

graphical and Descriptive, in a Series of Letters, p. 97.

23. For a general source on the Cherokees, see Ernest W. Winkler, "The Cherokee Indians in Texas," *Texas State Historical Association, Quarterly* 7 (1903): 95–165.

24. José María Sánchez, "A Trip to Texas in 1828," *Southwestern Historical Quarterly* 29 (1926): 286; Odom, "History of the Cattle Industry in East Texas," pp. 33–34; Z. N. Morrell, *Flowers and Fruits from the Wilderness*, p. 51.

25. MS census of the Tenaha District, 1835, in the Nacogdoches Archive, Texas State Library, Austin.

26. John H. Bounds, "The Alabama-Coushatta Indians of Texas," *Journal of Geography* 70 (1971): 178.

27. MS census of the districts of Jasper, Nacogdoches, Sabine, San Augustine, and Tenaha, 1835, in the Nacogdoches Archive, Texas State Library, Austin. See also Marion Day Mullins, "The First Census of Texas, 1829–1836," *Special Publications of the National Genealogical Society* no. 22 (1959).

28. MS Texas tax lists for Harrison, Houston, Jasper, Montgomery, Nacogdoches, Sabine, San Augustine, and Shelby counties, 1840 (the white population was estimated by multiplying the number of taxpayers times four); *Seventh Census of the United States, 1850*, pp. 503–4, including the counties listed above plus Angelina, Bowie, Cass, Cherokee, Newton, Panola, Polk, Rusk, Smith, Tyler, Upshur, and Walker.

29. Figures for county area were obtained from *Texas Almanac and State Industrial Guide, 1966–1967*, pp. 222, 301.

30. Fred Kniffen, "The Western Cattle Complex: Notes on Differentiation and Diffusion," *Western Folklore* 12 (1953): 183.

31. J. Marvin Hunter, *The Trail Drivers of Texas*, p. 114.

32. J. Villasana Haggard, "The House of Barr and Davenport," *Southwestern Historical Quarterly* 49 (1945–46): 84; Henderson K. Yoakum, *History of Texas*, 1: 136–37; Webb and Carroll, *Handbook of Texas*, 1:113, 467, 527; 2:766; MS Texas tax lists for Nacogdoches County, 1840.

33. Ford, *Texas Cattle Brands*, pp. 7–79,—for early descriptions of large herds owned by Piney Woods Anglos, see Dresel, *Houston Journal*, p. 81, and Parker, *Trip to the West*, p. 126; MS Texas tax lists for Houston, Jasper, Montgomery, Nacogdoches, Sabine, San Augustine, and Shelby counties, 1840; Seventh Census of the U.S., 1850, MS schedules of agriculture and free population for Angelina, Bowie, Cass, Cherokee, Harrison, Houston, Jasper, Montgomery, Nacogdoches, Newton, Panola, Polk, Rusk, Sabine, San Augustine, Shelby, Smith, Tyler, Upshur, and Walker counties, Texas.

34. *Seventh Census of the U.S., 1850*, pp. 503–4, 513–15.

35. Stanley A. Arbingast et al., *Atlas of Texas*, p. 142.

36. Wright, *My Rambles as East Texas Cowboy*, pp. 1, 2; Seventh Census of the U.S., 1850, MS free population schedule, Jasper County, Texas; MS Texas tax lists for Jasper County, 1840.

37. Webb and Carroll, *Handbook of Texas*, 2: 432; Seventh Census of the U.S., 1850, MS agriculture and free population schedules, Shelby County.

38. Ford, *Texas Cattle Brands*, pp. 31, 41.

39. Seventh Census of the U.S., 1840, MS free population schedule, Nacogdoches County, Texas, household no. 33; Ford, *Texas Cattle Brands*, p. 41.

40. Friedrich W. von Wrede, *Sketches of Life in the United States of North America and Texas*, p. 19; H. M. Smith, *Soil Survey of Polk County, Texas*, pp. 7, 10; John A. Caplen, as quoted in Francis E. Abernethy, ed., *Tales from the Big Thicket*, p. 110.

41. Wright, *My Rambles as East Texas Cowboy*, pp. 49, 52.

42. Ben Moore, Sr., *Random Shots and Tales of Texas*, p. 140; Wright, *My Rambles as East Texas Cowboy*, p. 5.

43. George B. Altgelt, "Present-Day Livestock Raising in the Gulf Coast Uplands—Use of Dogs in Herding Cattle," *Farm and Ranch* 57, no. 4 (15 February 1938): 4-5.

44. Moore, *Random Shots and Tales of Texas*, p. 193.

45. Frank X. Tolbert, "Tolbert's Texas," *Dallas Morning News*, 10 August 1974, p. 19A. Major breeders known to the author are located in Grimes and Van Zandt counties, bordering the Piney Woods on the west.

46. Wright, *My Rambles as East Texas Cowboy*, p. 54.

47. Ibid., pp. 15, 59.

48. Ibid., pp. 49, 59.

49. Ford, *Texas Cattle Brands*, p. 1-79.

50. MS Texas tax lists, 1840, and Seventh Census of the U.S., 1850, MS agriculture and population schedules, for the Piney Woods counties (see notes 28 and 33).

51. See, for example, Seventh Census of the U.S., 1850, MS free population schedules, Jasper County, household no. 135; Newton County, household no. 207; and Angelina County, household no. 41. For a rare example of a Spanish-surnamed "stock keeper," see Angelina County, household no. 42.

52. *Seventh Census of the U.S., 1850*, pp. 503-4; *Population of the United States in 1860; Compiled from the Original Returns of the Eighth Census*, pp. 484-86.

53. Dresel, *Houston Journal*, pp. 67-68; MS Texas tax lists, 1840, and Seventh Census of the U.S., 1850, MS agriculture and slave population schedules for the Piney Woods counties (see notes 17 and 33).

54. Wright, *My Rambles as East Texas Cowboy*, pp. 52, 59.

55. Andrew Davis, "Folk Life in Early Texas: The Autobiography of Andrew Davis," *Southwestern Historical Quarterly* 43 (1939-40): 323; James and McCrae, *Journal of a Tour in Texas*, p. 6.

56. Smith, *Soil Survey of Polk County*, p. 7.

57. Wright, *My Rambles as East Texas Cowboy*, pp. 2, 6; Smith *Soil Survey of Polk County*, pp. 7, 10; Abernethy, *Tales from the Big Thicket*, pp. 26, 62; Davis, "Folk Life in Early Texas," p. 323.

58. Juan N. Almonte, "Statistical Report on Texas," *Southwestern Historical Quarterly* 28 (1925): 215.

59. *Seventh Census of the U.S., 1850*, pp. 513-16.

60. Kennedy, *Texas*, p. 136.

61. Hunter, *Trail Drivers of Texas*, p. 949; Wright, *My Rambles as East Texas Cowboy*, p. 50.

Chapter 6

1. The first recognition of these two clusters was presented in D. W. Meinig, *Imperial Texas: An Interpretive Essay in Cultural Geography*, p. 66.

2. *Ninth Census of the United States, 1870*, 3: 251-59, for Atascosa, Bee, Bexar, DeWitt, Dimmit, Frio, Goliad, Gonzales, Guadalupe, Karnes, Kinney, La Salle, Lavaca, Live Oak, McMullen, Maverick, Medina, Nueces, Refugio, San Patricio, Uvalde, Victoria, Wilson, and Zavala counties, Texas.

3. *Seventh Census of the United States, 1850*, pp. 514-15, for Cameron-Starr-Webb counties; *Ninth Census of the U.S., 1870*, 3: 251-59, for Cameron, Duval, Encinal, Hidalgo, Starr, Webb, and Zapata counties, Texas.

4. Meinig, *Imperial Texas*, pp. 66-68; Rupert N. Richardson, *The Frontier of Northwest Texas, 1846-1876*, p. 153.

5. Terry G. Jordan, "The Texan Appalachia," *Annals, Association of American Geographers* 60 (1970): 409-27.

6. *Ninth Census of the U.S., 1870*, 3: 251-59, for Brown, Burnet, Coleman, Comanche, Coryell, Denton, Eastland, Erath, Hamilton, Hood, Jack, Johnson, Lampasas, Llano, McCulloch, Mason, Menard, Parker, San Saba, Stephens, Tarrant, Wise, and Young counties, Texas. Palo Pinto County also lay in the area, but marshals failed to take the census in 1870.

7. Meinig, *Imperial Texas*, p. 69.

8. Terry G. Jordan, *German Seed in Texas Soil: Immigrant Farmers in Nineteenth-Century Texas*, pp. 147-51; Marion M. Coleman, "The Polish Origins of Bandera, Texas," *Polish American Studies* 20 (January 1963): 21-27.

9. William T. Chambers, "Edwards Plateau: A Combination Ranching Region," *Economic Geography* 8 (1932): 67–80.

10. Cornelius C. Cox, "Reminiscences of C. C. Cox," *Texas State Historical Association, Quarterly* 6 (1902–1903): 205–7, 212.

11. "Stock-Raising," *Texas Almanac for 1861*, p. 149.

12. Kent Gardien, "Kokernot and His Tory," *Texana* 8 (1970): 282, 292–93.

13. J. Marvin Hunter, *The Trail Drivers of Texas*, pp. 611–12; A. Ray Stephens, *The Taft Ranch: A Texas Principality*, p. 9; and Gus L. Ford, ed., *Texas Cattle Brands: A Catalog of the Texas Centennial Exposition Exhibit, 1936*, p. 216.

14. Seventh Census of the United States, 1850, MS agricultural schedules for Bexar, Calhoun, Cameron-Starr-Webb, DeWitt, Goliad, Gonzales, Guadalupe, Medina, Nueces, Refugio, San Patricio, and Victoria counties.

15. *Seventh Census of the United States, 1850*, pp. 503–4, 514–15; *Ninth Census of the U.S., 1870*, 1: 63–64 and 3: 251–59.

16. *Texas Almanac for 1861*, p. 173; *Texas Almanac for 1867*, pp. 126, 197–99.

17. D. E. E. Braman, *Braman's Information about Texas*, p. 67.

18. Hunter, *Trail Drivers of Texas*, pp. 216, 217, 268, 568.

19. Sources on the Chisum family include: Richardson, *Frontier of Northwest Texas*, p. 153; Alexander W. Neville, *The History of Lamar County*, pp. 190–91; Rex W. Strickland, "Anglo-American Activities in Northeast Texas, 1803–1845" (Ph. D. diss., University of Texas, Austin, 1937), p. 321; Ed F. Bates, *History and Reminiscences of Denton County*, pp. 305–6; T. U. Taylor, *The Chisholm Trail and Other Routes*, pp. 47, 51; and MS Texas tax lists for Lamar County, 1846–54, in the Texas State Archives, Austin.

20. Data on the Waggoner family are from: C. L. Douglas, "Cattle Kings of Texas: D. Waggoner," *The Cattleman* 57 (July 1970): 75–78; MS Texas tax lists for Red River County 1839–48 and Hopkins County 1849–54; E. B. Fleming, *Early History of Hopkins County, Texas*, pp. 104–5; Seventh Census of the U.S., 1850, MS agricultural schedules for Hopkins County, Texas; Walter P. Webb and H. Bailey Carroll, eds., *The Handbook of Texas*, 2: 850–51.

21. Webb and Carroll, *Handbook of Texas*, 2: 87; Ford, *Texas Cattle Brands*, pp. 219–20.

22. Data on Gilbert are from: MS Texas tax lists for Fannin County, 1843 and 1848; Seventh Census of the U.S., 1850, MS population and agricultural schedules for Fannin County, Texas; Richardson, *Frontier of Northwest Texas*, p. 256; Floy Crandall Hodge, *A History of Fannin County, Featuring Pioneer Families*, p. 182; Webb and Carroll, *Handbook of Texas*, 1: 688.

23. Data on the Emberson family are from: Neville, *History of*

Lamar County, p. 80; MS Texas tax lists for Red River County 1838–40 and Lamar County 1842–49; Seventh Census of the U.S., 1850, MS agricultural and population schedules for Lamar County, Texas; and "History of Pilot Point Starts Ninety-six Years Ago," *Pilot Point Post Signal* (Pilot Point, Texas), vol. 63, no. 47 (24 July 1941): 8th un. p.

24. W. D. Wood, "Sketch of the Early Settlement of Leon County, Its Organization, and Some of the Early Settlers," *Texas State Historical Association, Quarterly* 4 (1900–1901): 211–12; MS Texas tax lists for Nacogdoches County, 1840; Seventh Census of the U.S., 1850, MS agricultural and population schedules for Leon County, Texas; Webb and Carroll, *Handbook of Texas*, 1: 527.

25. Andrew Davis, "Folk Life in Early Texas: The Autobiography of Andrew Davis," *Southwestern Historical Quarterly* 43 (1939–40): 326; MS Texas tax lists for Shelby County, 1840; Seventh Census of the U.S., 1850, MS agricultural and population schedules for Shelby and Navarro counties, Texas.

26. Ford, *Texas Cattle Brands*, p. 95.

27. Webb and Carroll, *Handbook of Texas*, 2: 432.

28. Sources on the Slaughter family include: David J. Murrah, "A Cattle Kingdom on Texas' Last Frontier: C. C. Slaughter's Lazy S Ranch" (M.A. thesis, Texas Tech University, Lubbock, 1970); Ford, *Texas Cattle Brands*, pp. 212–13; Webb and Carroll, *Handbook of Texas*, 2: 618; Eighth Census of the United States, 1860, MS agricultural schedules for Palo Pinto County, Texas; Tad Moses, "Early Day Cattlemen: A Compilation of Events, Names, Places and Dates of Early Southwest Cattle History," *The Cattleman* 34 (November 1947): 98.

29. Meinig, *Imperial Texas*, p. 69. See also: Robert M. Utley, *Longhorns of the Big Bend: A Special Report on the Early Cattle Industry of the Big Bend Country of Texas.*

30. Meinig, *Imperial Texas*, pp. 68–69.

31. See notes 19, 20, and 28 in this chapter for sources documenting the migrations of Chisum, Waggoner, and Slaughter. For the Kokernot family, see Moses, "Early Day Cattlemen," *The Cattleman* 34 (December 1947): 75.

32. Webb and Carroll, *Handbook of Texas*, 2: 780; Toni Frissell and Holland McCombs, *The King Ranch, 1939–1944: A Photographic Essay*, pp. 103–4; Jack Freeman, "Dogs Handy in Roundup," *Dallas Morning News*, 12 April 1975, p. 32A; Ben Moore, Sr., *Random Shots and Tales of Texas*, pp. 140, 193; Bates, *History and Reminiscences*, pp. 399–400; Gilbert J. Jordan, *Yesterday in the Texas Hill Country*, pp. 64, 66.

33. Dulcie Sullivan, *The LS Brand: The Story of a Texas Panhandle Ranch*, pp. 151–52, plates 7 and 8 following p. 64.

34. Philip Durham and Everett L. Jones, *The Negro Cowboys*, pp. 24, 92, 159; William C. Holden, *A Ranching Saga: The Lives of William Electious Halsell and Ewing Halsell*, 1: 27. MS schedules of the Tenth United States Census, 1880, for Wichita County, Texas, families no. 61 and 72. See also Philip C. Durham, "The Negro Cowboy," *American Quarterly* 7 (1955): 290–301.

35. Cox, "Reminiscences of C. C. Cox," p. 208; MS schedules of the Tenth Census, 1880—see table 6.2 for a list of the counties included; Alwyn Barr, *Black Texans: A History of Negroes in Texas, 1582–1971*, pp. 58, 91.

36. William E. Cureton, "Westward I Go Free: The Memoirs of William E. Cureton, Texas Frontiersman," *Southwestern Historical Quarterly* 81 (1977): 173.

37. Sullivan, *LS Brand*, p. 79.

38. Ford, *Texas Cattle Brands*, pp. 7–210.

39. Ibid., p. 168.

40. Ibid., pp. 25, 104.

41. Ibid., pp. 67, 155, 182.

42. Hortense W. Ward, "Indian Sign on the Spaniard's Cattle," *Texas Folk-Lore Society Publication* no. 19 (1944), pp. 94–105; Tad Moses, "Development of the Cattle Business in Texas," *Texas Almanac and State Industrial Guide, 1949–1950*, p. 258; Ford, *Texas Cattle Brands*, pp. 1–210.

43. W. H. Jackson and S. A. Long, *The Texas Stock Directory, or Book of Marks and Brands*.

44. Holden, *Ranching Saga*, 1: 43–44.

45. Cureton, "Westward I Go Free," p. 168.

46. James E. McCauley, *A Stove-Up Cowboy's Story*, p. 1; Francis E. Abernethy, ed., *Tales from the Big Thicket*, p. 115.

47. Holden, *Ranching Saga*, 1: 6; Webb and Carroll, *Handbook of Texas*, 2: 618.

48. *Ninth Census of the U.S., 1870*, 3: 251–59, for the counties listed in note 6.

49. Ibid., for the counties listed in note 2.

50. *Twelfth Census of the United States, Taken in the Year 1900*, 5: 481–85.

51. Sullivan, *LS Brand*, p. 166.

52. Américo Paredes, "The Bury-Me-Not Theme in the Southwest," *Texas Folk Lore Society Publication* no. 29 (1959), pp. 88–92.

53. Seventh Census of the U.S., 1850, MS free population schedules, Fort Bend County, Texas, household no. 58 and Jackson County, Texas, household no. 46.

54. Seventh Census of the U.S., 1850, MS free population and agricultural schedules for Bexar (11), Calhoun (2), DeWitt (1), Goliad (7), Gonzales (0), Guadalupe (0), Medina (6), Nueces (92),

Refugio (4), San Patricio (14), and Victoria (44) counties, Texas (the number of Mexican *vaqueros* in each county is shown in parentheses following the name of the county).

55. Moses, "Early Day Cattlemen," *The Cattleman* (November 1947), p. 85.

56. Walter P. Webb, *The Great Plains*, pp. 208–10.

57. *Ninth Census of the U.S., 1870*, 3: 251–59, for the counties listed in note 3.

58. Ibid., for the counties listed in note 2.

59. Sandra L. Myres, "The Ranching Frontier: Spanish Institutional Backgrounds of the Plains Cattle Industry," in *Essays on the American West*, pp. 29–30; Moses, "Early Day Cattlemen," *The Cattleman* (January 1948), p. 63.

60. Mody Boatright, "The Myth of Frontier Individualism," *Southwestern Social Science Quarterly* 22 (1941): 12–32.

61. Myres, "The Ranching Frontier," p. 28.

62. Cox, "Reminiscences of C. C. Cox," pp. 208–9.

63. Sullivan, *LS Brand*, pp. 39–40; Frederick W. Rathjen, *The Texas Panhandle Frontier*, pp. 101–3, 237.

64. Donald W. Meinig, "The Continuous Shaping of America: A Prospectus for Geographers and Historians," *American Historical Review* 83 (1978): 1190–91.

Bibliography

Primary Sources

Almonte, Juan N. "Statistical Report on Texas." Edited and translated by C. E. Castañeda. *Southwestern Historical Quarterly* 28 (1925): 177–222.

Archambeau, Ernest R. "The First Federal Census in the Panhandle, 1880." *Panhandle-Plains Historical Review* 23 (1950): 23–132.

Archives of Maryland, (Proceedings of the Council of Maryland, 1636–1667). Vol. 3. Baltimore: Maryland Historical Society, 1885.

Austin, Stephen F. "Journal on His First Trip to Texas." *Texas State Historical Association Quarterly* 7 (1903–1904): 286–307.

Banta, William, and J. W. Caldwell, Jr. *Twenty-Seven Years on the Texas Frontier*. Council Hill, Oklahoma: L. G. Park, 1933.

Barker, Eugene C., ed. *The Austin Papers*. Vol. 1, *Annual Report of the American Historical Association for the Year 1919*. Vol. 2, *Annual Report of the American Historical Association for the Year 1922*. Washington: Government Printing Office, 1924, 1928. Vol 3, Austin: University of Texas, ca. 1926.

Barrow, John. *Facts Relating to North-Eastern Texas, Condensed from Notes Made During a Tour through That Portion of the United States of America*. London: Simpkin, Marshall & Co., 1849.

Barry, James B. "The Diary of James Buckner Barry, 1860–1862." Edited by James K. Greer. *Southwestern Historical Quarterly* 36 (1932–33): 144–62.

Bartram, William. *The Travels of William Bartram*. Edited by Mark van Doren. N. p.: Macy-Masius Publishers, 1928. (First published 1791).

Bell, James G. "A Log of the Texas-California Cattle Trail, 1854." Edited by J. Evetts Haley. *Southwestern Historical Quarterly* 35 (1931–32): 208–37, 290–316.

Bollaert, William. *William Bollaert's Texas*. Edited by W. Eugene Hollon and Ruth Lapham Butler. Norman: University of Oklahoma Press, 1956.

191

Bolzius, Johann Martin. "Johann Martin Bolzius Answers a Questionnaire on Carolina and Georgia." Edited and translated by Klaus G. Loewald, Beverly Starika, and Paul S. Taylor. *William and Mary Quarterly* (third series) 14 (1957):218–61; 15 (1958):228–52.

Bonnell, George W. *Topographical Description of Texas*. Austin: Clark, Wing, and Brown, 1840.

Braman, D. E. E. *Braman's Information about Texas*. Philadelphia: J. B. Lippincott, 1858.

Brett, Bill. "Horse Penning: Southeast Texas, 1913." *Publications of the Texas Folklore Society*, no. 37 (1972), pp. 117–20.

Brooke, John. Quoted in *Report of the Commissioner of Patents for the Year 1855. Agriculture*. 34th Cong., 1st sess., Senate Executive Document no. 20, p. 26. Washington, D.C.: A. O. P. Nicholson, 1856.

Candler, Allen D., comp. and ed. *The Colonial Records of Georgia*. 6 vols. Atlanta: Franklin Printing and Publishing Co., 1904–1906.

Carman, Harry J., ed. *American Husbandry*. New York: Columbia, University Press, 1939.

Clark, R. K. "A Letter From Lamar County in 1844." Contributed by J. E. Pirie. *Southwestern Historical Quarterly* 53 (1949): 66–67.

Clark, Walter, comp. and ed. *The State Records of North Carolina*. Vol 23. Goldsboro, North Carolina: Nash Brothers, 1904.

Claus, Jacob. "Detailed Information and Account for those who are Inclined to America and are Interested in Settling in the Province of Pennsylvania." *Pennsylvania Magazine of History and Biography* 49 (1925): 115–40.

Clopper, J. C. "J. C. Clopper's Journal and Book of Memoranda for 1828." *Texas State Historical Association, Quarterly* 13 (1909–10): 44–80.

Compendium of the Enumeration of the Inhabitants and Statistics of the United States, as Obtained at the Department of State, from the Returns of the Sixth Census. Washington, D.C.: Thomas Allen, 1841.

Cox, Cornelius C. "Reminiscences of C. C. Cox." *Texas State Historical Association, Quarterly* 6 (1902–1903): 113–38, 204–35.

Crayon, Porte (Pseud. for David Hunter Strother). "Virginia Illustrated." *Harper's New Monthly Magazine* 10 (1854–55): pp. 1–25, 289–310.

Crèvecoeur, Michel-Guillaume St. Jean de. *Crèvecoeur's Eighteenth-Century Travels in Pennsylvania and New York*. Translated and edited by Percy G. Adams. Lexington: University of Kentucky Press, 1961.

————. *Journey into Northern Pennsylvania and the State of New York.* Translated by Clarissa S. Bostelmann. Ann Arbor: University of Michigan Press, 1964.

Cureton, William E. "Westward I Go Free: The Memoirs of William E. Cureton, Texas Frontiersman." Edited by William C. Pool. *Southwestern Historical Quarterly* 81 (1977): 155-90.

Davis, Andrew. "Folk Life in Early Texas: The Autobiography of Andrew Davis." Edited by R. L. Jones. *Southwestern Historical Quarterly* 43 (1939-40): 158-75, 323-41.

DeBow, J. D. B. *Statistical View of the United States... Being a Compendium of the Seventh Census.* Washington, D.C.: Beverly Tucker, 1854.

DeBrahm, William Gerard. *DeBrahm's Report of the General Survey in the Southern District of North America.* Edited and with an introduction by Louis De Vorsey, Jr. Columbia, South Carolina: University of South Carolina Press, 1971.

DeCordova, Jacob. *Texas: Her Resources and Her Public Men.* Philadelphia: E. Crozet, 1858.

DeWees, William B. *Letters from an Early Settler of Texas.* Compiled by Cara Cardelle. Louisville, Kentucky: Morton & Griswold, 1852.

Dor, John M. Letter to Col. B. R. Milam, dated 14 May 1831. In *Yanaguana Society Publications, Vol. 5: Texas Letters*, pp. 56-57. San Antonio: Yanaguana Society, 1940.

Dresel, Gustav. *Houston Journal: Adventures in North America and Texas, 1837-1841.* Edited and translated by Max Freund. Austin: University of Texas Press, 1954.

Egmont, John P. *The Journal of the Earl of Egmont.* Edited by Robert G. McPherson. Athens: University of Georgia Press, 1962.

Erskine, M. H. "A Cattle Drive from Texas to California: The Diary of M. H. Erskine, 1854." *Southwestern Historical Quarterly* 67 (1963-64): 397-412.

Eubank, Mary James. "A Journal of Our Trip to Texas, October 6, 1853." Edited by W. C. Nunn. *Texana* 10 (1972): 30-44.

Executive Document. 25th Cong. 2nd sess., document 351, serial 332. Washington, D.C.: n. p., ca. 1840.

"Exhibit of the Census of the State for the Year 1848." In *Journal of the House of Representatives of the State of Texas. Third Session*, pp. 33-34. Austin: Wm. H. Cushney, 1849.

Gammel, H. P. N., ed. *Laws of Texas.* Austin: Gammel Book Co., 1898.

[Glen, James]. *A Description of South Carolina.* London: R. & J. Dodsley, 1761.

Gordon, Clarence. "Report on Cattle, Sheep, and Swine, Supplementary to Enumeration of Live Stock on Farms in 1880." In *Report on the Productions of Agriculture as Returned at the Tenth Census*, pp. 951–1116. Washington, D.C.: Government Printing Office, 1883.

Gray, William F. *From Virginia to Texas, 1835: Diary of Col. Wm. F. Gray*. Edited by A. C. Gray. Houston: Gray, Dillaye & Co., 1909.

Gregg, Josiah. *Diary and Letters of Josiah Gregg, Southwestern Enterprises 1840–1847*. Edited by Maurice G. Fulton. Norman: University of Oklahoma Press, 1941.

Harris, Mrs. Dilue. "Reminiscences of Mrs. Dilue Harris." *Texas State Historical Association, Quarterly* 4 (1900–1901): 85–127, 155–89; 7 (1903–1904): 214–22.

Hawkins, Benjamin. "A Sketch of the Creek Country in the Years 1798 and 1799." In *Creek Indian History*. Georgia Historical Society, Collections and Transactions 3, pt. 1 (1938).

Holley, Mary Austin. *Texas*. Lexington, Kentucky: J. Clarke & Co., 1836.

_____. *Texas: Observations, Historical, Geographical and Descriptive, in a Series of Letters*. Baltimore: Armstrong & Plaskitt, 1833.

Hooton, Charles. *St. Louis' Isle, or Texiana*. London: Simmonds and Ward, 1847.

Houstoun, Mrs. Matilda Charlotte Fraser. *Texas and the Gulf of Mexico; or Yachting in the New World*. 2 vols. London: John Murray, 1844.

Ikin, Arthur. *Texas: Its History, Topography, Agriculture, Commerce, and General Statistics*. London: Sherwood, Gilbert, and Piper, 1841.

Imlay, Gilbert. *A Topographical Description of the Western Territory of North America*. 3rd ed. London: J. Debrett, 1797.

"Indian Removals." In *Senate Documents*, 25th cong. 1st sess., no. 512, 1, pp. 949–55. Washington, D.C.: n.p., ca. 1840.

Jackson, Ralph S. *Home on the Double Bayou: Memories of an East Texas Ranch*. Austin: University of Texas Press, 1961.

Jackson, W. H., and S. A. Long. *The Texas Stock Directory, or Book of Marks and Brands*. Vol. 1. San Antonio: Herald Office, 1865.

James, Joshua, and Alexander McCrae. *A Journal of a Tour in Texas*. Wilmington, North Carolina: T. Loring, 1835.

Journals of the Senate of the First Legislature of the State of Texas. Clarksville, Texas: Standard Office, 1848.

Kennedy, William. *Texas: The Rise, Progress, and Prospects of the Republic of Texas*. Fort Worth: Molyneaux Craftsmen, 1925 (original edition, London, 1841).

Kuykendall, J. H. "Reminiscences of Early Texans." *Texas State Historical Association, Quarterly* 6 (1902-1903): 236-53, 311-30; 7 (1903-1904): 29-64.

Lawrie, Arthur. "Lawrie's Trip to Northeast Texas, 1854-1855." Edited by V. E. Gibbens. *Southwestern Historical Quarterly* 48 (1944-45): 238-53.

Lincecum, Gideon. "Journal of Lincecum's Travels in Texas, 1835." Edited by A. L. Bradford and T. N. Campbell. *Southwestern Historical Quarterly* 53 (1949-50): 180-201.

Logan, William. "William Logan's Journal of a Journey to Georgia, 1745." *Pennsylvania Magazine of History and Biography* 36 (1912): 1-16.

Lubbock, Francis R. *Six Decades in Texas or Memoirs.* Edited by C. W. Raines. Austin: Ben C. Jones & Co., 1900.

Lundy, Benjamin. *The Life, Travels and Opinions of Benjamin Lundy, Including his Journeys to Texas and Mexico.* Philadelphia: William D. Parrish, 1847.

McCalla, William L. *Adventures in Texas, Chiefly in the Spring and Summer of 1840.* Philadelphia: The Author, 1841.

McCauley, James E. *A Stove-Up Cowboy's Story.* Dallas: Southern Methodist University Press, 1943.

McClintock, William A. "Journal of the Trip through Texas and Northern Mexico in 1846-1847." *Southwestern Historical Quarterly* 34 (1930-31): 20-37, 141-58, 231-56.

Manufactures of the United States in 1860, Compiled from the Original Returns of the Eighth Census. Washington, D.C.: Government Printing Office, 1865.

Marryat, Frederick. *Narrative of the Travels and Adventures of Monsieur Violet, in California, Sonora, and Western Texas.* 3 vols. London: Longman, Brown, Green & Longmans, 1843.

Merrens, H. Roy, ed. *The Colonial South Carolina Scene: Contemporary Views, 1697-1774.* Columbia: University of South Carolina Press, 1977.

Michaux, F. A. *Travels to the West of the Mountains, in the States of Ohio, Kentucky, and Tennessea.* London: D. N. Shury, 1805.

[Milligen-Johnston, George]. *A Short Description of the Province of South Carolina... Written in the Year 1763.* London: John Hinton, 1770.

Moore, A. W. "A Reconnoissance in Texas in 1846." *Southwestern Historical Quarterly* 30 (1927): 252-71.

Moore, Ben, Sr. *Random Shots and Tales of Texas.* Seagraves, Texas: Pioneer Book Publishers, 1977.

Moore, Francis, Jr. *Map and Description of Texas, Containing Sketches of its History, Geology, Geography and Statistics.*

Philadelphia: H. Tanner, Jr.; New York: Tanner & Disturnell, 1840.

Morrell, Z. N. *Flowers and Fruits from the Wilderness; or, Thirty-Six Years in Texas and Two Winters in Honduras.* Boston: Gould and Lincoln, 1873.

Morris, Thomas A. *Miscellany: Consisting of Essays, Biographical Sketches, and Notes of Travel.* Cincinnati: L. Swormstedt and A. Poe, 1852.

Muir, Andrew F., ed. *Texas in 1837, an Anonymous, Contemporary Narrative.* Austin: University of Texas Press, 1958.

Mullins, Marion Day. "The First Census of Texas, 1829–1836." *Special Publications of the National Genealogical Society*, no. 22 (reprinted from the 1959 volume of *The National Genealogical Register*). Washington, D.C.: National Genealogical Society, 1959.

Ninth Census of the United States, 1870. Vols. 1, 3. Washington, D.C.: Government Printing Office, 1872.

Northern Standard (newspaper). Clarksville, Texas. Vols. 1–5 (1842–48).

Nuttall, Thomas. *A Journal of Travels into the Arkansa Territory, During the Year 1819.* Philadelphia: Thomas Palmer, 1821.

Osburn, Mary M., ed. "The Atascosita Census of 1826." *Texana* 1 (1963): 299–321.

[Page, Frederic B.]. *Prairiedom: Rambles and Scrambles in Texas or New Estrémadura.* New York: Paine & Burgess, 1845.

Parker, Amos A. *Trip to the West and Texas.* Concord, New Hampshire: White & Fisher, 1835.

Parker, James W. *The Rachel Plummer Narrative.* N. p.: n.p., 1926.

Peña, José Enrique de la. *With Santa Anna in Texas: A Personal Narrative of the Revolution.* Translated and edited by Carmen Perry. College Station: Texas A & M University Press, 1975.

Population of the United States in 1860; Compiled from the Original Returns of the Eighth Census. Washington, D.C.: Government Printing Office, 1864.

Rabb, Mary Crownover, *Travels and Adventures in Texas in the 1820's, Being the Reminiscences of Mary Crownover Rabb.* Waco: Texian Press, 1962.

Rankin, Melinda. *Texas in 1850.* Boston: Damrell & Moore, 1850.

Report of the Commissioner of Patents for the Year 1855. Agriculture. 34th Cong. 1st sess. Senate Executive Document no. 20. Washington, D.C.: A. O. P. Nicholson, 1856.

Report of the Commissioner of Patents for the Year 1850. Part 2 Agriculture. Washington, D.C.: Office of Printers to House of Representatives, 1851.

Salley, Alexander S., Jr. *Narratives of Early Carolina.* New York: Barnes & Noble, 1967.

Sánchez, José María. "A Trip to Texas in 1828." Translated by Carlos E. Castañeda. *Southwestern Historical Quarterly* 29 (1926): 249–88.

Saunders, William L., ed. *The Colonial Records of North Carolina.* Vols. 1–4. Raleigh: P.M. Hale, 1886. Vols. 5–7. Raleigh: Josephus Daniels, 1887–90.

Sawyer, William E. "A Young Man Comes to Texas in 1852." *Texana* 7 (1969): 17–37.

Seventh Census of the United States, 1850. Washington, D.C.: A. O. P. Nicholson, 1853.

Sheridan, Francis C. *Galveston Island, Or, A Few Months Off the Coast of Texas.* Edited by Willis W. Pratt. Austin: University of Texas Press, 1954.

Shipman, Daniel. *Frontier Life..., 58 Years in Texas.* N.p.: n.p, 1879.

Smith, Edward. *Account of a Journey through North-Eastern Texas, Undertaken in 1849.* London: Hamilton, Adams & Co., 1849.

Smithwick, Noah. *The Evolution of a State.* Austin: Steck Co., 1935.

Smythe, D. Port. "D. Port Smythe's Journey Across Early Texas." Edited by Donald Day and Samuel W. Geiser. *Texas Geographical Magazine* 6, no. 2 (Fall 1942): 1–20.

Spenser, Edmund. "A View of the State of Ireland." In James Ware, *Two Histories of Ireland.* Dublin: Society of Stationers, 1633.

Sterne, Adolphus. *Hurrah for Texas! The Diary of Adolphus Sterne, 1838–1851.* Edited by Archie P. McDonald. Waco: Texian Press, 1969.

"Stock-Raising." In *Texas Almanac for 1861*, pp. 148–52. Galveston: Richardson, 1860.

Strother, David Hunter. *Virginia Illustrated.* New York: Harper & Brothers, 1857.

Telegraph and Texas Register. Columbia, Texas. 31 October 1835.

Texas Almanac for 1857. Galveston: Richardson, 1856.

Texas Almanac for 1861. Galveston: Richardson, 1860.

Texas Almanac for 1867. Galveston: Richardson, 1866.

Texas in 1840, or the Emigrant's Guide to the New Republic. New York: W. W. Allen, 1840.

Thirteenth Census of the United States Taken in the Year 1910. Vol. 7, Agriculture. Washington, D.C.: Government Printing Office, 1913.

Twelfth Census of the United States, Taken in the Year 1900. Vol. 5, "Agriculture, Part 1." Washington, D.C.: United States Census Office, 1902.

A Visit to Texas; Being the Journal of a Traveller through Those Parts Most Interesting to American Settlers. New York: Goodrich & Wiley, 1834.

White, Gifford E., ed. *The 1840 Census of the Republic of Texas*. Austin: Pemberton Press, 1966.

Woodman, David, Jr. *Guide to Texas Emigrants*. Boston: M. Hawes, 1835.

Woodmason, Charles. *The Carolina Backcountry on the Eve of the Revolution: The Journal and Other Writings of Charles Woodmason, Anglican Itinerant*. Edited by Richard J. Hooker. Chapel Hill: University of North Carolina Press, 1953.

Wrede, Friedrich W. von. *Sketches of Life in the United States of North America and Texas*. Translated by Chester W. Geue. Waco: Texian Press, 1970.

Wright, Solomon Alexander. *My Rambles as East Texas Cowboy, Hunter, Fisherman, Tie-Cutter*. Austin: Texas Folklore Society, 1942.

Secondary Sources

Abernethy, Francis E., ed. *Tales from the Big Thicket*. Austin: University of Texas Press, 1966.

Aitken, Robert. "Routes of Transhumance on the Spanish Meseta." *Geographical Journal* 106 (1945): 59–69.

Allen, H. C. *Bush and Backwoods: A Comparison of the Frontier in Australia and the United States*. East Lansing: Michigan State University Press, 1959.

Altgelt, George B. "Present-Day Livestock Raising in the Gulf Coast Uplands—Use of Dogs in Herding Cattle." *Farm & Ranch* 57, no. 4 (15 February 1938): 4–5.

Ames, Susie M. *Studies of the Virginia Eastern Shore in the Seventeenth Century*. Richmond, Va.: Dietz Press, 1940.

Andreae, Bernd. *Betriebsformen in der Landwirtschaft*. Stuttgart: Eugen Ulmer, 1964.

Arbingast, Stanley A., et al. *Atlas of Texas*. 5th ed. Austin: University of Texas Bureau of Business Research, 1976.

Arbos, Philippe. "The Geography of the Pastoral Life: Illustrated with European Examples." *Geographical Review* 13 (1923): 559–75.

Arnade, Charles. "Cattle Raising in Spanish Florida, 1513–1763." *Agricultural History* 35 (1961): 116–24.

Arrington, Fred. *A History of Dickens County*. Quanah, Texas: Nortex Offset Publications, 1971.

Atkinson, J. H. "Cattle Drives from Arkansas to California Prior to the Civil War." *Arkansas Historical Quarterly* 28 (1969): 275–81.

Atwood, Elmer Bagby. *The Regional Vocabulary of Texas*. Austin: University of Texas Press, 1962.

Barker, Eugene C. *The Life of Stephen F. Austin.* Nashville and Dallas: Cokesbury Press, 1925.

Barr, Alwyn. *Black Texans: A History of Negroes in Texas, 1528–1971.* Austin: Pemberton Press, 1973.

Bates, Ed. F. *History and Reminiscences of Denton County.* Denton, Texas: McNitzsky, 1918.

Bennett, Carmen Taylor. *Our Roots Grow Deep: A History of Cottle County.* Floydada, Texas: Blanco Offset Printing, 1970.

Bidwell, Percy W., and John I. Falconer. *History of Agriculture in the Northern United States, 1620–1860.* Washington: Carnegie Institution, 1925.

Bishko, Charles Julian. "The Peninsular Background of Latin American Cattle Ranching." *Hispanic American Historical Review* 32 (1952): 491–515.

Blake, R. B. "Beef Trail." In *The Handbook of Texas.* Edited by Walter P. Webb and H. Bailey Carroll, vol. 1, p. 138. Austin: Texas State Historical Association, 1952.

———. "Gil Antonio Ibarvo." In *The Handbook of Texas,* Edited by Walter P. Webb and H. Bailey Carroll vol. 1, p. 873. Austin: Texas State Historical Association, 1952.

Boatright, Mody. "The Myth of Frontier Individualism." *Southwestern Social Science Quarterly* 22 (1941): 12–32.

Boesch, Hans. "Nomadismus, Transhumanz und Alpwirtschaft." *Die Alpen* 6 (1951): 202–7.

Bogue, Allan G. *From Prairie to Corn Belt.* Chicago: University of Chicago Press, 1963.

Bolton, Herbert E. *Bolton and the Spanish Borderlands.* Edited by John F. Bannon. Norman: University of Oklahoma Press, 1964.

———. "The Spanish Abandonment and Re-Occupation of East Texas, 1773–1779." *Texas State Historical Association, Quarterly* 9 (1905): 67–137.

Bounds, John H. "The Alabama-Coushatta Indians of Texas." *Journal of Geography* 70 (1971): 175–82.

Brand, Donald D. "The Early History of the Range Cattle Industry in Northern Mexico." *Agricultural History* 35 (1961): 132–39.

Branda, Eldon S., ed. *The Handbook of Texas, A Supplement.* Vol. 3 Austin: Texas State Historical Association, 1976.

Browder, Virginia. *Donley County, Land O' Promise.* Quanah, Texas: Nortex Press, 1975.

Brown, Ralph H. *Historical Geography of the United States.* New York: Harcourt, Brace & Co., 1948.

———. "Texas Cattle Trails: Notes on Three Important Maps." *Texas Geographic Magazine* 10, no. 1 (1946): 1–6.

Bruce, Philip A. *Economic History of Virginia in the Seventeenth Century.* 2 vols. New York: Macmillan, 1907.

Burnett, Edmund C. "Hog Raising and Hog Driving in the Region of the French Broad River." *Agricultural History* 20 (1946): 86–103.

Carrier, Lyman. *The Beginnings of Agriculture in America.* New York: McGraw-Hill, 1923.

Carter, Jeff. *In the Tracks of the Cattle.* Sydney, Australia: Angus and Robertson, 1968.

Carter, William T., et al. *Soil Survey of Red River County, Texas.* United States Dept. of Agriculture, Bureau of Soils. Washington, D.C.: Government Printing Office, 1923.

Casey, Clifford B. *Mirages, Mysteries and Reality: Brewster County, Texas.* Seagraves, Texas: Pioneer Book Publishers, 1972.

Chambers, William T. "Edwards Plateau: A Combination Ranching Region." *Economic Geography* 8 (1932): 67–80.

Chevalier, François. *Land and Society in Colonial Mexico—The Great Hacienda.* Berkeley: University of California Press, 1963.

Chisholm, Michael. *Rural Settlement and Land Use.* London: Hutchinson, 1962.

Clark, Pat B. *The History of Clarksville and Old Red River County.* Dallas: Mathis, Van Nort & Co., 1937.

Coleman, Marion M. "The Polish Origins of Bandera, Texas." *Polish American Studies* 20 (January 1963): 21–27.

Combs, Joe F. "Cattle Raising in the Coastal Area One of the Oldest Industries to Claim Attention of Texans. *Coastal Cattleman* 2, no. 1 (May 1936): 3, 9.

Connor, Seymour V. "Early Ranching Operations in the Panhandle: A Report on the Agricultural Schedules of the 1880 Census." *Panhandle-Plains Historical Review* 27 (1954): 47–69.

Cotter, John L., and J. Paul Hudson. *New Discoveries at Jamestown: Site of First Successful English Settlement in America.* Washington, D.C.: Government Printing Office, 1957.

Crist, Raymond E. "Cattle Ranching in the Tropical Rainforest." *Scientific Monthly* 56 (1943): 521–27.

Croker, Thomas C., Jr. "The Longleaf Pine Story." *Journal of Forest History* 23 (1979): 32–43.

Cruikshank, J. W., and I. F. Eldredge. *Forest Resources of Southeastern Texas.* Forest Service, United States Department of Agriculture, Miscellaneous Publication no. 326. Washington, D.C.: Government Printing Office, 1939.

Culbertson, Gilbert M. "The Creek Indians in East Texas." *East Texas Historical Journal* 14 (Fall 1976): 20–25.

Dacy, George H. *Four Centuries of Florida Ranching.* St. Louis: Britt Publishing Co., 1940.

Dale, Edward E. *The Range Cattle Industry: Ranching on the Great Plains from 1865 to 1925.* 2nd ed. Norman: University of Oklahoma Press, 1960.

Daus, F. A. "Transhumación de montaña en Neuquen." *Gaea* 8 (1948): 383-426.

Davies, Elwyn. "The Pattern of Transhumance in Europe." *Geography* 26 (1941): 155-68.

Deffontaines, Pierre. *Contribution à la Géographie pastorale de l'Amérique latine.* Rio de Janeiro: Centro de Pesquisas de Geografia do Brasil, 1964.

Denevan, William M. "Cattle Ranching in the Mojos Savannas of Northeastern Bolivia." *Yearbook of the Association of Pacific Coast Geographers* 25 (1963): 37-44.

Dillard, J. L. "The Lingua Franca in the American Southwest." *Revista Interamericana Review* 3 (1973): 278-89.

Dobie, J. Frank. "The First Cattle in Texas and the Southwest, Progenitors of the Longhorns." *Southwestern Historical Quarterly* 42 (1939): 171-97.

――――. *The Longhorns.* Boston: Little, Brown & Co., 1941.

Doran, Michael F. "Antebellum Cattle Herding in the Indian Territory." *Geographical Review* 66 (1976): 48-58.

Douglas, C. L. "Cattle Kings of Texas: Burk Burnett of the Four Sixes." *The Cattleman* 57, no. 3 (August 1970): 99-102.

――――. "Cattle Kings of Texas: D. Waggoner and Son." *The Cattleman* 57, no. 2 (July 1970): 75-78.

Dunbar, Gary S. "Colonial Carolina Cowpens." *Agricultural History* 35 (1961): 125-30.

――――. *Historical Geography of the North Carolina Outer Banks.* Baton Rouge: Louisiana State University Press, 1958.

Dunn, Edgar S., Jr. *The Location of Agricultural Production.* Gainesville: University of Florida Press, 1954.

Durham, Philip C. "The Negro Cowboy." *American Quarterly* 7 (1955): 291-301.

――――, and Everett L. Jones. *The Negro Cowboys.* New York: Dodd, Mead, 1965.

Evans, E. Estyn, "Culture and Land Use in the Old West of North America." *Heidelberger Studien zur Kulturgeographie* 15 (1966): 72-80.

――――. *Irish Folk Ways.* London: Routledge & Kegan Paul, 1957.

――――. *The Personality of Ireland: Habitat, Heritage and History.* Cambridge: At the University Press, 1973.

Ewald, Ursula. "The von Thünen Principle and Agricultural Zonation in Colonial Mexico." *Journal of Historical Geography* 3 (1977): 123-33.

Faulk, Odie B. "Ranching in Spanish Texas." *Hispanic American Historical Review* 45 (1965): 257-66.

Fiedler, Gisela. "Kulturgeographische Untersuchungen in der Sierra de Gredos, Spanien." *Würzburger Geographische Arbeiten*, no. 33, 1970.

"The First Cattle Ranch in Texas." *Frontier Times* 13 (1936): 304-8.

Fleming, E. B. *Early History of Hopkins County, Texas.* N.p.: n.p., 1902.

Ford, Gus L., ed. *Texas Cattle Brands: A Catalog of the Texas Centennial Exposition Exhibit.* Dallas: Clyde C. Cockrell, 1936.

Francis, Ruth Garrison. "The Coastal Cow Country—The Saga of James Taylor White, First." *Coastal Cattleman* 6, no. 7 (September 1940): 21-23.

Frazier, Evelyn M., and William E. Fripp. "Names in Colleton County." *Names in South Carolina* 12 (Winter 1965): 11-12.

Freeman, Jack. "Dogs Handy in Roundup." *Dallas Morning News.* Dallas, Texas. 12 April 1975, p. 32A.

Fribourg, André. "La Transhumance en Espagne." *Annales de Géographie* 19 (1910): 231-44.

Frissell, Toni, and Holland McCombs. *The King Ranch, 1939-1944: A Photographic Essay.* Dobbs Ferry, New York: Morgan & Morgan; Fort Worth, Texas: Amon Carter Museum, 1975.

Fritz, Henry E. "The Cattlemen's Frontier in the Trans-Mississippi West: An Annotated Bibliography." *Arizona and the West* 14 (1972): 45-70, 169-90.

Fry, Virginia K. "Reindeer Ranching in Northern Russia." *Professional Geographer* 23 (1971): 146-51.

Fugate, Francis L. "Origins of the Range Cattle Era in South Texas." *Agricultural History* 35 (1961): 155-58.

Gardien, Kent. "Kokernot and His Tory." *Texana* 8 (1970): 269-94.

Gates, Paul W. "Cattle Kings in the Prairies." *Mississippi Valley Historical Review* 35 (1948): 379-412.

———. "Hoosier Cattle Kings." *Indiana Magazine of History* 44 (1948): 1-24.

Gersmehl, Phil. "Factors Leading to Mountaintop Grazing in the Southern Appalachians." *Southeastern Geographer* 10, no. 1 (1970): 67-72.

Goodwin, Gary C. *Cherokees in Transition: A Study of Changing Culture and Environment Prior to 1775.* University of Chicago, Department of Geography, Research Paper no. 181. Chicago: 1977.

Gough, Lysius. *Spur Jingles and Saddle Songs: Rhymes and Miscellany of Cow Camp and Cattle Trails in the Early Eighties.* Amarillo, Texas: Russell Stationery Co., 1935.

Graebner, Norman A. "History of Cattle Ranching in Eastern Oklahoma." *Chronicles of Oklahoma* 21 (1943): 300-11.

Gray, Lewis C. *History of Agriculture in the Southern United States*. Gloucester, Mass.: Peter Smith, 1958.

Grimes, Roy, ed. *Three Hundred Years in Victoria County*. Victoria, Texas: Advocate, 1968.

Grothe, Randy Eli. "106 Dogs, a Man and a Bear." *Dallas Morning News*. Dallas, Texas. 26 March 1977, p. 36E.

Guice, John D. W. "Cattle Raisers of the Old Southwest: A Reinterpretation." *Western Historical Quarterly* 8 (1977): 167–87.

Haggard, J. Villasana. "The House of Barr and Davenport." *Southwestern Historical Quarterly* 49 (1945–46): 66–88.

Haldane, A. R. B. *The Drove Roads of Scotland*. London: Thomas Nelson and Sons, 1952.

Haley, James Evetts. *The XIT Ranch of Texas*. 2nd ed. Norman: University of Oklahoma Press, 1953.

Halverson, L. H. "The Great Karroo of South Africa." *Journal of Geography* 29 (1930): 287–300.

Hammett, A. B. J. *The Empresario Don Martin De Leon*. Waco: Texian Press, 1973.

Hamrick, Alma Ward. *The Call of the San Saba: A History of San Saba County*. Austin: San Felipe Press, 1969.

Hancock, William Keith. "Evolution of the Settlers' Frontier, Southern Africa." Chap. 1 in *Survey of British Commonwealth Affairs* vol. 2 pt. 2 London: Oxford University Press, 1942.

———. "Perspective View." Chap. 1 in *Survey of British Commonwealth Affairs*, vol. 2, pt. 1. London: Oxford University Press, 1940.

Hanes, Bailey C. *Bill Pickett, Bulldogger: The Biography of a Black Cowboy*. Norman: University of Oklahoma Press, 1977.

Harper, Minnie T., and George D. Harper. *Old Ranches*. Dallas: Dealey and Lowe, 1936.

Haskett, Bert. "Early History of the Cattle Industry in Arizona." *Arizona Historical Review* 6 (October 1935): 3–42.

Henlein, Paul C. "Cattle Driving from the Ohio Country, 1800–1850." *Agricultural History* 28 (1954): 83–95.

———. *Cattle Kingdom in the Ohio Valley, 1783–1860*. Lexington, Ky.: University of Kentucky Press, 1959.

———. "Early Cattle Ranges of the Ohio Valley." *Agricultural History* 35 (1961): 150–54.

———. "Shifting Range-Feeder Patterns in the Ohio Valley Before 1860." *Agricultural History* 31 (1957): 1–12.

Hilliard, Sam B. *Hog Meat and Hoecake: Food Supply in the Old South, 1840–1860*. Carbondale and Edwardsville: Southern Illinois University Press, 1972.

Hodge, Floy Crandall. *A History of Fannin County, Featuring Pioneer Families*. Hereford, Texas: Pioneer Publishers, 1966.

Hofmeister, Burkhard. "Wesen und Erscheinungsformen der Transhumance." *Erdkunde* 15 (1961): 121–35.

Holden, William C. *A Ranching Saga: The Lives of William Electious Halsell and Ewing Halsell.* 2 vols. San Antonio: Trinity University Press, 1976.

Holmes, Jack D. L. "Livestock in Spanish Natchez." *Journal of Mississippi History* 23 (1961): 15–37.

Homer. *The Odyssey of Homer.* Translated by Richmond Lattimore. New York: Harper & Row, 1965.

Horvath, Ronald J. "Von Thünen's Isolated State and the Area around Addis Ababa, Ethiopia." *Annals, Association of American Geographers* 59 (1969): 308–23.

Hunter, J. Marvin. *The Trail Drivers of Texas.* Nashville: Cokesbury Press, 1925.

Hunter, Lillie Mae. *The Book of Years: A History of Dallam and Hartley Counties.* Hereford, Texas: Pioneer Book Publishers, 1969.

Huson, Hobart. *Refugio: A Comprehensive History of Refugio County from Aboriginal Times to 1953.* 2 vols. Woodsboro, Texas: Rooke Foundation, 1953.

Johannessen, Carl. "Savannas of Interior Honduras." *Ibero-Americana,* no. 46 (1963).

Jones, R. L. "The Beef Cattle Industry in Ohio Prior to the Civil War." *Ohio Historical Quarterly* 64 (1955): 168–94.

Jordan, Gilbert J. *Yesterday in the Texas Hill Country.* College Station: Texas A & M University Press, 1979.

Jordan, Terry G. "Early Northeast Texas and the Evolution of Western Ranching." *Annals, Association of American Geographers* 67 (1977): 66–87.

———. *German Seed in Texas Soil: Immigrant Farmers in Nineteenth-Century Texas.* Austin: University of Texas Press, 1966.

———. "The Origin and Distribution of Open-Range Cattle Ranching." *Social Science Quarterly* 53 (1972): 105–21.

———. "The Origin of Anglo-American Cattle Ranching in Texas: A Documentation of Diffusion from the Lower South." *Economic Geography* 45 (1969): 63–87.

———. "Population Origins in Texas, 1850," *Geographical Review* 59 (1969): 83–103.

———. "The Texan Appalachia." *Annals, Association of American Geographers* 60 (1970): 409–27.

———. "Texan Influence in Nineteenth-Century Arizona Cattle Ranching." *Journal of the West* 14 (1975): 15–17.

———, and Gilbert J. Jordan. *Ernst and Lisette Jordan: German Pioneers in Texas.* Austin: Von Boeckmann-Jones Co., 1971.

Kish, George. "Transhumance in Southern Italy." *Michigan Academy of Sciences, Arts, Letters, Papers* 39 (1953): 301–7.

Kniffen, Fred B. *Louisiana: Its Land and People*. Baton Rouge: Louisiana State University Press, 1968.

———. "A Spanish (?) Spinner in Louisiana." *Southern Folklore Quarterly* 13 (1949): 192–99.

———. "The Western Cattle Complex: Notes on Differentiation and Diffusion." *Western Folklore* 12 (1953): 179–85.

Kocher, A. E., and W. S. Lyman. *Soil Survey of Franklin County, Texas*. United States Dept. of Agriculture, Bureau of Soils. Washington, D.C.: Government Printing Office, 1909.

Kollmorgen, Walter M. "The Woodsman's Assaults on the Domain of the Cattleman." *Annals, Association of American Geographers* 59 (1969): 215–39.

LeBon, J. W., Jr. "The Catahoula Hog Dog: A Folk Breed." *Pioneer America* 3, no. 2 (1971): 35–45.

Lefebvre, Th. "La transhumance dans les Basses-Pyrénées." *Annales de Géographie* 37 (1928): 35–60.

Love, Clara M. "History of the Cattle Industry in the Southwest." *Southwestern Historical Quarterly* 19 (1916): 370–99; 20 (1916): 1–18.

McCormick, Andrew P. *Scotch-Irish in Ireland and in America*. New Orleans: n.p., 1897.

McDonald, Forrest, and Grady McWhiney. "The Antebellum Southern Herdsman: A Reinterpretation." *Journal of Southern History* 41 (1975): 147–66.

Malone, P. V. *Sam Houston's Indians—The Alabama—Coushetti*. San Antonio: Naylor Co., 1960.

Mantesanz, José. "Introducción de la ganadería en Neuva España, 1521–1535. *Historia Mexicana* 14 (1964): 522–66.

Mason, Julian. "The Etymology of 'Buckaroo.'" *American Speech* 35 (1960): 51–55.

Mather, E. Cotton. "Five Major Ranch Types of the Central Great Plains." *Annals, Association of American Geographers* 46 (1956): 262.

———. "The Production and Marketing of Wyoming Beef Cattle." *Economic Geography* 26 (1950): 81–93.

Matley, Ian M. "Transhumance in Bosnia and Herzegovina." *Geographical Review* 58 (1968): 231–61.

Mealor, W. Theodore, Jr., and Merle C. Prunty. "Open-Range Ranching in Southern Florida." *Annals, Association of American Geographers* 66 (1976): 360–76.

Meinig, Donald W. "The Continuous Shaping of America: A Prospectus for Geographers and Historians." *American Historical Review* 83 (1978): 1186–1217.

———. *Imperial Texas: An Interpretive Essay in Cultural Geography*. Austin: University of Texas Press, 1969.

Merrens, H. Roy. *Colonial North Carolina in the Eighteenth Century*. Chapel Hill: University of North Carolina Press, 1964.

Minkel, Clarence W. "Names in the Mapping of Original Vegetation." *Names* 5, no. 3 (1957): 157-61.

Moore, John H. *Agriculture in Ante-Bellum Mississippi*. New York: Bookman Associates, 1958.

Morris, John W. "Arbuckle Mountain Ranching Area." *Economic Geography* 23 (1947): 190-98.

Morrisey, Richard J. "The Early Range Cattle Industry in Arizona." *Agricultural History* 24 (1950): 151-56.

―――. "The Northward Expansion of Cattle Ranching in New Spain, 1550-1600." *Agricultural History* 25 (1951): 115-21.

―――. "The Shaping of Two Frontiers." *Américas* 3, no. 1 (January 1951): 3-6, 41-42.

Moses, Tad. "Development of the Cattle Business in Texas." In *Texas Almanac and State Industrial Guide, 1949-1950*, pp. 256-67. Dallas: A. H. Belo, 1949.

―――. "Early Day Cattlemen: A Compilation of Events, Names, Places, and Dates of Early Southwest Cattle History." *The Cattleman* 34 (November 1947): 25-28, 85-100; (December 1947): 27-28, 70-76; (January 1948): 39-40, 60-67; (February 1948): 23-25, 60-71.

Muir, Andrew F. "The Free Negro in Jefferson and Orange Counties, Texas." *Journal of Negro History* 35 (1950): 183-206.

Müller, E. "Die Herdenwanderungen im Mittelmeergebiet." *Petermanns Geographische Mitteilungen* 84 (1938): 364-70.

Murray, Myrtle. "Home Life on Early Ranches of Southwest Texas." *The Cattleman*. A series of articles, beginning in vol. 24, no. 8 (January 1938), and ending in vol. 27, no. 7 (December 1940).

Myres, Sandra L. "The Ranching Frontier: Spanish Institutional Backgrounds of the Plains Cattle Industry." In *Essays on the American West*, ed. Harold M. Hollingsworth and Sandra L. Myres, pp. 19-39. Austin: University of Texas Press, 1969.

―――. *The Ranch in Spanish Texas, 1691-1800*. El Paso: Texas Western Press, 1969.

―――. "The Spanish Cattle Kingdom in the Province of Texas." *Texana* 4 (1966): 233-46.

Neville, Alexander W. *The History of Lamar County*. Paris, Texas: North Texas Publishing Co., 1937.

Newell, J. A. "Early Cattle Raising in East Texas." *The Cattleman* 20, no. 9 (February 1934): 9-13.

Oberste, William H. *Texas Irish Empresarios and Their Colonies*. Austin: Von Boeckmann-Jones, 1953.

O'Connor, Mrs. Thomas. "Martín DeLeón" and "DeLeón's Colony." In *The Handbook of Texas*, edited by Walter P. Webb and H. Bailey Carroll, vol. 1, pp. 484–85. Austin: Texas State Historical Association, 1952.

Owsley, Frank L. "The Pattern of Migration and Settlement on the Southern Frontier." *Journal of Southern History* 11 (1945): 147–76.

———. *Plain Folk of the Old South*. Baton Rouge: Louisiana State University Press, 1949.

Paddock, B. B., ed. *A Twentieth Century History and Biographical Record of North and West Texas*. 2 vols. Chicago and New York: Lewis Publishing Company, 1906.

Paredes, Américo. "The Bury-Me-Not Theme in the Southwest." *Texas Folk Lore Society Publication* 29 (1959): 88–92.

Patteson, Ikie Gray. *Loose Leaves: A History of Delta County, Texas*. Dallas: Mathis Publishing Company, 1935.

Peet, Richard. "Influences of the British Market on Agriculture and Related Economic Development in Europe Before 1860." *Transactions, Institute of British Geographers* no. 56 (1972), pp. 1–20.

———. "The Spatial Expansion of Commercial Agriculture in the Nineteenth Century: A von Thünen Explanation." *Economic Geography* 45 (1969): 283–301.

———. "Von Thünen Theory and the Dynamics of Agricultural Expansion." *Explorations in Economic History* 8 (1970–71): 181–201.

Pelzer, Louis. *The Cattlemen's Frontier: A Record of the Trans-Mississippi Cattle Industry*. Glendale, Calif.: Arthur H. Clark Co., 1936.

Perry, T. M. *Australia's First Frontier: The Spread of Settlement in New South Wales, 1788–1829*. Melbourne: Melbourne University Press, 1963.

Pilot Point Post Signal. Pilot Point, Texas. Special edition of 24 July 1941. Article on the 8th un. p. In the Special Materials section, Willis Library, North Texas State University, Denton.

Planhol, Xavier de. "Le Chien de Berger: Développement et Signification Géographique d'une Technique Pastorale." *Bulletin de l'Association de Géographes Français*, no. 370 (1969), pp. 355–68.

Pollock, N. C., and Swanzie Agnew. *An Historical Geography of South Africa*. London: Longmans, 1963.

Porter, K. W. "The Cowkeeper Dynasty of the Seminole Nation." *Florida Historical Quarterly* 30 (1952): 341–49.

———. "The Founder of the Seminole Nation, Secoffee or Cowkeeper." *Florida Historical Quarterly* 27 (1949): 362–84.

Post, Lauren C. *Cajun Sketches from the Prairies of Southwest Louisiana.* Baton Rouge: Louisiana State University Press, 1962.

———— . "Cattle Branding in Southwest Louisiana." *McNeese Review* 10 (1958): 101–17.

———— . "The Domestic Animals and Plants of French Louisiana in the Literature with References to Sources, Varieties, and Uses." *Louisiana Historical Quarterly* 16 (1933): 554–86.

———— . "The Old Cattle Industry of Southwestern Louisiana." *McNeese Review* 9 (1957): 43–55.

———— . "The Upgrading of Beef Cattle on the Great Plains." *California Geographer* 2 (1961): 23–30.

Prunty, Merle C. "Some Geographic Views of the Role of Fire in Settlement Processes in the South." *Tall Timbers Fire Ecology Conference, Proceedings,* 1964: 161–68.

Quelle, O. "Die kontinentalen Viehstrassen Südamerikas." *Petermanns Geographische Mitteilungen* 80 (1934): 114–17.

Ramsdell, Charles. "Espiritu Santo: An Early Texas Cattle Ranch." *Texas Geographic Magazine* 13, no. 1 (1949): 21–25.

Rathjen, Frederick W. *The Texas Panhandle Frontier.* Austin: University of Texas Press, 1973.

Ray, John B. "Trade Patterns along Zane's Trace, 1797–1812." *Professional Geographer* 22 (1970): 142–46.

Remington, Frederic. "Cracker Cowboys of Florida." *Harper's New Monthly Magazine* 91 (1895): 339–45.

Rice, Thomas D., and E. B. Watson. *Soil Survey of Titus County, Texas.* United States Dept. of Agriculture, Bureau of Soils. Washington, D.C.: Government Printing Office, 1910.

Richardson, Rupert N. *The Frontier of Northwest Texas, 1846 to 1876: Advance and Defense by the Pioneer Settlers of the Cross Timbers and Prairies.* Glendale, Calif.: Arthur H. Clark, 1963.

Richardson, T. C. "Cattle Trails of Texas." *Texas Geographic Magazine* 1, no. 2 (1937): 16–29.

Richtofen, Walter, Baron von. *Cattle-Raising on the Plains of North America.* Edited by Edward Everett Dale. Norman: University of Oklahoma Press, 1964.

Roach, Hattie. *The Hills of Cherokee.* N.p.: n.p., 1952.

Robinson, K. W. "Population and Land Use in the Syndey District: 1788–1820." *New Zealand Geographer* 9 (1953): 144–60.

Rostlund, Erhard. "The Geographic Range of the Historic Bison in the Southeast." *Annals, Association of American Geographers* 50 (1960): 395–407.

Russell, Traylor. *History of Titus County, Texas.* 2 vols. Waco: W. M. Morrison, 1965–66.

———. "Kendall Lewis." *Texana* 9 (1971): 17-32.

St. Clair, Gladys. *A History of Hopkins County, Texas.* Waco: Texian Press, 1965.

Salley, A. S., Jr. *The History of Orangeburg County, South Carolina.* Orangeburg, R. Lewis Berry, 1898.

Sauer, Carl O. *The Geography of the Ozark Highland of Missouri.* Geographic Society of Chicago, Bulletin no. 7. Chicago: 1920.

———. *Geography of the Pennyroyal.* Frankfort, Kentucky: Kentucky Geological Survey, 1927.

Schoenmann, L. R., et al. *Soil Survey of Bowie County, Texas.* United States Dept. of Agriculture, Bureau of Soils. Washington, D.C.: Government Printing Office, 1921.

Sharp, Paul F. "Three Frontiers: Some Comparative Studies of Canadian, American, and Australian Settlement." *Pacific Historical Review* 24 (1955): 369-77.

Simonett, David S. "Climate and Cattle Production in North Australia." *Australian Geographer* 6, no. 2 (1953): 15-24.

Smith, H. M. *Soil Survey of Polk County, Texas.* United States Dept. of Agriculture, Bureau of Chemistry and Soils, Series 1930, no. 36. Washington, D.C.: Government Printing Office, 1935.

Smither, Harriet. "The Alabama Indians of Texas." *Southwestern Historical Quarterly* 36 (1932): 83-108.

Sorre, Max. "La notion de genre de vie et sa valeur actuelle." *Annales de Géographie* 57 (1948): 97-108, 193-204.

Spencer, J. E., and Ronald J. Horvath. "How Does an Agricultural Region Originate?" *Annals, Association of American Geographers* 53 (1963): 74-92.

Stephens, A. Ray. *The Taft Ranch: A Texas Principality.* Austin: University of Texas Press, 1964.

Strickland, Rex W. "Miller County, Arkansas Territory, the Frontier That Men Forgot." *Chronicles of Oklahoma* 18 (1940): 12-34, 154-70; 19 (1941): 37-54.

———. "William Becknell." In *The Handbook of Texas*, edited by Walter P. Webb and H. Bailey Carroll, vol. 1, p. 134. Austin: Texas State Historical Association, 1952.

Sullivan, Dulcie. *The LS Brand: The Story of a Texas Panhandle Ranch.* Austin: University of Texas Press, 1968.

Taylor, T. U. *The Chisholm Trail and Other Routes.* San Antonio: Naylor Co., 1936.

Templin, E. H., and R. M. Marshall. *Soil Survey of Hunt County, Texas.* Washington, D.C.: United States Dept. of Agriculture, Bureau of Chemistry and Soils (Series 1934, no. 14) and Texas Agricultural Experiment Station, 1939.

———. I. C. Mowery, J. W. Huckabee, et al. *Soil Survey of Fannin County Texas.* United States Dept. of Agriculture, Bureau of Chemistry and Soils, in cooperation with the Texas Agricultural Experiment Station, Series 1938, no. 10. Washington, D.C.: Government Printing Office, 1946.

Texas Almanac and State Industrial Guide, 1966-1967. Dallas: A. H. Belo Corp., 1965.

Thompson, James W. *A History of Livestock Raising in the United States, 1607-1860*. United States Dept. of Agriculture, Bureau of Agricultural Economics, Agriculture History Series, no. 5, Washington, D.C.: November, 1942.

Thompson, John. "Production, Marketing, and Consumption of Cattle in El Salvador." *Professional Geographer* 13 (September 1961): 18-22.

Thünen, Johann Heinrich von. *Von Thünen's Isolated State*. Translated by Carla M. Wartenberg. Oxford: Pergamon Press, 1966.

Tolbert, Frank X. "Tolbert's Texas." *Dallas Morning News*. 10 August 1974, p. 19A.

Towne, Charles W., and Edward N. Wentworth. *Cattle and Men*. Norman: University of Oklahoma Press, 1955.

Trewartha, Glenn T. *An Introduction to Climate*. New York: McGraw-Hill, 1954.

Turner, Frederick Jackson. *The Frontier in American History*. New York: Henry Holt & Co., 1921.

———. "The Significance of the Frontier in American History." *Annual Report of the American Historical Association for the Year 1893*. Washington, D.C.: Government Printing Office, 1894.

Utley, Robert M. *Longhorns of the Big Bend: A Special Report on the Early Cattle Industry of the Big Bend Country of Texas*. Santa Fe, New Mexico: United States Department of the Interior, National Park Service, Region 3, 1962.

Vandiver, Frank E. "Texas and the Confederate Army's Meat Problem." *Southwestern Historical Quarterly* 47 (1944): 225-33.

Vidal de la Blache, Paul. "Les genres de vie dans la géographie humaine." *Annales de Géographie* 20 (1911): 193-212.

Wagoner, J. J. *History of the Cattle Industry in Southern Arizona, 1540-1940*. Tucson: University of Arizona Press, 1952.

Wahlenberg, W. G. *Longleaf Pine: Its Use, Ecology, Regeneration, Protection, Growth, and Management*. Washington, D.C.: Charles Lathrop Pack Forestry Foundation and the Forest Service, United States Dept. of Agriculture, 1946.

Waibel, Leo. "Die Viehzuchtgebiete der südlichen Halbkugel." *Geographische Zeitschrift* 28 (1922): 54-74.

Ward, Hortense W. "Ear Marks." *Texas Folk-Lore Society Publication*, no. 19 (1944), pp. 106-16.

———. "Indian Sign on the Spaniard's Cattle." *Texas Folk-Lore Society Publication*, no. 19 (1944), pp. 94-105.

Watson, E. B., and Risden T. Allen. *Soil Survey of Morris County, Texas*. United States Dept. of Agriculture, Bureau of Soils. Washington, D.C.: Government Printing Office, 1910.

Webb, Walter Prescott. *The Great Plains*. Boston: Ginn and Co., 1931.

_____, and H. Bailey Carroll, eds. *The Handbook of Texas*. 2 vols. Austin: Texas State Historical Association, 1952.

Webster's New International Dictionary of the English Language. 2nd ed. Unabridged. Springfield, Mass.: G. & C. Merriam, 1955.

Wheeler, David L. "The Beef Cattle Industry in the Old Northwest, 1803-1860." *Panhandle-Plains Historical Review* 47 (1974): 28-45.

_____. "The Beef Cattle Industry in the United States: Colonial Origins." *Panhandle-Plains Historical Review* 46 (1973): 54-67.

Whitaker, James W. *Feedlot Empire: Beef Cattle Feeding in Illinois and Iowa, 1840-1900*. Ames: Iowa State University Press, 1975.

White, G. Langdon. "Cattle Raising: A Way of Life in the Venezuelan Llanos." *Scientific Monthly* 83 (September 1956): 122-29.

Whitelaw, Ralph T. *Virginia's Eastern Shore: A History of Northampton and Accomack Counties*. 2 vols. Richmond: Virginia Historical Society, 1951.

Wilhelm, Eugene J. "Animal Drives—A Case Study in Historical Geography." *Journal of Geography* 66 (1967): 327-34.

_____. "Animal Drives in the Southern Highlands." *Mountain Life and Work* 42, no. 2 (Summer 1966): 6-11.

Wilhelmy, Herbert. "Die Weidewirtschaft im heissen Tiefland Nordkolumbiens." *Geographische Rundschau* 6 (1954): 41-54.

Williams, Robert E. "Cattle in the Southeastern United States, or The Original Wild West." *Corral Dust* 10, no. 2 (Spring 1965): 4-6.

Wilson, James A. "Cattlemen, Packers, and Government: Retreating Individualism on the Texas Range." *Southwestern Historical Quarterly* 74 (1971): 525-34.

_____. "West Texas Influence on the Early Cattle Industry of Arizona." *Southwestern Historical Quarterly* 71 (1967): 26-36.

Winkler, Ernest W. "The Cherokee Indians in Texas." *Texas State Historical Association, Quarterly* 7 (1903): 95-165.

Winston, James E. "Notes on Commercial Relations between New Orleans and Texan Ports, 1838-1839." *Southwestern Historical Quarterly* 34 (1930): 91-105.

Wolfenstine, Manfred R. *The Manual of Brands and Marks*. Norman: University of Oklahoma Press, 1970.

Wood, Peter H. *Black Majority: Negroes in Colonial South Carolina from 1670 through the Stono Rebellion*. New York: Alfred A. Knopf, 1974.

_____ . " 'It Was A Negro Taught Them,' A New Look at African Labor in Early South Carolina." *Journal of Asian and African Studies* 9 (1974): 160–189.

Wood, W. D. "Sketch of the Early Settlement of Leon County, Its Organization, and Some of the Early Settlers." *Texas State Historical Association, Quarterly* 4 (1900–1901): 203–17.

Woodward, Arthur. "Saddles in the New World." *Quarterly of the Los Angeles County Museum* 10 (Summer 1953): 1–5.

Wright, Celia M. *Heritage from the Past: Sketches from Hopkins County History.* Sulphur Springs, Texas: Shining Path Press, 1959.

Yoakum, Henderson K. *History of Texas from Its First Settlement in 1685 to Its Annexation to the United States in 1846.* 2 vols. Austin: Steck Co., 1935 (originally published in 1855).

Unpublished Material

Adams, Leann Cox. "Winning Hand: Burk Burnett of the 6666 Ranch." Master's thesis, Texas Christian University, 1969.

"Appendix to Empresario Contracts." Vol. 54 in MS Spanish and Mexican Records, General Land Office of Texas, Austin, Texas.

Béxar Archives, 1820–35. Austin, University of Texas Archives.

Brand and mark registries, MS, Fannin, Hopkins, and Lamar counties, Texas. Available at the courthouses in Bonham, Sulphur Springs, and Paris.

Census of the Austin Colony. MS, "Censo y Estadistica, Estado de Coahuila y Texas, Departamto. de Bexar, Villa de San Felipe de Austin, Año de 1830." Nacogdoches Archive, Texas State Library, Austin, Texas.

Census of the Austin Colony. MS, "Censo y Estadistica, Estado de Coahuila y Texas, Departamto. de Bexar, Villa de San Felipe de Austin, Año de 1831." Nacogdoches Archive, Texas State Library, Austin, Texas.

Censuses of the districts of Jasper, Nacogdoches, Sabine, San Augustine, and Tenaha, 1835, MS. Nacogdoches Archive, Texas State Library, Austin, Texas.

Census of the town and district of Nacogdoches, 1793, MS in part 6 of the Béxar Archives. University of Texas Archives, Austin.

Coon, David L. "The Development of Market Agriculture in South Carolina, 1670–1785." Ph.D. dissertation, University of Illinois, 1972.

Crow, Corrinne E. "Settlement Patterns and Subsequent Social Development of Red River County, 1814–1849." Master's thesis, East Texas State University, 1972.

Eighth Census of the United States 1860. MS schedules for free population, slave population, and agriculture for the State of Texas. Microfilm copies at Willis Library, North Texas State University, Denton, Texas.

Graf, LeRoy. "The Economic History of the Lower Rio Grande Valley, 1820-1875." Ph. D. dissertation, Harvard University, 1942.

"History of Grazing in Texas." MS, Historical Records Survey, Work Projects Administration (fourteen boxes of clippings and manuscripts), University of Texas Archives, Austin, Texas.

Israel, Kenneth D. "The Cattle Industry of Mississippi, Its Origin and Its Changes Through Time Up to 1850." Ph.D. dissertation, University of Southern Mississippi, 1970.

Laing, Wesley N. "Cattle in Early Virginia." Ph.D. dissertation, University of Virginia, 1954.

LeBon, Joseph W., Jr. "The Catahoula Hog Dog: A Cultural Trait of the Upland South." Master's thesis, Louisiana State University, 1970.

Lobb, C. Gary. "The Historical Geography of the Cattle Regions along Brazil's Southern Frontier." Ph.D. dissertation, University of California at Berkeley, 1970.

McArthur, Daniel E. "The Cattle Industry of Texas, 1685-1918." Master's thesis, University of Texas, Austin, 1918.

McCarty, H. A. MS biographical material on Solomon and Daniel Waggoner, provided by H. A. McCarty, manager of the Waggoner Estate, 3942 Paradise, Vernon, Texas, 1978. The material was originally part of a speech given by Mr. McCarty; MS in possession of Terry G. Jordan.

Mealor, William T., Jr. "The Open-Range Ranch in South Florida and Its Contemporary Successors." Ph.D. dissertation, University of Georgia, 1972.

Mitchell, Robert D. "The Upper Shenandoah Valley of Virginia during the Eighteenth Century." Ph.D. dissertation, University of Wisconsin, Madison, 1969.

Morrisey, Richard J. "The Establishment and Northward Expansion of Cattle Ranching in New Spain." Ph.D. dissertation, University of California at Berkeley, 1949.

Murrah, David Joe. "A Cattle Kingdom on Texas' Last Frontier: C. C. Slaughter's Lazy S Ranch." Master's thesis, Texas Tech University, 1970.

Myres, Sandra L. S. "The Development of the Ranch as a Frontier Institution in the Spanish Province of Texas, 1691-1800." Ph.D. dissertation, Texas Christian University, 1967.

Odom, Max Clifton. "A History of the Cattle Industry in East Texas." Master's thesis, University of Texas, Austin, 1958.

Osburn, John D. "A History of Present Red River County Area through 1845." Master's thesis, Southern Methodist University, 1954.

Peebles, Ruth. "The Westward Migration of the Alabama and Coushatta Indians." Master's thesis, Sam Houston State University, 1968.

"The Reign of King Hog: New Perspectives on the Antebellum Southern Livestock Industry." Session at the annual meeting of the Organization of American Historians, New Orleans, Louisiana, April 1979.

Seventh Census of the United States, 1850. MS schedules for free population, slave population, and agriculture for the State of Texas. Microfilm copies at Willis Library, North Texas State University, Denton, Texas.

Shields, Carla Smith. "Spanish Influences on East Texas Place Names and Vocabulary." Master's thesis, East Texas State University, 1966.

Sparks, Barbara E. H. "The History of Grazing in Texas: An Analytical Inventory of the Findings of the Historical Records Survey." Master's thesis, Southwest Texas State University, 1973.

Strickland, Rex W. "Anglo-American Activities in Northeast Texas, 1803–1845." Ph.D. dissertation, University of Texas, Austin, 1937.

Tarpley, Fred A. "A Word Atlas of Northeast Texas." Ph.D. dissertation, Louisiana State University, 1960.

Tenth Census of the United States, 1880. MS schedules of population, for the State of Texas. Microfilm copies at Willis Library, North Texas State University, Denton, Texas.

Texas tax lists, Republic of Texas and State of Texas, 1837–60. MS, Texas State Archives, Austin, Texas.

Warburton, Margaret Rose. "A History of the O'Connor Ranch, 1834–1939." Master's thesis, Catholic University of America, 1939.

Whitaker, James W. "Cattle Raising and Trade in Western North Carolina, 1820–1860: A Micro-Study." Paper read at the annual meeting of the Organization of American Historians, New Orleans, Louisiana, 14 April 1979.

White, Wayne R. "The Historical Geography of Marion County, Texas, 1830–1890: An Example from the Era of Steamboat Navigation on Inland Waters." Master's thesis, University of Texas, Austin, 1964.

Index

Acadians. *See* Cajuns
Africa, 19; cattle exported from, 14, 38; herders in, 2, 3, 4, 14-15; slaves from, 14, 29, 42; transhumance in, 10
Alabama: brands in, 147; French in, 47; herding in, 49; Indians in, 49; settlement of, 46; as source of Texas settlers, 77-78, 90, 101, 113, 115, 147
Alabama-Coushatta Indians, 111
Alexandria, Louisiana, 72
Allen, H. C., 5
Anglo-Americans, 13, 16, 17, 23; as bearers of herding culture, 25-58, 65-81, 86-98, 101-2, 111-23, 125-50, 154-57; as cowboys, 29, 32, 35, 57, 74-75, 98, 99, 122, 143, 145, 146; early cattle herding by, 25-58; settlement by, 43-58, 62-65, 77-79, 86-87, 111-12, 129-31; in Texas, 59-157
Appalachian Mountains: droving in, 30; herding in, 29, 35-36, 51, 85; vegetation of, 35
Argentina, 10, 16, 21
Arkansas, 87; French in, 47; herding in, 47; as source of Texas settlers, 87, 90; transhumance in, 57
Arkansas Post, 47
Arkansas River, 47
Asheville Basin, 36, 40, 53-54, 55
Atascosita District, 63, 64, 66, 69, 76
Austin Colony: cattle in, 65-66, 72, 87; cowhunts in, 70; crops in, 76; ethnic groups in, 78; hogs in, 76; settlement of, 62-63
Austin, Stephen F., 62, 65, 77
Austin, Texas, 72
Australia, 3, 4-5, 15, 21
Azores, 3

Barbados, 41
Barbed wire, 1, 22, 102, 147
Barr, William, 112

Barrens, 40, 54. *See also* Pine barrens
Bartram, William, 49
Bath, North Carolina, 52
Beef, 41, 65, 72, 95, 101, 123
Big Bend, 139
Big Thicket, 106, 117
Biloxi, Mississippi, 47
Bishko, Charles Julian, 8
Blackland Prairie, 85, 103, 116, 134, 137-39, 147
Blacks: as cattle drovers, 30; as cattle raisers, 47, 74, 110, 143; as cowboys, 14, 29, 30, 50, 57, 74, 98, 122, 143-46; as herders in Africa, 14; in South Carolina, 29, 40; in Texas, 74, 98, 122, 143-46
Bluegrass Basin, 40, 54, 56
Boers, 4, 10
Boone, Daniel, 54
Boonslick, Missouri, 55, 89
Branding, 57; in colonial America, 25, 26, 27; in Europe, 9, 27; in the Middle East, 9; in Texas, 71, 92-94, 120, 122
Brands: diffusion of, 147; in Texas, 88, 92-94, 108, 120, 122, 144, 147; in Virginia, 27, 28
Brazil, 3
Brazos River, 61, 65, 70, 72, 73, 127
Bulldogging, 33
Bullwhip. *See* Whips
Burning, range. *See* Fire

Cajuns, 47, 49, 50, 64, 80
California, 5, 23, 95
Cape Fear River, 52
Cape Verde Islands, 3
Cattle: in Africa, 14, 15, 38; branding of, 9, 25-28, 57, 71, 92-94, 120, 122, 144, 147; breeds, 6, 10, 12, 25, 37-38, 48, 72-73, 100, 117, 118, 122, 147-49, 154-55; care of, 10-13, 25-27; control of, 9-10, 25, 30-36, 38, 47, 57, 73-74, 91-92, 118-21,

215